Deciphering Ancient Minds

DAVID LEWIS-WILLIAMS AND SAM CHALLIS

Deciphering Ancient Minds

THE MYSTERY OF SAN BUSHMAN ROCK ART

With 98 illustrations, 29 in colour

 Thames & Hudson

First published in the United Kingdom in 2011 by
Thames & Hudson Ltd, 181A High Holborn, London WC1V 7QX

Copyright © 2011 Thames & Hudson Ltd, London

British Library Cataloguing-in-Publication Data
A catalogue record for this book is available from the British Library

ISBN 978-0-500-05169-6

Printed in China by Toppan Leefung

Contents

Preface

Early in the 20th century the French philosopher Lucien Lévy-Bruhl wrote numerous books and articles that were influential in their time but are now almost entirely forgotten. Two of his books were *Les Fonctions mentales dans les sociétés inférieures* (1912) and *La Mentalité primitive* (1922). As these titles suggest, he, and indeed many others at that time, were fascinated by the way in which people living in small-scale, pre-industrial societies thought. He believed that 'primitive' people used different categories and processes of thought from people in complex, modern societies. As far as he could determine, 'primitive' people were essentially mystical and superstitious, and their 'pre-logical' beliefs in mystical things sometimes vitiated their ability to reason and draw logical inferences from observations. For Lévy-Bruhl, there was a 'primitive mentality' and a 'higher mentality'. He did not mean that 'primitive' people lacked (genetically, as we say today) a capacity for rational thought, but rather that their thinking, moulded by their small-scale societies, was more symbolic, more allusive than modern Western thought.

Lévy-Bruhl was an armchair anthropologist. When more practically minded anthropologists, such as Sir Edward Evans-Pritchard and Bronislaw Malinowski, began to live among people in small-scale societies, ideas changed. These social (cultural) anthropologists grew up and were trained in the context of 19th-century colonialism and its aftermath. As the West expanded its influence into the most remote parts of the world, they began to study what they called 'primitive societies'.[1] They soon discovered that so-called 'primitive' thinking was in fact highly complex and well adjusted to the people's social circumstances. They tried to discover how seemingly irrational beliefs functioned in the context of a whole culture. As a result of this hands-on, 'functionalist' research, it is now widely recognized that Lévy-Bruhl overemphasized the supposed lack of logic among 'simple' people and underestimated the amount of irrationality in the supposedly more sophisticated thought of his own culture. Towards the end of his life, he himself began to realize that his distinction between 'primitive mentality' and 'higher mentality' was too rigid. He wrote: 'There is a mystical mentality which is more marked and more easily observable among "primitive peoples" than in our own societies, but it is present in every human mind.'[2]

Nevertheless, Lévy-Bruhl's ideas persist among the general public today, and, as a result, words like 'primitive' and 'superstitious' spring into many Western people's minds when they try to think themselves back via the small-scale societies that anthropologists have studied and on into the deep, prehistoric past. (By 'prehistoric' we mean times before written records.) In contemplating the prehistoric past, modern people often imagine a truly dark age of unremitting struggle against the forces of nature, imminent starvation, brutality and an all-pervading fear of the unknown, be it the unknown of tomorrow, or the unknown that lies behind a distant mountain range or, in an even more terrifying sense, unknown beings and forces suspected to lurk in every nook of daily life.

Here we encounter a problem that has, at least in part, been created by social anthropology. Many of the earlier anthropologists believed that the nearest they could come to prehistoric thinking was in their dealings with people who preserved a pre-industrial, pre-literate way of life into the 19th and early 20th centuries – people like the indigenous Australian population and the southern African San (Bushmen). We shall, of course, never be able to speak to ancient prehistoric people and, by definition, they left no written records, so, for a while, that seemed a reasonable line of enquiry. But today alarm bells sound. There are numerous problems, some quite subtle. Finding out about prehistoric minds is indeed a formidable challenge.[3] Still, we do sometimes – very rarely – discover a chink in the wall of time. Through that chink we hear the voices of people who lived at least part of their lives in pre-agricultural, pre-literate times. If we are extraordinarily lucky, we hear these voices speaking in their own language, not just in Western translations that rearrange statements so that they become more intelligible to modern readers. In the process of translation, the desire for intelligibility becomes a distorting filter that eliminates some of the elusiveness (and allusiveness) of the original thought patterns. Yet, ultimately, there is no other way to proceed. We therefore need some sort of trade-off.

In this book our trade-off involves working with a prehistoric language as far as is possible. Even though we are writing in modern English, we try to examine prehistoric words and see how, and in what contexts, people used them. Like the practical field anthropologists of the 20th century we vacate our armchairs and abandon purely philosophical musings.

1 *The three registers of the Rosetta Stone have parallels in the study of southern African San rock paintings.*

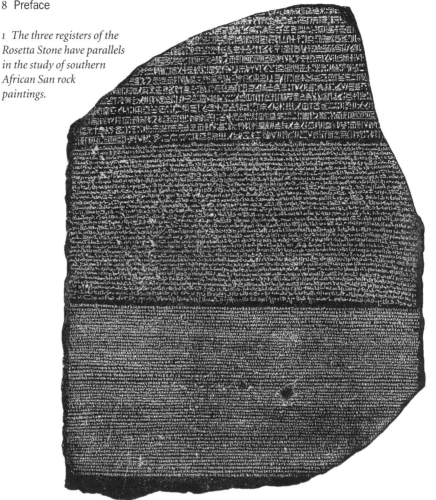

Three registers

By an astonishing stroke of good fortune, we have something like a multi-component Rosetta Stone, the famous inscribed stone that was named after a village in the western Egyptian delta where it was found (Fig. 1). In 1822 the French linguist Jean François Champollion was able to decipher Egyptian hieroglyphics because the Rosetta Stone was engraved with a message in three scripts: at the top was a hieroglyphic text, below it was demotic, cursive ancient Egyptian, and in the lowest register was an intelligible Greek translation.

In this book we deal with equivalents of Champollion's three registers. The people of whom we write are the pre-agricultural, hunter-gatherer San of southern Africa. Today they are well known; they and the Aboriginal people of Australia have become iconic – epitomes of vanished prehistoric times.

The anthropologist Alan Barnard[4] describes the San as 'a pervasive image in anthropology, well beyond Bushman or hunter-gatherer specialists'.

The three 'registers' of the San legacy are:

1 highly detailed, though enigmatic, pictures (rock paintings and engravings) of the people's beliefs and religious experiences.

2 19th-century phonetic texts running to over 12,000 pages of a now-extinct prehistoric language in which ancient people speak, in their own words and idioms, of their beliefs, rituals, life histories and their hunting and gathering economy, and even more voluminous 20th- and 21st-century records of the Kalahari San.

3 transliterations of those texts into English that, word by word, give patterned clues to often elusive concepts.

In the paintings, we can actually *see* how the San who used the prehistoric words imagined their spirit world. Though less well known, these spiritual panoramas rival in complexity, detail and variety the Ice Age painted caverns of western Europe, ancient Egyptian art and the intricately carved Maya temples and stelae.

Many of the San images that we decipher date back to times long before 19th-century researchers compiled the phonetic texts. Some have been dated to almost 3,000 years before the present;[5] others, from southern Namibia, were made as much as 27,000 years ago.[6] Although we cannot date every individual image, we can see that the painting tradition is very ancient, not just in general terms but in specific, decipherable features that clearly dovetail with practices and beliefs described in the texts.[7] The older images are thus an extension to the texts: they take us back from the violence of the 19th century when the texts were recorded to hunter-gatherer times long before there was any Western or other influence. While we may legitimately doubt the appropriateness of 'prehistoric' to describe the material provided by 19th-century San informants, we can be confident that many of the images are indeed prehistoric. In this way, rock paintings, indigenous language texts and English translations come together on our 'Rosetta Stone' to give us access to a now-lost thought world that is breathtaking in its intricacies.

Debilitating misunderstandings

Three fundamental points must be made at the outset of this exploration in decipherment. All three may appear, at first glance, to be serious limitations, but, as will become apparent, all are in fact positive features that, with the use of appropriate methods, have the potential to open up new avenues of insight.

The first, put starkly, is that San rock paintings and engravings constitute (at least to many Western eyes) the most exquisite rock art in the world – but also one that has for various reasons been grossly undervalued. So provocative a claim demands substantiation. We argue that the sheer beauty of San rock paintings derives from the cameo-like size of many images and their amazing details: there is nothing 'crude' or 'primitive' about these delicate images. Often an antelope's head, mouth, nose and subtle shading of the animal's coat are meticulously delineated (Pls 5, 8–11, 13, 19, 29).

This beauty has turned out to be a two-edged sword. The problem with beauty is that it gives the impression that the images were made for aesthetic reasons. Indeed, one of the early (and more attractive) Western explanations for San rock art was *l'art pour l'art* – 'art for art's sake'. Today, most researchers allow that the artists probably did take extreme care with and pleasure in their creations, though we cannot gauge their pleasure with any certainty. Nevertheless, that was not the reason why they made the images: the aesthetic explanation does not tell us why the painters selected certain subjects for repeated depiction and ignored others. Their art was not a record of daily events, heroic deeds or the natural world around them.

Our second initial point robustly contests the notion that San rock art is 'simple' and crude, little more than a series of stick figures. The complexity of the art extends beyond the glorious depictions of antelope and other creatures (birds, fish, snakes and, rarely, insects) to human figures, and it is here that we encounter a strong indication that this was not *l'art pour l'art*. People, fully delineated, are shown in every conceivable posture: running, walking, sitting, dancing, lying down, somersaulting and, though far less frequently than is usually assumed, hunting. Within human figures the cameo-principle also applies. The figures' clothing (antelope-skin cloaks, caps and so forth) and artefacts (such as bows, arrows, spears, digging sticks and beads) are depicted as they go about their various activities, some of which are related in mysterious ways to animals. Interspersed with these images are depictions of antelope-headed beings, fantastic creatures and other puzzling forms: what can they mean? So much infinite care went into the creation of this great variety of images that we cannot avoid concluding that they were immensely important to their makers and far from simple.

The third misunderstanding has proved as misleading as the first two. The egregious misapprehension that San rock art is simple and rather crude is frequently linked to the notion that knowing about it is also a simple and straightforward matter: everyone can plainly see what it is all about. If superficial inspection does not provide explanations, all that is needed, so the canard goes, is for researchers to ask a few present-day San what the images mean. As we explain in Chapter 1, the situation is far more complex. The southern San, known from 19th-century records, are culturally and linguistically extinct. The surviving San live in the Kalahari Desert (see Fig. 2), whereas the art is found largely much farther to the south. As we shall see, the Kalahari San were not painters driven into the inhospitable desert in comparatively recent times by 'stronger' people: on the contrary, they have lived in the Kalahari for millennia and they speak languages different from those that were spoken by the people who made the art. They themselves have no tradition of making rock art. Showing the modern San copies of the art or taking them hundreds of kilometres to the painted sites produces disappointing results. Yet – and this is the key point – the modern-day San entertain similar religious beliefs and perform the same rituals as the now-extinct painters did.

The 19th-century southern San's own explanations of the images that we decipher in later chapters are often oblique: they have come down to us in the people's own thought categories and idioms, not in recensions prepared by anthropologists who believed (probably wrongly) that they knew all about so seemingly explicit an art. The virtual absence of fully intelligible, direct explanations of images leaves us with what we may call 'pristine' (albeit initially opaque) indigenous statements that draw us into the long-gone minds of San rock painters.

Notable beauty, complexity and a supposed ease of explanation have unfortunately combined to marginalize San rock art. Archaeologists and anthropologists working in other parts of the world have often failed to notice the importance of San rock art as an avenue into ancient minds.

A route to understanding

As we try to decipher San rock art, we ask: does a pattern emerge, one that ties together texts, translations and images? In Chapter 1, we begin this quest by examining the colonial milieu in which the San phonetic texts and some of the paintings were recorded. Can we avoid falling into the traps that bedevilled the work of the early social anthropologists who sought 'primitive mentalities'? We also need to ask how 'pristine' the 19th-century San people were whose own accounts of their thought and way of life we study.

Chapter 2 focuses on two key texts that have been preserved in the now-extinct /Xam San language. At first glance they seem opaque, or, at any rate, naïve. But, when we dig deeper, we find that the words the San used lead us to the very heart of their religious experiences, beliefs and rituals. We feel rather as Champollion must have felt when he analysed and deciphered the individual elements contained within an Egyptian hieroglyphic cartouche (an elongated oval ring containing a royal name). Our research strategy in some ways follows his procedure. The first cartouche he cracked was inscribed on the temple at Abu Simbel in Nubia. It was the name of Ramesses II. With that clue in mind, he was able to move on to decipher the only cartouche remaining on the Rosetta Stone (the hieroglyphic register on the stone is badly damaged): it contained the name Ptolemy. Here was the key: accepting Thomas Young's earlier discovery that hieroglyphics were phonetic, Champollion achieved the breakthrough that became the foundation for all subsequent Egyptology. Similarly, we find that the elements making up some key /Xam words and phrases come together to denote immensely powerful San concepts that we can find commonly illustrated in their art throughout southern Africa. In the art, words spring vividly to life.

Having established the overall framework of San religious thought, we proceed in Chapter 3 to unravel what the 19th-century recorders translated as 'deeds and things of sorcery'. We find that, while some of these 'things' were material objects, others were conceptual: they existed only in the minds of the San. Yet some of these curious conceptual things are not left to our imagination: the San painted them in remarkably explicit panels of images. The texts *tell* us what the images mean, and the images *show* us what the words mean.

This complementarity becomes even clearer in Chapter 4. When the 19th-century /Xam San were asked to comment on certain copies of rock paintings, an unsuspected domain of San belief and ritual suddenly opened up. It all began in the 1870s, when an early colonial traveller copied an enigmatic rock painting that seemed to him to depict mermaids. He then linked it to a myth recorded in the same area from a San man. But was he correct in making this association? Another San man gave an altogether different explanation of the painting. At once we need to ask how reliable such explanations are.

In Chapter 5 we take the matter further, though this time the two indigenous explanations of the paintings on which we focus are in closer accord. Two San men living in different parts of southern Africa responded with similar explanations to paintings of strange animals of no known species. As a result, we need not dismiss these curious creatures as vaguely 'mythical'. On the contrary, they were conceptual rather than material 'things of sorcery'. We now know that these 'animals of the mind' had a name in the /Xam language, a name that, like a cartouche, can be analysed and deciphered element by element.

In Chapter 6 we take decipherment into another dimension. We have managed to track down many of the sites in which 19th-century colonial copyists worked and have examined what remains of the paintings. Now, 140 years after the copies were made, we find that they themselves stand in need of decipherment. We have identified errors in copying that, paradoxically, led the San to reveal rich vistas of religious experience and symbolism.

Chapter 7 addresses a thorny problem. The pre-literate cultures around the world are, as anthropologists have shown, rich in mythology, so rich that some early writers, like Lévy-Bruhl, believed that pre-literate people thought in terms of myths rather than logically. Having come this far in our decipherment of San texts and images, we now ask two important questions: First, can what we have learned about San cosmology, ritual and image-making help us to decipher specific San myths? Second, what was the relationship between San mythical narratives and painted images? In answer to these questions, we show that myths are decipherable by the same techniques that we have employed in our approach to texts and rock paintings: the actual prehistoric words hold vital clues.

In Chapter 8 we enquire about the land in which the painters lived. We find that, for them, the mountains, valleys and mists were charged with spirituality. Often what has become known as 'landscape archaeology' relies on archaeologists' own responses to the environment. By contrast, we tap into the thoughts of the prehistoric San themselves and explore their landscape from the point of view of insiders. To expand our conclusions, we examine the Dinwoody rock art of Wyoming, North America. We find that, in both regions, the rock art images were situated in meaningful landscapes.

Our final chapter comes back to the questions we asked right at the beginning. Were ancient ways of thinking fundamentally different from modern Western ways? Was the thinking of the San whose words and pictures we have examined simple and 'primitive'? Certainly, if we revert to our image of the Rosetta Stone, we have found that what is inscribed on our southern African equivalent is no less complex, no less fascinating than the hieroglyphs of ancient Egypt.

We must bear in mind that what we have found out about San thinking is not a blueprint for *all* prehistoric peoples. Apart from our comparison of San rock art with the North American Dinwoody images, we have been writing about only one instance of ancient thought. Nevertheless, we suspect that the elusiveness and fluidity of San 'religious' rather than 'practical' thought, so foreign to Western scientific ways of thinking, was widespread in the deep, prehistoric past. We say 'suspect' because we cannot prove such a conclusion. Some early social anthropologists may have been right in a general sense: instances like that of the San do bring us a little closer to prehistoric minds. But those anthropologists were certainly wrong in believing that 'primitive people' were simple-minded and naïve.

A Note on Pronunciation

Many of the San words in this book contain sounds unfamiliar to English speakers. In addition to the more usual phonetic representations, the following symbols are used for the clicks that are a distinctive feature of the Khoisan language family, which comprises the many San (Bushman) and the Khoekhoen languages. The Khoekhoe were formerly known by the highly pejorative word 'Hottentot'. We take the descriptions of these sounds from Lorna Marshall's book *The !Kung of Nyae Nyae* (1976):[1]

/ **Dental click** The tip of the tongue is placed against the back of the upper front teeth; in the release, it is pulled away with a fricative sound. English speakers use a similar sound in gentle reproof.

! **Alveolar-palatal click** The tip of the tongue is pressed firmly against the back of the alveolar ridge where it meets the hard palate and is very sharply snapped down. A loud pop results. English speakers use this sound to imitate horses' hoofs on paving.

≠ **Alveolar click** The front part of the tongue, more than the tip, is pressed against the alveolar ridge and drawn sharply downward when released.

// **Lateral click** The tongue is placed as for the alveolar click. It is released at the sides by being drawn in from the front teeth. Horse riders sometimes use lateral clicks to signal their steeds to start or go faster.

X In San orthography, X indicates a guttural sound as in the Scottish *loch*.

In Bantu language (e.g., isiZulu, isiXhosa) orthography, clicks, which derive from Khoisan languages, are represented as follows:

$$/ = c$$
$$! = q$$
$$// = x$$

Readers who experience difficulty with the clicks are advised simply to omit them.

CHAPTER 1

Back in Time

Before the cattle were unyoked, we saw a female figure emerge from
a hole in the face of the cliff bearing what we at first thought to be a sick
child but on a nearer approach proved to be a diminutive and emaciated
old woman, the mother of her dutiful and, to do her no more than
justice, affectionate bearer …
Accompanying her to a low cave formed by an enormous block of stone
with a flattened undersurface now blackened by smoke and soot, we found
two men of something between the Bushman and Hottentot tribes, one in
an old felt hat and sheepskin cloak, smoking tobacco out of the shankbone
of a sheep, the other in a red coat, lying outstretched upon his back and fast
asleep, with an old musket, marked G R Tower, carefully covered beside
him. A few thorn bushes served to narrow the entrance of the cave
and partially to screen its inmates from the weather …
A few animals, nearly obliterated, were still visible upon the walls of
their dwelling, proving it to have been an ancient habitation of their race;
and the men told me they had seen drawings of the unicorn but had never
known any one who could testify to the existence of the living animal.[1]

In this extract from his diary, the British artist and explorer Thomas Baines
describes the appalling conditions in which many San people lived at the
middle of the 19th century. He had sailed to the Cape of Good Hope in 1842
and, after working in Cape Town as a coach painter, embarked on an extensive
journey through the interior of the subcontinent. On this journey, he compiled what is today an invaluable collection of paintings that depict not only
scenery but also indigenous people. In 1858 he accompanied David Living-
stone along the Zambezi river, where he was one of the first Westerners to see
the Victoria Falls.

The encounter that Baines describes took place near the present-day town
of Aliwal North (Fig. 2). The San whom he met and painted were bereft of the
land and animals that had sustained them for millennia (Pl. 2). They drifted
from place to place, clinging to what little they could derive from the Western
civilization that had engulfed them. Next to the man whom he found sleeping
in the rock shelter lay a musket engraved with the name of its former owner;
traded tobacco provided the other man with some solace. The San, together

1 A line of eland antelope moves past low cliffs with painted rock shelters and up into the San spiritual hinterland that lies beyond the high peaks.

2 In the 18th and 19th centuries travellers and explorers, such as the artist Thomas Baines, came across the impoverished remnants of San groups.

3 Today, San groups living on the fringes of more complex economies still practise the trance, or healing, dance. As the women clap the rhythm, the feet of the dancing men make a rut in the sand.

4 In the Drakensberg mountains large rock shelters beneath sandstone cliffs were occupied by the San, and they made their paintings there.

5 (Above) On a rock in the shelter shown in Plate 4 the San painted a multitude of eland. Why did they think it necessary to depict so many eland?

6 (Below) In this dance clapping women stand on either side of dancing men who bend forward and support their weight on dancing sticks.

7 (Above) A painting of a circular trance dance. The curved line may represent the dance rut or a hut in which there is a sick person and three clapping women. The pointing finger indicates the shooting of supernatural potency.

8, 9, 10, 11 (Overleaf, clockwise from top left) The eland was believed to have more supernatural potency than any other animal. The San painted it in various ways: in lateral views (8, 9), with its head turned to look backward (10), and lying down (11).

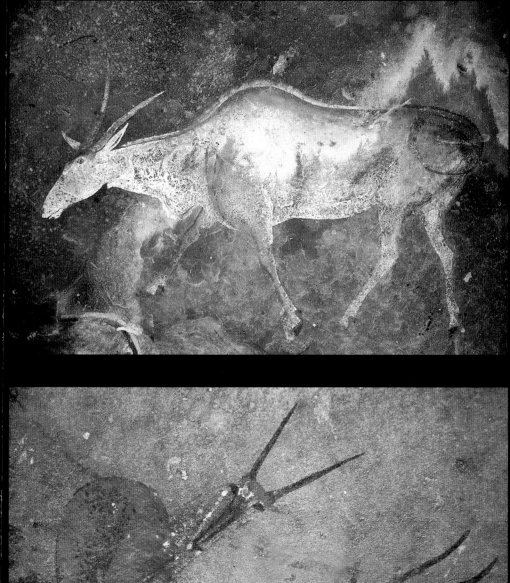

14 (Opposite) Joseph Orpen's article 'A glimpse into the mythology of the Maluti Bushmen', published in 1874, illustrated four groups of San rock art images. The Sehonghong rain-capture scene [see p. 111] is in the top right corner of the fold-out.

15 (Below) The high Drakensberg over which Orpen's expedition climbed in 1873.

16, 17, 18 (Overleaf) Three of George Stow's 1870s copies of rain-animals. It was through these copies that the Bleek family first learned of San beliefs about rain-making. In Plate 18 a man bleeds from the nose as he holds his arms in the backward posture.

19 (Overleaf, below right) A San man apprehends a rain-animal in a way that is comparable to the action depicted in Plate 18.

12, 13 Transformation is a theme in San rock art. Flying creatures are common. Above (12), a figure with a white face has emanations from the back of its neck. Its arms have white feathers. The 'swift-person' below (13) has a forked tail and complex wavy lines in its body.

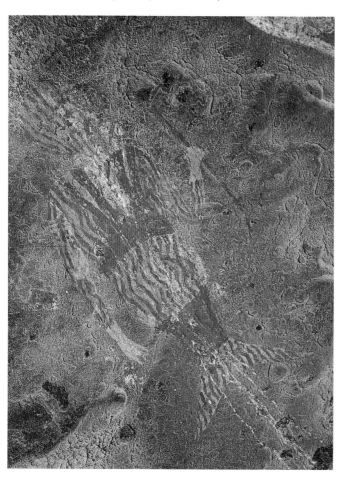

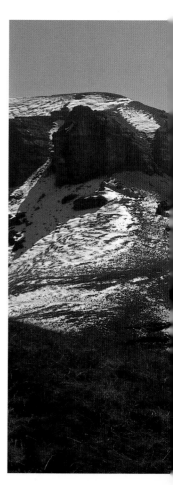

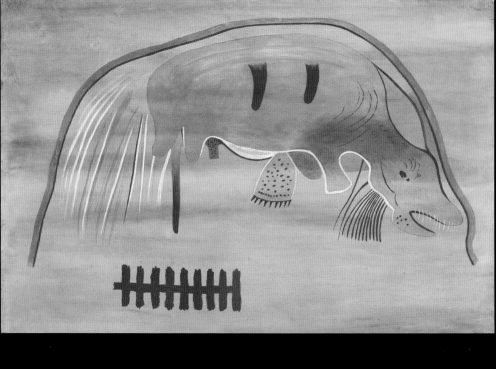

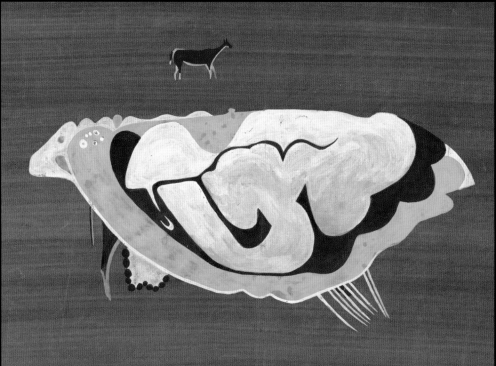

20, 21 George Stow's copy of the complex panel shown in Plate 21, below. Stow rearranged many of the images. In the painting itself a tusked serpent can be seen emerging from a facet in the rock face (Fig. 37).

22, 23, 24 In a hollow beneath a boulder a San artist painted a lion with a long tail pursuing a number of men (Fig. 40). One of the antelope-headed flying figures is shown in Plate 24. It bleeds from the nose.

25 (Right) A coloured photograph of eland and a dead rhebok around which people dance. A swarm of bees can be seen. A 'thread of light' leads from a hartebeest on the right to a flying creature on the left.

26, 27 (Below, left and right) A 'freezingly cold mist', here seen from above and from below, lies between the level of the rock shelters and the summits of the high Drakensberg. It was 'the rain's breath' and guarded the place where the San trickster-deity lived with his vast herds of eland.

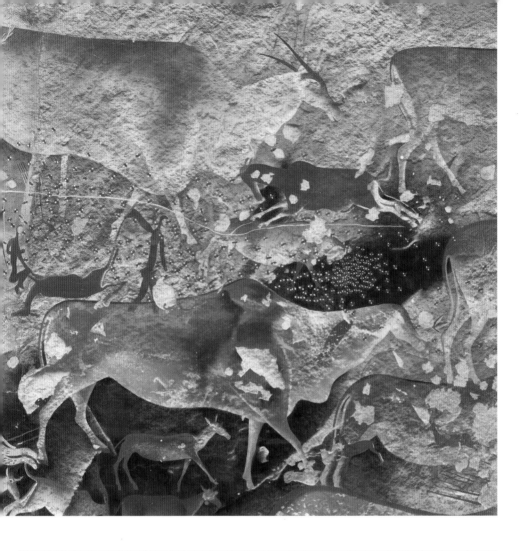

28 (Above) A hilltop in the semi-arid terrain where the /Xam San lived. A waterhole can be seen in the left-hand end of the ravine. Rock engravings are in the foreground; they overlook the waterhole.

29 A transformed San shaman stands next to an upside-down buck, a source of supernatural potency. He has blood coming from his nose and antelope hoofs. He holds a long stick and a flywhisk. A 'thread of light' hangs around his body. He is in the San spirit realm.

with the pastoral Khoekhoe (formerly known as Hottentots), who had for the most part lost their herds and flocks, were caught between two ways of life.

On the rock wall behind the people were the remains of San paintings. Though blackened by smoke and soot, the few remaining images pointed to a rich cultural heritage – but Baines himself was unimpressed by them. He thought the artists were 'ignorant of perspective' and in 'want of skill'.[2] The poverty of the San in material things tended to persuade early travellers that they were equally poor in culture and belief, and therefore unworthy of respect.

Nevertheless, Baines did not consider the San whom he met to be poverty-stricken simply because they were, by tradition, nomadic hunter-gatherers. True, mobile people cannot carry much in the way of goods on their long treks. There was more to it, however. The 19th-century San were the victims of two centuries of harassment and dispersal. We read that the young woman in the group had no option but to carry her frail mother on her back. She had no extended family to help her. Even her daughter had been 'detained in servitude' by a group of people known as Bergenaars – mountain robbers, as Baines explained. The whole San social system had broken down.

2 Map of southern Africa showing places mentioned in the text. The San groups indicated speak, or spoke, mutually unintelligible languages.

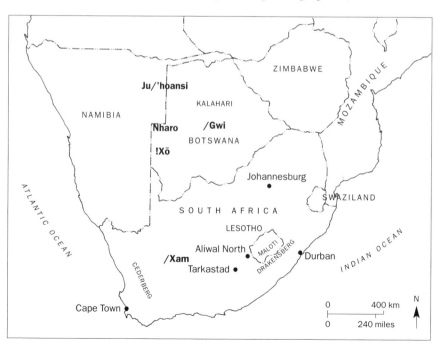

The Bergenaars, a mixed-race group, lived very largely through banditry and stock theft, as did many other culturally and racially heterogeneous groups throughout southern Africa, and indeed the people whom Baines himself met.[3] The remnant communities of San had no recourse but to steal cattle and sheep. They therefore joined creolized groups like the Bergenaars and defended their land with their traditional bows and arrows and with newly acquired muskets. Early on, they became feared for their lethal poisoned arrows and their cunning cattle rustling.

This state of affairs gave the colonists the excuse they sought to eradicate the hunters. In the 1770s, the Swedish naturalist and traveller Anders Sparrman wrote: 'Does a colonist at any time get view of a Boshiesman [as the San were then known], he takes fire immediately, and spirits up his horse and dogs in order to hunt him with more keenness and fury than he would a wolf or any other wild beast.'[4] No quarter, no negotiation. Another Swedish naturalist, Carl Peter Thunberg, writing at the end of the 18th century, was appalled by the treatment that the San received at the hands of the colonists. One commando raised to exterminate the Sneeuberg San 'killed 400 Boschiesmen; of this party seven had been wounded by arrows, but none died'.[5]

Those who were taken alive by the colonists were no better off. Louis Anthing, who was commissioned in the 1860s by the Parliament of the Cape of Good Hope to investigate the atrocities that were being committed, was shocked by what he found:

Those who went into the service of the new comers did not find their condition thereby improved. Harsh treatment, and insufficient allowance of food, and continued injuries inflicted on their kinsmen are alleged as having driven them back into the bush, from whence hunger again led them to invade the flocks and herds of the intruders, regardless of the consequences, and resigning themselves, as they say, to the thought of being shot in preference to death and starvation.[6]

Some British colonists (Britain having finally taken full control of the Cape in 1814) tried to blame the Dutch farmers for this state of affairs, but the missionary John Phillip found otherwise:

While England boasts of her humanity, and represents the Dutch as brutes and monsters, for their conduct towards the Hottentots and Bushmen, a narrow inspection … will bring to light a system … perhaps exceeding in cruelty anything recorded in the facts you have collected, respecting the atrocities committed under the Dutch Government.[7]

Materially poor, culturally rich

The San were an autochthonous people. As archaeological evidence testifies, they and their ancestors lived for many millennia throughout the whole of the subcontinent.[8] Then, about 2,000 years ago, they had to contend with an influx of other peoples.[9] First, there were Khoekhoe herders in the western, central and coastal regions and, later, Bantu-speaking black farmers along the east coast and the highveld of the interior. Then a more comprehensive threat came in 1652, when the Dutch established a settlement at the Cape of Good Hope. Domestic herds and their colonial owners soon spread into the interior of southern Africa. Thereafter, the San survived in the shrinking interstices of land between the more populous and resource-hungry agricultural economies. In the semi-arid parts of the central interior and in the mountains in the south-east, the San managed to sustain viable communities into the 19th century. By turns, these communities had both good and bad relations with the peoples moving into the subcontinent.

Many settlers, especially missionaries, believed that the San did not have the mental capacity to understand any form of religion. Nevertheless, some colonists did take the trouble to enquire into San beliefs. One of these was Sir James Edward Alexander. A Scottish soldier and traveller, a man of independent financial means, he journeyed up the western side of what are now South Africa and Namibia hoping 'to discover some of the secrets of the great and mysterious continent of Africa'.[10] In particular, he hoped 'to promote trade, to civilize the native tribes that might be visited, and to extend a knowledge of our holy religion' (ibid.). He began his long trek in 1835, a time when the colonists entertained a very low opinion of the 'Boschmans', as the San were then known.

Alexander, however, discovered that the San were not entirely without religious concepts, albeit very rudimentary ones:

During the journey I had often endeavoured to find out traces of religion among the Boschmans and others; but I had hitherto been very unsuccessful.... [A]mong the Boschmans I had discovered nothing to indicate the faintest trace of religion, but now I did in a singular way.... 'Numeep, the Boschman guide, came to me labouring under an attack of dysentery.

I asked him what had occasioned the disease; and he said it was from having dug for water at the place called Kuisip ... without having first made an offering ... to Toosip, the old man of the water.

'Do you say any thing to him when you put down your offering at the water-place?'

'We say, "Oh! Great father! Son of a Boschman – give me food; give me the flesh of the rhinoceros, of the gemsbok, of the wild horse [zebra or quagga], or what I require to have."'

I was very glad he had been ill; for owing to this, I found out a trace of worship among a very wild people.[11]

That Alexander hardly understood this 'trace of worship' is today clear. But he at least saw beyond the people's material poverty. Little by little and very slowly, the view that the San were irredeemably 'primitive' began to break down in more educated colonial circles, though not in rural districts.

Today, numerous San linguistic groups still live in the Kalahari Desert, where their ancestors lived for thousands of years. They include the Ju/'hoansi (formerly !Kung), /Gwi, !Kō, and Nharo. These present-day San are not descendants of people who were recently driven into the desert by other people. They are descended from the aboriginal human populations of the African subcontinent.[12] They have become one of the most thoroughly studied of the world's small-scale, hunter-gatherer societies.[13]

By comparing the beliefs and rituals of these desert people with what was recorded for the groups, like the /Xam, that lived farther to the south in the 19th century, we are able to see that, notwithstanding regional variations, certain beliefs and rituals were widespread, probably pan-San. These commonalities included complex hunting observances, girls' puberty rites and the central, all-important healing, or trance, dance.[14] Where basic parallels are demonstrable, it is therefore possible to supplement the 19th-century southern ethnographic record by recourse to more recent research in the Kalahari.

Comparisons of this kind highlight the large number of mutually unintelligible San languages.[15] When four young Ju/'hoan boys from the northern Kalahari were brought to Cape Town in 1879, it was found that their language was unintelligible to the southern /Xam San people.[16] Many San languages have unfortunately died out in comparatively recent times. One of these, the /Xam language, was chosen for the new, post-apartheid South African national motto: !Ke e: /xarra //ke – People who are different come together.[17]

In the 19th century, a gradual (though unfortunately still incomplete) reassessment of the San was initiated by a small group of people whose work provides the foundation for our investigation of what the San themselves said and thought about the paintings they made in their rock shelters. This group comprised the Bleek family, Joseph Orpen and George Stow.

A remarkable family

Today the history of the Bleek family is well known. Indeed, a scholarly industry has grown up around its various members.[18] Wilhelm Bleek (1827–1875) was a German philologist, who came to southern Africa in 1855 to compile a Zulu grammar. While he was working on the Zulu language in the British colony of Natal he heard about the San. He wrote: 'During the first few months of this year [1856] the Bushmen descended from their impregnable hiding places in the Kahlamba mountains [Drakensberg] to steal cattle again.'[19] After a brief but linguistically productive sojourn in Natal, Bleek moved to Cape Town in 1856 to become a court interpreter and, later, curator of the valuable library owned by the British governor, Sir George Grey.

Bleek's life took a momentous turn soon after he moved to the Cape. He learned that some San men, convicted of sheep-stealing and even murder, had been taken to a jail in Cape Town. He saw this as an opportunity to study their little-known language. He realized that Zulu and other Bantu languages were not in any danger, but that the San languages, quite different from those Bantu languages, were threatened with extinction as a result of the frontier conditions we have described. Eventually, Bleek persuaded Sir George Grey's successor, Sir Philip Wodehouse, to allow some of the San convicts who spoke the /Xam language to live with him in his suburban house. There were six major /Xam informants – 'teachers' would be a better word – from the central Cape and, later, four young boys from the Kalahari Desert. The names of the /Xam informants will crop up in subsequent chapters: /A!kunta, //Kabbo, /Han ≠kasso, ≠Kasin, !Kweiten-ta-//ken and Diä!kwain (Fig. 3). The symbols indicating clicks are explained in the introductory Note on Pronunciation (p. 15).

Wilhelm Bleek was joined by his sister-in-law Lucy Lloyd (1834–1914). Although she had no formal training, she proved to be a talented linguist. While Bleek concentrated principally on working out /Xam grammar, Lloyd took down statements in phonetic script and prepared parallel English transliterations. All in all, Bleek and Lloyd compiled over 12,000 manuscript pages of personal histories, word lists, myths, and accounts of rituals – an astonishing compendium of information (Fig. 6). (The references that we give to the notebooks should be understood as follows: the initial B or L indicates whether the notebook was compiled by Bleek or Lloyd. The first numerals are the numbers that Bleek and Lloyd assigned to the informants; the next numeral is the number of the notebook; the final numeral is the page number, the notebook pages being numbered consecutively through the whole series.)

3 /Xam San people whom the Bleek family interviewed in the 1870s.
Left: *Diä!kwain.* Right: *//Kabbo.* Below: *A group of /Xam prisoners at the Cape Town Breakwater Jail.*

Neither Bleek nor Lloyd was able to visit San people in their homeland. The colonial frontier conditions and Bleek's commitments in Cape Town did not allow for what would in any case have been a long and hazardous journey. There were therefore many aspects of /Xam daily life they were not able to observe. Nor were they able to see any rock paintings first-hand in the rock shelters where they were painted or engravings on open rock surfaces near waterholes. They had to depend entirely on copies made by other people.

After Bleek died in 1875, Lloyd continued with the work, eventually publishing *Specimens of Bushman Folklore* in 1911. It made public only small parts of the manuscript notebooks. By that time, Bleek's daughter Dorothea (1873–1948) had become involved in the work, and after Lloyd's death in 1914 she continued to publish sections of the vast manuscript collection. Dorothea died in 1948, bringing to an end one of the world's greatest ethnographic enterprises. Today the entire collection has been electronically scanned and is available to researchers worldwide.[20]

Joseph Millerd Orpen

The Bleek family's research received a considerable boost in 1874. In that year Joseph Millerd Orpen (1828–1923), a British representative in the Eastern Cape, sent a package to the editor of the *Cape Monthly Magazine* in Cape Town. He had co-led an expedition into southern Lesotho in an unsuccessful attempt to capture the renegade chief of the Hlubi, a sub-section of the Zulu nation. This man, Langalibalele (his name means Scorching Sun), had escaped over the Drakensberg escarpment into a maze of valleys and ranges that constitute the Maloti mountains of present-day Lesotho.

Orpen's package contained what became a key document in our understanding of the southern San belief system.[21] It told how he had met a young San man by the name of Qing, and how this man became his guide to a number of painted rock shelters, some 600 km (370 miles) to the east of where the Bleek family's informants lived.[22] Orpen also sent the editor copies that he had made of four rock paintings on which Qing had given fascinating if somewhat enigmatic comments (Pl. 14).

The editor sent the copies and, a few days later, the text of Orpen's article to Bleek, who, in turn, showed them to his /Xam informants. Immediately, new vistas opened up. Bleek was able to compare his informants' remarks with those that Orpen had recorded. He found that certain mythological figures were present in the tales of both regions, though the myths differed.[23]

A prominent part of the unity discernible between the /Xam collection and Qing's myths is the presence of the San trickster-deity. 'Cagn' is Orpen's Bantu-language transcription of the name that the Bleek family gave as '/Kaggen'. In his 'Remarks' on Orpen's article Bleek wrote that Cagn 'is not only the same as the chief mythological personage in the mythology of the Bushmen living in the Bushmanland of the Western Province, but his name has evidently the same pronunciation'.[24] Depending on the orthography used, the dental click can be given as a 'c' or as a solidus (/). We retain the two spellings of the name to distinguish between the being's appearances in Bleek's and Orpen's collections.

George William Stow

Another key figure in the study of San thought and rock art was also in contact with the Bleek family. He was George William Stow (1822–1882).

Stow came to South Africa from England in 1843 and eventually became a self-taught but respected geologist. He was well known in colonial intellectual circles. In the 1860s and 1870s, he developed an interest in the San and made many copies of rock paintings and engravings in what is now the region encompassed by the eastern Free State and the Eastern Cape provinces of South Africa. A large section of his book *The Native Races of South Africa*[25] is devoted to the San and, at the time of his death, he claimed he was collecting copies of rock paintings to include in a 'history of the manners and customs of the Bushmen, as depicted by themselves'.[26]

Bleek's first glimpse of Orpen's copies made him long to see 'that splendid collection of Bushman paintings which Mr. C. G. Stowe [sic] is said to have made'.[27] Bleek's wish was soon fulfilled, and a portion of Stow's collection arrived in Cape Town – sadly, just before Bleek died in 1875. After Stow's death in 1882, Lucy Lloyd purchased the entire collection from his widow. Continuing the work of her brother-in-law, she sought San comments on a number of Stow's copies.

Lloyd also obtained the manuscript of Stow's *The Native Races of South Africa*. She invited George McCall Theal, the Keeper of the Archives of the Cape Colony and Colonial Historiographer, to edit the huge manuscript. She also selected and prepared a number of Stow's copies of rock paintings and engravings for inclusion in the book. Theal remarked that 'they are reproduced by chromolithography, so that they are indistinguishable from the originals, except that most of them have been reduced in size'.[28] He could not have known that subsequent developments in printing techniques would, in the 21st century, lead to more accurate reproductions of Stow's copies (see Pls 16–18, 20; see Figs 7, 12, 17, 21, 46).[29] Much edited, Stow's book was published in 1905.

In the late 1920s Dorothea Bleek was faced with a dilemma. Lloyd had died in 1914, but the entire collection of Stow's copies of rock paintings had remained in the Bleek family unseen, except by specially privileged visitors to their home in Cape Town. Understandably, Dorothea was anxious to publish the rest of Stow's collection. Before doing so, she tried to track down the original paintings in the rock shelters where Stow had copied them over 60 years earlier, as have others since then.[30] For the most part she was successful in finding the sites, but others still remain lost. Once in the sites, Dorothea discovered that Stow had, in most instances, done a certain amount of re-arranging of the images to suit the size and rectangular shape of the paper on which he was reproducing them. She noted some of his interventions in her commentary on the plates in what became one of the great monuments of southern African rock art research: *Rock Paintings in South Africa: from Parts of the Eastern Province and Orange Free State, Copied by George William Stow, with an Introduction and Descriptive Notes by Dorothea F. Bleek.*[31]

Unfortunately, Stow's contribution to our understanding of San rock art has been misconstrued and has indeed become misleading. At the root of the problem is the failure of later rock art researchers to distinguish between the copies that he made, his comments on them and the further comments that Bleek and Lloyd elicited from their 19th-century /Xam San informants. In addition to rearranging images, Stow also omitted what we now know are highly significant paintings and deliberately or accidentally falsified other images to suit his preconceived ideas about the original narrative purpose of the art. Writers have used Stow's copies on the false assumption that they are accurate and that his comments on them derived from personal contact with San people.[32] In fact, he had next to no direct contact with indigenous interpretations of the paintings. By his own account, he thought that the art was a 'history' of the San people 'written' by themselves. In at least one instance he completely forged a copy to provide an illustration of a hunting practice that he believed the San must have depicted somewhere – if only he could find it. It purports to depict a man disguised as an ostrich; he appears to be hunting a flock of those birds. Stow inexplicably faked what is his most influential copy and thereby precipitated a modern-day *cause célèbre* that ranks alongside other infamous archaeological frauds.[33]

Knowing the problems posed by Stow's copies, one is tempted simply to ignore them. Researchers are, however, tied to them, because it was on these copies that the Bleek family obtained indispensable comments by San people. This is why we considered it essential to find the rock shelters whenever possible and to compare Stow's copies with the original paintings. Then, having checked Stow's copies in the actual rock shelters, we began to decipher what the informants said and to compare Bleek and Lloyd's transliterations with the /Xam San words that the informants used. This is how the three registers of our 'Rosetta Stone' are interconnected: taken together, they lead us into the thought world of the San.

Three registers

1: THE ART

Southern African rock art is more varied than this book may at first suggest. This is because we concentrate on San comments on San rock paintings and ignore other rock art traditions. The incoming Khoekhoe herders and the Bantu-speaking farmers also made their own rock art, though their sites are neither as prolific nor as widespread as those of the San.[34] Some researchers have investigated interaction between the San and other peoples and the ways in which this interaction may be reflected in the art.[35]

San paintings are found on the walls of open rock shelters (Pl. 4; Fig. 4). They are principally concentrated in the mountainous rim of the interior plateau: the Cederberg in the west and the Drakensberg and Maloti ranges in the east (Fig. 2). Fewer images, generally of a less fine kind, occur in the interior. As we shall see, the images found in the mountains comprise what we may (tendentiously) call 'realistic' images of animals and human beings, as well as a rich repertoire of more mysterious images. Often the human figures seem to be performing recognizable activities, such as walking in a line and dancing, and this has led researchers to follow Stow and mistakenly to consider the paintings a narrative of daily life.[36] This is one of the misconceptions that our decipherments of San comments on the art challenge.

It is difficult to date the paintings. We do, however, know that in certain parts of southern Africa they were being made up to the end of the 19th century. At the other end of the time scale, the oldest date that we have for images comes from southern Namibia: excavated pieces of stone with painted representational images were dated to 27,000 years BP.[37] More recent work

4 *A Drakensberg rock shelter in which the San painted many images. The peaks in the background reach 10,000 ft (3,000 m).*

based on AMS radiocarbon dating techniques has shown that depictions of eland antelope in the Drakensberg were being made about 2,900 years ago.[38] The images that we discuss in this book belong to this more recent period, that is, from about 3,000 years ago to the end of the 19th century.

The paintings were made with naturally occurring ochres, the colours of which could be altered by heating. Ochre and other pigments were mixed with various media that sometimes included animal blood and fat (Chapter 8). The paint was applied with a brush made from antelope hairs, or in some cases, with a finger. Much of the art is amazingly fine: many images are exquisite cameos. The head of an antelope, for instance, may be no larger than a single joint of a finger, yet the eye, mouth and ears are meticulously depicted (Pls 8–11; Fig. 5).

Apart from the paintings, there is also engraved San rock art – 'petroglyphs', as these images are sometimes known. They were either scored or pecked through the outer patina of rocks to leave a lighter-coloured image. Engraved rocks are found principally in the interior of the subcontinent.[39] They are scattered on low hilltops. We refer to them briefly in Chapter 3; later we consider the role they seem to have played in rain-making (Chapters 4 and 6). Quite different engravings depicting the settlement layouts of Bantu-speaking agriculturalists have also been found. They occur in the eastern parts of South Africa.[40]

In our Preface we acknowledged the doubtful use of 'prehistoric' to describe the statements of 19th-century San informants but nevertheless suggested that the art took us back into indisputably prehistoric times. Questions that now arise are: Did the meanings of specific categories of images change over time? How far back can we project 19th-century indigenous interpreta-

5 A fine example of a painted eland head. The artist has shown the mouth, nose, eye, tuft of red hair on the forehead and other details. The head, including horns, is approximately 10 cm (3.9 in) long. Colours: see Plate 9.

tions? In answer to these difficult questions, we can say that even though we can detect regional and stylistic differences, and changes in religious emphasis through time, the core religious ceremony – the healing, or trance, dance – is always present. Painted stones found in southern Cape and Drakensberg excavations and dated to around 2,000 years ago bear images of diagnostic dance postures that suggest the trance dance still observable in the Kalahari.[41] We discuss this dance in Chapter 2. Some of the dance images are indistinguishable from paintings on the walls of open rock shelters that have been dated stylistically to the last few hundred years.[42] The anthropologist Alan Barnard has written, 'As with all Bushmen, the medicine dance is the central rite of their religious practice.'[43] We suspect that, although there were temporal and regional variations in emphasis within the San rock art tradition,[44] the geographically widespread nature of the principal San ritual (the trance dance) and the dated southern Cape stones point to the high antiquity of the main San beliefs and rituals.

Contemplating the new, and often significantly more accurate, copies that we and others[45] have been able to make of the paintings that Stow copied, we wonder whether the Bleek family's San commentators would have said anything different if they had seen the originals in the rock shelters. On the other hand, do some of the striking images that they never saw because Stow omitted them actually confirm their interpretations? Generally, though not in every instance, we have found that it is now possible to construct more detailed explanations than those that the 19th-century San offered. These advances have been possible because researchers have been able to expand their knowledge of San thought exponentially since the middle of the 20th century by consulting the present-day Kalahari San and by detailed analysis of the Bleek and Lloyd Collection.

All in all, the detailed 'fit' between the art and what 19th-century San people said about the images and, moreover, their beliefs in general, demonstrate beyond reasonable doubt the relevance of those indigenous explanations to the rock art. Indeed, parallels between the 19th-century explanations and the painted images recall the complementarity between the registers of the Rosetta Stone.

2: SAN TEXTS

The 19th-century San texts that we decipher are key to our enquiry into the thinking of the San rock painters, but they pose many problems, more than we can discuss fully here. Questions arise concerning the informants themselves and the ways in which their explanations were recorded. We need to ask: Did the informants understand what they were being asked? Were they simply guessing? How can we judge the reliability of their comments? Did they have first-hand knowledge of rock art?

As we have seen, the /Xam informants who came from the Northern Cape were interviewed by Wilhelm Bleek and Lucy Lloyd. The work was laborious. Lloyd described how //Kabbo 'watched patiently until a sentence had been written down, before proceeding with what he was telling'.[46] She found that 'he much enjoyed the thought that the Bushman stories would become known by means of books'.[47] The informants soon adjusted to the unfamiliar circumstances of dictation. Lloyd wrote of Diä!kwain: 'It was difficult for him to dictate at 1st, which is probably why I could not get this properly and as he 1st told it to me. I have now heard again that this is the right story.'[48]

Today we cannot tell to what extent the manner of dictation affected what the /Xam people had to say. In their homeland, the tales were dramatized and acted out; the narrators could give free rein to their histrionic skills. Sitting in a Victorian suburban garden was a different matter altogether. The recording process was also punctuated with questions that Bleek and Lloyd put to the people. Unfortunately, those questions were not recorded, so we do not know to what extent the narratives were shaped by the recorders.

Some of the /Xam informants had worked for colonial farmers and had acquired Dutch names, but that contact seems to have been fairly recent. /Han≠kasso said that his father, Ssounni, 'possessed no Dutch name, because he had died before the Boers were in that part of the country'.[49] //Kabbo (whose acquired Dutch name was Jantje Toorn) still lived for part of the year at a waterhole called //Gubo or Blauputs, its recently acquired Dutch name. It had been 'owned' by his grandfather and father.[50] He still moved seasonally to another waterhole.[51]

When these people were shown copies of rock art, they never doubted that they were looking at pictures made by their own people. Diä!kwain made it clear that his father had made rock engravings of gemsbok (large antelope) and quagga (a type of zebra) at a place called !Kánn 'before the time of the boers'.[52] The Cape informants' familiarity with rock paintings, as distinct from rock engravings, was further attested by a myth that Lloyd obtained from /Han≠kasso. It begins thus:

Little girls they said, one of them said, 'It is //hára, therefore I think I shall draw a gemsbok with it.' Another said, 'It is tò therefore I think I will draw a springbok with it.' Then she said, 'It is hára therefore I think I will draw a baboon with it.'[53]

Clearly, /Han≠kasso was familiar with the practice of painting and, moreover, he had some knowledge of the ingredients used in the preparation of paint. /Hára is black specularite and tò red haematite.

In the region of the Maloti, we have no doubt that Qing was knowledgeable, though not omniscient. Orpen described him as a young man who had 'escaped from the extermination of their remnant of a tribe in the Malutis'. He was 'the son of their chief' and 'had never seen a white man but in fighting'.[54] Confused by what seemed to him muddled accounts of myths, Orpen blamed 'imperfect translation'. He was not able to record Qing's actual words phonetically, as did Bleek and Lloyd; we have only his summary translation. As we see in later chapters, however, we have new reasons for believing that not only was the translation reliable but also that Qing had an intimate knowledge of the beliefs and rituals of his people.

The Bleek family was in a better position. They had the ability to record the actual /Xam San words in phonetic script. But even that approach was not plain sailing. As we have seen, the Cape informants were familiar with the practice of making rock art, but they were unfamiliar with the conventions of the art of the more eastern regions of the subcontinent where Stow and Orpen worked and where the copies were made. Consequently, many of their explanations are puzzling and researchers have ignored them, believing the informants to be ignorant and uncomprehending. In turning away from these San explanations, researchers have missed a pivotal opportunity. The situation is paradoxical though not hopeless. To be sure, the copies are, to varying degrees, inaccurate and, moreover, the informants were unfamiliar with some of their conventions. Yet the comments that they offered drew on a fund of authentic San beliefs and practices, and indeed led Bleek and Lloyd into otherwise unknown areas of San belief. A central element of this book is therefore our attempt to draw a distinction between Stow's questionable work and the /Xam people's comments; we then extract otherwise missed information from the people's actual words. As we shall see, appropriately analysed, apparently opaque comments can afford valuable insights into the decipherment of San images.

One way of assessing an informant's explanations is to ask whether what he said illuminates *other* panels of images that (a) confirm the overall context of what is depicted and (b) expand what we learned from the informant's initial comments. In the recent case of a woman of San descent living in the Eastern Cape, we found that she described practices that are recorded in the San ethnography but about which she could not have known except by an authentic San tradition. Where her testimony paralleled what we know from other sources, she was able to expand our knowledge. At one point, however, she used what she said was her own San language but was in fact isiXhosa minus prefixes and suffixes. We must remember that informants are ordinary human beings who may enjoy the attention that researchers give them and the social distinction that remains with them after the researchers have departed. Being human, they sometimes try to please and to retain their hold on the researchers' interest.

We should also remember that, even as we speak to people in pre-literate societies, we change them: our questions sometimes direct them to aspects of their lives and contradictions in their beliefs about which they do not usually think. Furthermore, what they say in answer to our questions is sometimes shaped by what they think we want to hear or are in a position to comprehend. They may therefore filter out things that they themselves do not think necessary to understand. And, of course, they do not even mention things they consider so obvious that they cannot imagine anyone not knowing about them. Perhaps most importantly, scholars now point out that the so-called 'primitive societies' studied by anthropologists had long histories. We should not assume that such societies experienced no change for thousands of years: they were not human fossils.

Nevertheless, we should surely notice that, whatever changes people in recent so-called 'primitive societies' went through in their deep past, they remained within what we may loosely call a prehistoric framework until the time of their contact with the expanding West or other peoples. Even when this happens, and an important component of a society changes (say, its economy), it does not follow that the people's *entire* way of thinking changes. Writing of the Kalahari San, anthropologists Jacqueline Solway and Richard Lee make a significant point: 'The evidence for long-established trade relations between foragers and others has been glossed by some as evidence for the fragility of the foraging mode of production. But if it was so fragile, why did it persist?… The majority of the world's foragers are, for whatever reason, people who have resisted the temptation (or threat) to become like us.'[55] We should also remember that Christianity has lasted for 2,000 years, Judaism and Buddhism even longer. Christianity and Judaism persisted through the fall of the Roman Empire, the medieval period and the industrial revolution, yet, whatever happened around them, Christians and Jews steadfastly continued to believe in certain named supernatural beings and their interventions in daily human life. Change is complex. Major economic and political change beyond the ebb and flow of daily human relations is a piecemeal, stop-go process. It is a researcher's task to sort out what changed in the past and what did not. Both change and continuity in the past must be demonstrated, not simply assumed.

Ultimately, researchers have to consider each San explanation of a rock painting individually. Each must be analysed and assessed. None can be taken at face value.

3: ENGLISH TRANSLATIONS

The Bleek family was meticulous and tried to be 'scientific'. On the right-hand notebook pages Bleek and Lloyd used two columns, one for the phonetic transcription and one for the English transliteration. The left-hand pages were, for the most part, reserved for additional notes and explanations (Fig. 6).

At first, the informants assisted the process of translation by giving Cape Dutch words that they had learned. They also soon picked up some English. They thus had a foot in two worlds: they were thoroughly familiar with their own heritage, but they had also seen the encroaching Western way of life.

6 *A double page from one of Lucy Lloyd's notebooks (L.V.22); it is dated 21 June 1874. The right-hand page carries the phonetic /Xam text and an English transliteration. The entry concerns the capture of a 'water-cow'.*

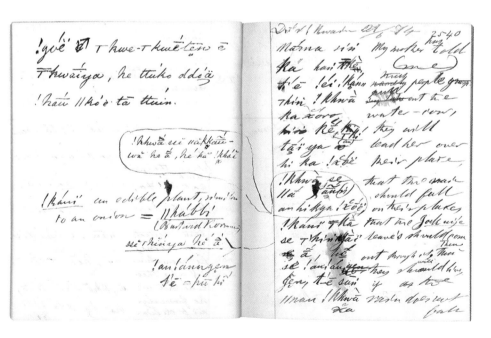

Finally, we must remember that Bleek and Lloyd were learning the /Xam language with its clicks and tones that are utterly unfamiliar to Westerners. One of the techniques they used to find the /Xam words for various things was to show the informants illustrated books, point to the things depicted and then ask for the relevant /Xam words. This sort of identification covered animals and different kinds of people. Bleek and Lloyd also took informants to the museum in Cape Town where they gave the /Xam words for various species. These strategies had a significant outcome. When they were shown copies of rock paintings, the /Xam were caught between identifying the things depicted and, as was sometimes more clearly the case, providing a summary of San beliefs about those things. In deciding between what needed mere identification and what called for more complex explanations and interpretations, some informants were caught in a dilemma. This seems to be why some comments are simple identifications of what is depicted, whereas others are, at least for our purposes, more interesting and complex.

Recurrent 'sorcery'

Overall, Bleek and Lloyd's informants gave what we may call prosaic identifications of images in the copies 12 times. It seems in these instances that they were responding in the same way that they had responded to other pictures which they had been shown to elicit the /Xam words for various things. They simply identified what they saw depicted and added nothing further.

By contrast, they referred more frequently to what the researchers called 'sorcery' than to anything else (Chapters 2 and 3). Along with 'sorcery', we include rain-making (Chapters 4 and 5). On four occasions they recalled a myth of which the copies reminded them; in two of these instances the myth involved the rain in a mystical way. In total, the informants referred to 'sorcery', rain-making and myths 15 times. This total shows that they did not see the art as a naïve narrative of daily life but rather as something with power and religious connotations. This is certainly the case with the first comment that we decipher. It helps us to grasp what Bleek and Lloyd meant by 'sorcery'.

CHAPTER 2

Dance of Life, Dance of Death

The people know that he is the one who always dances first,
because he is a great sorcerer.[1]

These simple yet evocative words are among the first San comments on rock paintings that we have chosen to decipher. They take us directly to the heart of the people's religious experience, belief and ritual. By comparison with the fascinating but enigmatic comments that we discuss in subsequent chapters, these words appear to be fairly straightforward and descriptive. They are none the less important. At the outset we therefore emphasize that the more puzzling comments to which we shall later come can be understood only in the context of the all-embracing San network of belief and ritual. Isolated, ad hoc attempts to understand what the informants were saying in their more convoluted explanations are doomed to failure and, worse, to the erroneous conclusion that they did not really know what they were talking about.

Even seemingly prosaic San explanations of rock paintings may have hidden depths. Always, we need to dig below the narrative surface of what they were saying by analysing the original texts word by word. Fortunately, in the instance with which we begin, we have not only an English translation of what the informant, a /Xam man named Diä!kwain, said but also the actual /Xam words that he used – unlike other instances in which only the translations and not the /Xam texts have been preserved. We can therefore explore nuances of meaning of which the 19th-century translators, unfamiliar as they were with the whole sweep of San thought, were unaware. They were groping their way into an unknown 'thoughtscape' on which we today have a wider perspective.

In 1930, Dorothea Bleek published a small portion of the first text we discuss and placed it alongside George William Stow's copy of the relevant rock painting. This juxtaposition of Diä!kwain's comments with a rock painting is valuable enough. But, if we go back to Lucy Lloyd's manuscripts, we find an extended verbatim /Xam language text that continues after the published portion. All in all, the full 20 pages of verbatim text provide information about San beliefs and religious practices that extends beyond what is depicted in the specific rock painting copy that Diä!kwain was shown. Indeed, as we proceed in subsequent chapters, we shall see that San thought and religious practices were not compartmentalized. The links between San ideas and ways of speaking that we detect as we decipher their words take us directly into ancient minds.

In 1875, when Lloyd wrote down Diä!kwain's explanations, she was compiling a text that Wilhelm Bleek and she herself struggled to understand. A century later, the situation changed. In the 1970s, Diä!kwain's /Xam words, combined with other evidence, led to profound changes in our understanding of what the painted images meant to those who made them and originally looked at and – importantly – used them. But at the time when Lloyd asked her informants about the paintings, Westerners considered many of the images on the walls of rock shelters utterly bizarre and incomprehensible. Puzzling images were ascribed to primitive naivety, not to complexity. Even when, in the 20th century, the Kalahari San plainly performed some of the rituals in their presence, Westerners did not notice the relationship between them and what was painted in the rock shelters.

The first clues came as long ago as the 1830s. The Protestant missionaries Thomas Arbousset and François Daumas were shocked to witness a San dance in what is now Lesotho. Somewhat grudgingly, Arbousset wrote, 'I could almost fancy that there may be mixed with it something of a religious rite, but I would not push this supposition too far.'[2] Indeed, he was more inclined to think of the dance as an 'amusement' or, satirically, as a 'ball':

This is the only amusement known to the Baroas [San]; it is only practised when they have eaten and are filled, and it is carried on in the middle of the village by the light of the moon. The movements consist of irregular jumps; it is as if one saw a herd of calves leaping, to use a native comparison. They gambol together till all be fatigued and covered with perspiration. The thousand cries which they raise, and the exertions which they make, are so violent that it is not unusual to see some one sink to the ground exhausted and covered with blood, which pours from the nostrils; it is on this account that this dance is called *mokoma*, or the dance of *blood*.

When a man falls thus out of breath in the middle of the ball, the women gather around him, and put two bits of reed across each other on his back. They carefully wipe off the perspiration with ostrich feathers, leaping backwards and forwards across his back. Soon the air revives him; he rises, and this in general terminates the strange dance.[3]

The tone of this description reflects the general colonial milieu in which Wilhelm Bleek and Lloyd worked: more than any other indigenous people the San seemed impervious to missionary endeavours. Their seemingly bloody rituals were little short of disgusting.

Yet, amid all this revulsion, it became clear that dancing was very important to the San. It was more than an 'amusement'. To be sure, they enjoyed dancing, but there seemed to be more to it than mere pleasure. George Stow found unmistakeable evidence for dancing in every camp and, significantly for our enquiry, every large rock shelter, the very locations where he found rock paintings:

The universality of this custom was shown by the fact that, in the early days, in the centre of every village or kraal, or near every rock-shelter, and in every great cave, there was a large circular ring where either the ground or grass was beaten flat and bare, from the frequent and constant repetition of their terpsichorean exercises.[4]

These dance circles, or ruts in the sand, are still found in the Kalahari, where they are frequently in the centre of a camp (Pl. 3). The San return to the same spot every time they hold a dance and their circular movements help to preserve the ruts for the duration of their stay in one place.

Dances and dancers

Today we know that what appeared to Arbousset and Daumas as chaotic and 'irregular jumps' was in fact a structured and meaningful ritual. This more perceptive understanding begins to emerge in what Diä!kwain said when he saw Stow's copy of a rock painting that used to be in a rock shelter near the small present-day town of Tarkastad (Fig. 7). Unfortunately, the original panel of images was destroyed in the 1970s when the rock was blasted away to widen a road. Stow's copy is all that remains. It shows a line of six human figures in rather ungainly postures; they lack the elegance and animation of so many San rock paintings. The leading figure carries a stick.

The actual /Xam words that Diä!kwain used are preserved in Lloyd's notebook numbered L.V.22.5755 (Fig. 8). The English translation that we now give, though prepared by Lloyd in 1875, was not published until 1930, when Dorothea Bleek included it in her selection of Stow's copies. There are some slight differences in punctuation between Dorothea's published transcription and the original notebook version, and the second parenthesis is in fact a note that Lloyd made on the adjacent page:

They seem to be dancing, for they stand stamping (?) with their legs. This man who stands in front (1st figure to the right of beholder) seems to be showing the people how to dance; that is why he holds a stick. He feels that he is a great man, so he holds the dancing stick, because he is the one who dances before the people, that they may

Nos. 1. 2. & 3
From Riet Poort - Tarka
5th April 1867
GWS

7 Above: *George Stow's 1867 copy of a rock painting showing a San dance. The human figures, rendered in black, are crudely done compared with most San rock paintings.*

8 Below: *The page in Lucy Lloyd's notebook that begins Diä!kwain's explanation of George Stow's copy of a painting showing a San dance (Fig. 7).*

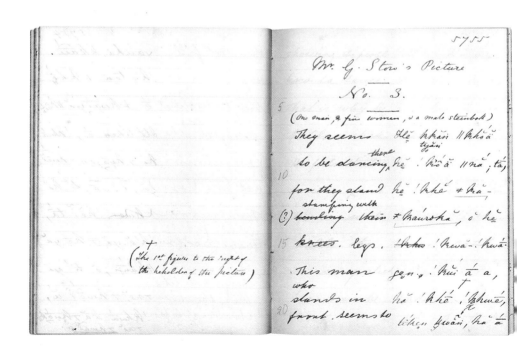

dance after him. The people know that he is the one who always dances first, because he is a great sorcerer. That is why he dances first, because he wants the people who are learning sorcery to dance after him. For he is dancing, teaching sorcery to the people. That is why he dances first, for he wants the people who are learning sorcery to dance as he does. For when a sorcerer is teaching us, he first dances the 'ken dance, and those who are learning dance after him as he dances.[5]

We begin by considering a number of /Xam words that are key to understanding not only this particular text but also San rock art in general: these words form the foundation for much of what we consider here and in later chapters.

The first is the word that Diä!kwain used to describe the man who is leading the dance: *!gi:xa*. Problematically, Lucy Lloyd translated it as 'sorcerer'. (She and Dorothea Bleek spelled the word 'sorceror'; we use the more acceptable spelling throughout.) In the 19th century, Western writers knew little about the religious specialists of other cultures. They therefore tended to transfer their own terms, such as 'priest' or 'magician', in inappropriate ways. By the middle of the 20th century, when anthropologists had studied many cultures around the world and a vast array of ethnography was available, the magical and derogatory connotations of 'sorcerer' were clearly unsuitable in the San context. By that time, too, the southern African San of the Kalahari Desert had become one of the most studied small-scale societies in the world, and an understanding of their religious specialists had advanced beyond anything that Bleek and Lloyd could possibly have achieved.[6]

Anthropologists of the 20th century used a number of English words to translate San words for religious specialists – though never 'sorcerer'. These words include:

- 'healers' (because one of their principal tasks was, and still is, curing the sick)[7]
- 'medicine people' (again, because they heal people)
- 'trancers' or 'trance performers' (because they perform their spiritual tasks in an altered state of consciousness)[8]
- 'shamans'. This Central Asian word seems appropriate because San practitioners use comparable techniques to perform a range of tasks similar to those performed by 'classic' Asian shamans.[9]

We need not now debate the relative merits of these terms; as the anthropologists who use them will readily admit, they are all unsatisfactory to some degree.[10] To avoid the repetition of click-laden words and to take cognizance of the commonality of such practitioners across the globe, we and other writers have used the word 'shaman' in many publications.[11] We do so again now without implying an exact equivalence with religious specialists in Central Asia. We merely mean a person who, on behalf of the community, enters an altered state of consciousness to heal the sick, see into the future, control the weather, visit the supernatural realm, and so forth. At the same time, the differences between San and Asian shamans are numerous, though we believe peripheral to the core activities that they perform. For instance, in Asia there is usually only one shaman per community, whereas among the San up to half the men and a third of the women in a camp may be shamans. Some older San women also become shamans. Then, too, Asian shamans use elaborate dress and paraphernalia, but San shamans dress like anyone else, though in the dance they wear rattles on their ankles and carry fly whisks. Despite these, we believe, minor differences, we have decided to retain the use of 'shaman' in this book.

As a way into the somewhat arcane religious beliefs locked up in the San text we have quoted, we begin by teasing apart the /Xam word that Diä!kwain used and that Lloyd translated as 'sorcerer': *!gi:xa*. Like an Egyptian cartouche, it is an amalgam of definable elements. The first syllable of *!gi:xa* requires close attention because an understanding of what it signifies is fundamental to San thought and, as we shall see, rock paintings. In her posthumously published *Bushman Dictionary* Dorothea Bleek defined *!gi:* as 'magic power, sorcery'.[12] The examples of its use that she provided are especially interesting because they show that *!gi:* can have both positive and negative connotations. We have added the square brackets:

> [T]he sorcerers [*!giten,* in this instance Lloyd omitted the colon] *are wont to say, they intend to take away my magic power [!gi:].*
>
> [T]hey worked sorcery [*!gi:*], and they killed my grandmother with sorcery [*!gi:*].[13]

In the first example, the 'sorcerers' may be dead rather than living. Certain dead 'sorcerers' were believed to become malevolent spirits; not all dead 'sorcerers' were necessarily evil. Either way, living or dead, their intention was to use their *!gi:* malevolently to rob the speaker of his own *!gi:*, which was presumably good and which he used for healing and protecting people. In the second example, *!gi:* is clearly used malevolently. The dictionary entry for *!gi:* also gives an example that refers to a specific kind of 'sorcerer': 'he had been a rain sorcerer (*!khwa:-ka !gi:xa*)'. We return to the idea of specialist 'rain sorcerers' in Chapters 4 and 5.

Today, we prefer to translate *!gi:* as 'supernatural potency', rather than Bleek's 'magic power, sorcery'. But what are its characteristics? A reading of the /Xam texts shows that *!gi:* is an invisible (at least to ordinary people) essence that resides in powerful animals, things and, significantly, certain people – those known as *!gi:ten*. They can manipulate it for benign or evil ends. In intense concentrations it can be dangerous and should be avoided. The anthropologist Lorna Marshall likened potency to electricity: it can be beneficial, but in intense concentrations it can be dangerous. At a trance dance, the women's sharp, rhythmic clapping activates potency. Some of that potency may come from a recently killed large animal, such as an eland (*Taurotragus oryx*), the antelope believed to have more potency than any other creature. In the Kalahari today, San people sometimes say that they are dancing 'eland potency'. In fact, their shamans individually claim to possess different kinds of potency. They say that their particular potency is giraffe potency, or honey potency, or sun potency, or, the most desired kind, eland potency. There is no discernible difference between these potencies, though San shamans readily acknowledge that some of them are more powerful than others. The name of the potency refers more to its source than its quality.

In addition to dancing after an eland kill, the southern San sometimes made rock paintings (Chapters 7 and 8). They took some of the animal's blood and mixed it into their paint. The painting itself then became a reservoir of potency to which dancing shamans could turn when they wished to increase the level of their potency.[14] The paintings were not merely pictures. Rather, many were potency-filled things that played a role in subsequent rituals.

The second syllable of the /Xam word *!gi:xa*, namely xa, means 'full of'.[15] In another example of this suffix, *!kwa:xa* means 'full of wrath', 'wrathful'.[16] A San *!gi:xa* is someone who is full of potency. The man leading the dance in Figure 7 was thus a *!gi:xa:* filled with supernatural power.

All San linguistic groups believe in the existence of supernatural potency and special people who can control it. Though there may be minor regional emphases, the overall concept is indisputably pan-San. The Kalahari Ju/'hoansi, for instance, call potency *n/om*, and speak of a *n/om k"au*, an 'owner' of *n/om* (pl. *n/om k"ausi*). The Nharo, another Kalahari group, speak of a *tsô.khùè*, the first syllable being their word for 'medicine' or potency.[17] Interestingly, despite considerable differences between the Kalahari Ju/'hoan and southern /Xam languages, the Ju/'hoansi use *!gi:xa* (*g!aeha* in Ju/'hoan orthography) to mean an especially powerful shaman, or *n/om k"au*, who routinely travels to the spirit realm and is known as a powerful healer. This is further evidence that not only the concepts but also some of the words used to denote them are spread over enormous distances.[18] Although the San words differ from language to language, they all refer to the same essence and the people who have the ability to manipulate it.

Nor need we doubt that the concept of potency and specialists who learn to control it is ancient: all the various San linguistic groups who made southern African rock art would certainly have embraced the general idea, if with minor regional and temporal emphases. Whether they expressed the concept in their rock art is another question altogether. Mere assertion will not do. As we shall see, all interpretations of rock art images must be supported by pointing to precise elements in the art and relating those images to the testimonies of the San themselves.

In his response to Stow's copy, Diä!kwain qualified *!gi:xa* by adding an epithet: *!kerri*. It means 'old', 'big', 'grown-up', 'great', as numerous other contexts of its use confirm.[19] In Diä!kwain's view the dance was thus being led by a *!gi:xa !kerri*, a special 'sorcerer', not just anyone.

Learning 'sorcery'

Exactly what sort of dance did the rock painter depict? What is the *!gi:xa !kerri* doing? Is this a dance merely for pleasure or is it more significant? Diä!kwain explained:

> For he is dancing, teaching sorcery to the people…. For when a sorcerer is teaching us, he first dances the 'ken dance, and those who are learning dance after him as he dances.

In the Kalahari today that is still exactly what happens. Young men wishing to become shamans dance behind a powerful older shaman.[20] They absorb potency from him and so learn to enter the altered state of consciousness we call trance – *!kia* (*!aia*) in the Ju/'hoansi language. An equivalent /Xam word does not seem to have been recorded. When a San shaman enters trance, he trembles violently and falls to the ground, sometimes cataleptic. His *!gi:* is said to 'boil' up his spine; climactically, his spirit is believed to leave his body via a 'hole' in the top of his head and go on out-of-body travel. Megan Biesele describes the transformation that a trancer experiences: 'Men who go into trance become able to contact the gods and the ancestors, who are suddenly visible to them beyond the circle of firelight.'[21]

When this happens, people say that the shaman has 'died'. The Nharo, for instance, use the word //ó (also //óa) to mean both 'to die' and 'to enter trance'.[22] In trance, a San shaman's spirit is believed to leave his body and to travel to the spirit world, just as it does in death. The only difference is that a shaman's spirit returns to his body. Everyone present agrees that the dance is performed to secure the life of the community and of individuals who may be ill, but in it the shamans 'die' to achieve this renewal of life.

In Lloyd's translation of Diä!kwain's statement we read that the dance depicted is a 'ken dance. In the manuscript, we see that the actual /Xam word that he used was //ke:n. In the version published alongside Stow's copy Dorothea Bleek substituted an apostrophe for the lateral click, probably because she felt that readers would find the click too difficult to pronounce. What does //ke:n mean? The /Xam people from whom Bleek and Lloyd obtained so much information used three words with closely related, if not identical, meanings: !gi: (which we have already discussed), //ke:n and /ko:öde. In the *Bushman Dictionary*, Bleek translated //ke:n as 'magic, sorcery' and /ko:öde as 'magic things, magic doings, magic power'.[23]

Are the three words synonyms? This is a difficult question. The only way we can answer it is to examine the contexts in which /Xam people used the words. We give two examples. In a passage that deals with the death of a /Xam shaman, Diä!kwain said that 'our mothers' had taught them about this potency. He continued:

> *He takes the magic power [/**ko:öde**], he shoots it back to the place where people are. For the people are those whom he wants to take away with his sorcery [//**ke:n**], for the thought of them while he was among men … a sorcerer is a being who when he dies, wishes to fall heavily taking his sorcery [!**gi:**].*[24]

Here, it seems that the three words were interchangeable. In another context, Diä!kwain used two of the words when he was speaking about locusts, a desired food that was drawn into the web of mystical things. He said that shamans control the appearance of locusts. They:

> *charm them with magical doings [//**ke:n-ka didi**] … locusts only go about because of magical doings [/**ko:öde**].*[25]

In this sentence, //k:en and /ko:öde appear to be synonyms. Even though in some instances the phonetic /Xam language transcriptions of the informants' comments cannot now be traced (if indeed they ever existed), we can be sure that they used one of the three words we have discussed: !gi:, //k:en and /ko:öde.

Bleek and Lloyd's 'sorcery', then, is the manipulation of supernatural potency for a variety of ends, some good, some malign. Whichever word people used, potency was an invisible essence that permeated the San world and that people struggled to control.

We can now enquire more closely about what Diä!kwain called the //ke:n dance. He used the phrase '!kōä //ke:n', that is, 'dances //ke:n'; the word !kōä means 'to dance, tread or step'.[26] In the Kalahari, we can still observe potency being activated by 'stamping' dance steps. There is, however, much more to the dance than 'stamping'.

The 'dance of blood'

We do not have to rely entirely on Diä!kwain's comments on Stow's copy. In the same general region of southern Africa that Arbousset and Daumas visited, but nearly 30 years later, the young San man named Qing told Joseph Orpen about this dance. Qing's description makes an interesting comparison with what the two missionaries saw and what Diä!kwain independently said. Like Diä!kwain, Qing was not just describing a social custom; he, too, was responding to rock paintings. Indeed, it is important to notice that both Diä!kwain and Qing linked the rock paintings on which they were asked to comment to the dance.

For the present, we need note that Qing described some key features of the dance and then went on to give one of the reasons why the people perform it:

> It is a circular dance of men and women, following each other, and it is danced all night. Some fall down; some become as if mad and sick; blood runs from the noses of others whose charms are weak, and they eat charm medicine, in which there is burnt snake powder. When a man is sick, this dance is danced round him, and the dancers put both hands under his arm-pits, and press their hands on him, and when he coughs the initiated put out their hands and receive what has injured him – secret things.[27]

In sum, Qing said that the design and intentions of the dance were that:
 – It was circular.
 – It healed people by laying hands on them.
 – Dancers fell down in what we call a trance.
 – The noses of the dancers bled.

In the Kalahari today medicine dances are still circular (Pl. 3; Fig. 9). Although Diä!kwain did not mention a circular form, we wonder whether the

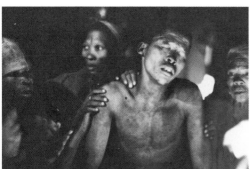

9 Ju'/hoan San trance, or healing, dances photographed in the Kalahari Desert in the 1950s. The leading man carries a stick in both photographs. In the upper photograph a man carries a fly whisk and is being restrained. The dance rut in the sand can be seen in both photographs. Left: A San man in trance.

line of dancers in Stow's copy, and indeed in many other rock paintings of people in a long line, was a way of depicting a circular dance without using perspective. In a Kalahari dance and in Qing's account people dance one behind the other and this pattern could be represented by a line of painted figures. Qing spoke of men and women following one another. For the most part, Kalahari women sit around a central fire as the men, shamans and ordinary men as well, circle around them in groups of half a dozen or so; only a few women sometimes join the line of dancing men for a short while before returning to their places.

In the Kalahari, a central fire is considered essential to a dance. Its heat activates potency and contributes to the 'boiling' of potency up the spines of the shamans as they enter trance. Around the fire, the tight circle of seated women provides the clapping of the complex rhythms of 'medicine songs'. Like the central fire itself, the songs, too, contain potency and are named after the 'strong' things we have mentioned – eland, honey, sun, gemsbok, giraffe and so forth.[28] The men, up to half of whom may be shamans, dance in a circle, now clockwise, now anticlockwise: it is their pounding steps that make the rut in the sand.

Overall, the Kalahari San dance is a nest of concentric circles. Around the fire, the seated women are in a circle. Around them, the men dance in a circle. And beyond them spirits of the dead lurk in the encircling darkness where the firelight does not reach. In the centre are activated potency and healing, beyond, in the darkness, are malevolent spirits of the dead who seek to shoot 'arrows of sickness' into people.

When they begin to enter trance, Kalahari San shamans take the sweat from their armpits and rub it on people, just as, speaking of San in the south-eastern mountains, Qing himself described. Everyone is cured: the San believe that physical, mental and social ills may be in a person without that person being aware of it. Through their fluttering hands, they draw the sickness out of those whom they are curing and into their own bodies. Finally, with a shriek, the shamans expel the sickness from their bodies via a supposed 'hole' at the nape of the neck. Only shamans can see the sickness flying back to the spirit realm whence it came.[29] It is reasonable to conclude that paintings showing sickness being expelled (Pl. 12, Fig. 10), and other things that only shamans can see, were probably painted by shamans themselves who were depicting their own religious experiences. The paintings showed ordinary people what they could not themselves see, and presented novice shamans with what they could expect to see.

10 A San rock painting (with inset tracing) showing a man who has fallen to his knees in a trance dance. He has hoofs in place of feet. He bleeds from the nose, and sickness, invisible to ordinary people, can be seen leaving the back of his neck. Uniquely, he holds what appears to be a head or skull. Colours: dark red, white.

One of Qing's most striking statements concerns what was, for the San, a powerful substance: '[B]lood runs from the noses of others whose charms are weak.' Decades earlier, Arbousset and Daumas also referred to the importance of blood; they wrote: '[I]t is on this account that this dance is called *mokoma*, or the dance of *blood*.'[30] Many readers have wrongly concluded that *mokoma* means 'dance of blood'. It seems that the missionaries, too, may have misunderstood the SeSotho word *mokoma*. (SeSotho is the language spoken by the Basotho Bantu-speaking people; *mokoma* is not a San word.) It does not mean blood. In modern orthography *mokôma*, or *mokômê*, means 'great physician or doctor'.[31] The dance may have been popularly known as 'the dance of *blood*', but the Basotho recognized that it was a healing dance. Their word *mokoma* shows not only that the dance featured specialist healers but also that the Basotho people themselves held San healers in high regard.

What then was the function of blood in the dance? The southern San believed that blood kept sickness at bay. A shaman therefore smeared his nasal blood on the people whom he was healing. A /Xam shaman said, '[H]e (the sorcerer) thinks, that other magic things may again come to kill the man, therefore he anoints the man with the blood of his nose.'[32]

In the continuation of his account of Stow's copy (the Lloyd notebook pages that Dorothea Bleek omitted), Diä!kwain gave more information about a 'sorcerer's' blood:

> When a sorcerer is teaching us, when his nose bleeds, he sneezes the blood from his nose into his hand, he makes us smell the blood from his nose, for he wishes its scent to enter our gorge (?), that our gorge may feel as if it were rising, because the blood of his nose is making it rise. And when the blood has made our gorge rise, our gorge feels cool, as if water which is cold were in it. For however hot a place may be, the blood from a sorcerer's nose feels like cold water, because he is a sorcerer he is cold.[33]

Here, it is clear that potency was believed to reside in a 'sorcerer's' blood. The novice obtains potency from his mentor via his blood. Mention of a person's 'gorge' is interesting. The Ju/'hoansi speak of the *gebesi*, the stomach and diaphragm that contract painfully when shamans enter trance – a function of their 'boiling' potency. This causes them to bend their torsos over at right angles to their legs. When one of us (David Lewis-Williams) was in the Kalahari with the anthropologist Megan Biesele in 1974, a Ju/'hoansi man explained this point. He adopted the bending-forward posture and, in addition, held his arms in a backward position. He said that this position is adopted 'when *n/om* is going into your body, when you are asking God for *n/om*'.[34] The position is important, though not sustained for long. Significantly, there are many rock paintings of men in just this posture (Fig. 11). It depicts the transitional moment when a shaman crosses over into the spirit realm.

As we have pointed out, the present-day Ju/'hoansi experience a rising sensation starting in the stomach or lower spine at the onset of trance. A century earlier, Diä!kwain gave his own understanding of this sensation. He told Lloyd that it seemed as if a shaman's 'vertebral artery would break', and that when a shaman was experiencing out-of-body travel his 'vertebral artery has risen up'.[35] Here we again run into the problem of translating San words into

11 *San dancers in the arms-back posture adopted when asking God for supernatural potency. The tracing shows a part-antelope, part-human figure in the same posture. Colours: dark red, white.*

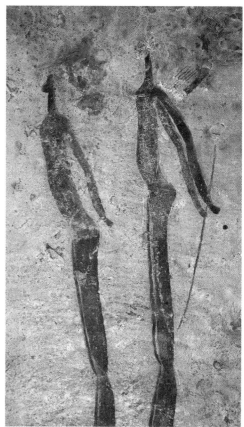

English. Lloyd's translation of the /Xam word *!khāūä* as 'vertebral artery' was probably an error arising from her lack of familiarity with San trance rituals and experiences. In trying to explain the word to Lloyd, Diä!kwain probably ran his hand up and down his spine, and, possibly, spoke about his blood heating up. Used as a verb (as many /Xam nouns can be), the word *!khāūä* means 'to boil'.[36] It was probably the southern San's metaphor to describe the rising sensation experienced in the region of the spine as a shaman goes into trance. The identical 'boiling' metaphor is still used by the Ju/'hoansi. Small wonder, then, that Richard Katz entitled his book about Ju/'hoan healing *Boiling Energy*.[37]

Caps and respect

These ideas about San shamans and what they experience when they enter trance are complex enough, but Diä!kwain enlarged on them when he commented on another painting. It is in a site in the Eastern Cape Province (Fig. 12). We have checked Stow's copy, which he made on two sheets of cartridge paper, against what remains of the original. Although almost everything else in the shelter has been badly damaged, Stow's copy can be seen to be reasonably accurate in most regards. As he copied it, the panel comprises a scatter of 31 images. Many of them appear to have antelope heads. Some are women. Lloyd's phonetic transcription of Diä!kwain's comments shows that the published English version is reliable.[38] Although he explicitly refers to the *//ke:n* dance, he speaks of rather puzzling pieces of clothing and concepts: 'caps', 'rings' and 'respect':

12 *Half of George Stow's copy of a rock painting of people who 'mean to tread the 'ken'. Some wear antelope head caps. The bodies of others fuse with antelope heads. Colours: dark red, black, yellow ochre.*

The things which the people here have put on are caps which they have made for
themselves of young gemsboks' heads. They have cut the horns out: they mean to
tread the 'ken with them. At the time when they do the 'ken they wear such caps.
The rings which they have put on are the 'ken's rings. They do this when they mean
to try us, they put on this dress because they want to see whether we shall laugh at
them. That is why they put on such things, for they intend to observe us, to see if we
are people who laugh at a person who is different. That is why they do this; they have
dressed themselves up oddly for us, for they wish to see if we know manners. And if
we do not laugh at them, they talk to our people about it. They say 'Do you know
that the children whom we see do not mock us? It seems as if they knew manners,
for they show respect to us. We had just put on things about which we thought that
they would laugh at us.'[39]

The key point to notice here is that Diä!kwain again identified the group as
a *//ke:n* dance, even though they are not shown dancing in a line or circle:
'They mean to tread the 'ken' (*!kōä //ke:n*). It is possible that various choreo-
graphies were followed.[40] Significantly, Diä!kwain says nothing about hunting
disguises, a common explanation that researchers have advanced for human
figures that seem to have antelope heads. This painting is one of the exceptional instances in which the figures are clearly wearing some sort of
headdress. Most comparable paintings show the antelope head blending in a
non-realistic way with the human body (Fig. 13).

The making of caps with antelope ears or small horns was a practice
adopted by /Xam shamans (Fig. 14). People believed that a springbok would
follow a shaman wearing such a cap and lead the whole herd into the hunters'
ambush.[41] It is not clear whether this supernatural hunting practice is explicitly illustrated in the painting that we are discussing. The large number of
figures apparently wearing horned caps seems to count against this interpretation. On the other hand, Diä!kwain indisputably related the wearing of the
antelope caps to the *//ke:n*, or trance, dance. It therefore seems likely that, in
this painting, the wearing of antelope caps referred in some way to harnessing
antelope potency and guiding antelope herds, not to hunting disguises.

The 'rings' to which Diä!kwain referred may have been merely decorative,
though they were clearly considered important and he called them the *//ke:n*'s
rings. In an additional note,[42] he explained that they were made from an edible
root called *//gwi*.

More puzzling is Diä!kwain's claim that the dancers want to see whether
the people will laugh at them. What could he have meant? Today, there is often
much laughter at a San trance dance, particularly in its early stages. Children

13 Opposite above: An antelope-headed figure bleeds from the nose. He is wearing an antelope skin kaross painted in white and has an extra finger. Colours: dark red, white.

14 Opposite below: A bowman wearing a cap with antelope ears. He has sectioned arrows thrust between his back and his kaross. A quiver slung over his shoulder holds the arrows in place. Colours: dark red, yellow ochre, white.

sometimes weave in and out of the dancers, mimicking them. No one seems to care. We suspect that what Diä!kwain had in mind here was not this sort of relaxed behaviour but rather an outright rejection, or ridiculing, of the shamans' abilities. Indeed, some /Xam shamans complained that they did not receive the respect that was their due. For instance, Diä!kwain said that shamans who specialized in making rain (Chapters 4 and 5) complained that people soon forgot that in times of drought they had been begging the rain shamans to help them: 'That is why the medicine men will not always make rain fall for them.'[43]

Respect and respectful behaviour were valued by the San, but they did not express respect in a way that Westerners would find appropriate. Being a shaman was no joking matter: on the contrary, it was a dangerous business. In a continuation of the passage about the 'great sorcerer' leading the line of dancers, Diä!kwain explained:

> *A man who is a sorcerer takes care of himself, because he is a sorcerer.... For other sorcerers will kill him, if he does not take care of himself, when he meets them.... As he is lying asleep, they come upon him sleeping there.... That is why we sometimes hear a sorcerer shivering at night; when other sorcerers come to him, then he shivers because the others want to see whether his veins are still alive.*[44]

These threatening 'sorcerers' may be either dead shamans or shamans on out-of-body travel from another camp. In San thought, evil and sickness come from outside the immediate community. The protective shivering (*!khauken*) of which Diä!kwain spoke is the trembling that a /Xam person experienced when in trance.[45] It is a central component of San trance experience. In the statement about the shaman who lies asleep, he trembles (that is, enters trance while he is asleep) to protect himself. For the San, sleep and trance are not clearly distinguished from one another. Both states take a person into the spirit realm.

Fragments of the dance

So far we have discussed rock paintings of trance dances that are fairly complete. We therefore need to emphasize a key point that modern Westerners easily overlook when they try to decipher a complex rock art panel of many images, all apparently jumbled together (Pls 5, 20, 21, 25). San rock art is not a faithful, photographic, representation of daily life. To be sure, there are depictions of many items that everyone encounters in daily life, such as bows and arrows and animals. But these items are often arranged next to one another in unrealistic juxtapositions. Sometimes, one finds depictions of bows, bags and fly whisks quite separate from human beings, or small depictions of people next to large paintings of eland. Clearly, the whole panorama of images in an extensive panel was not intended to be a realistic 'set piece'. We have explained how some images were reservoirs of potency rather than simply 'pictures'.

Now, we point out one of the non-realistic ways in which painters referred to the trance dance. We call it synecdoche – a part stands for a whole.[46] Often, painters depicted only single human figures in recognizable dancing postures. Although the trance dance was central to San religion, depictions of complete dances are fairly rare. Instead, painters deployed what we call 'fragments of the dance'. These include:

- human figures bending forward at the waist as their potency boils and their gebesi contracts (Fig. 15a, c)
- blood falling from the nose of a figure (Fig. 15b)
- figures in an arms-back dancing posture in which shamans ask god for more potency (Fig. 15c)
- clapping figures that activate potency (Fig. 15d)
- fly whisks that people use only in the dance (Fig. 15a, e)
- dance rattles (Fig. 15c)

Sometimes only one of these fragments, say, a person bleeding from the nose, may be part of a group of people. Its presence clearly implicates the whole group: they are all, though perhaps in different ways, implicated in what the dance means to the San. Similarly, a fragment of the dance, say a single woman clapping, positioned in the midst of a number of depictions of eland, is appropriate in a conceptual rather than a realistic way. In this example, the fragment links people to animals in the context of the dance: the clapping woman can be seen as activating the potency of eland. Westerners tend to seek clear, unambiguous, comprehensive depictions of the dance and, as a result, are often misled into thinking that the dance rarely occurs in San

15 *Fragments of the dance. (a) The bending forward posture and fly whisks. (b) Bleeding from the nose. (c) The bending forward posture and dancing rattles. (d) Women in the clapping posture. (e) An unrealistic cluster of fly whisks. Colours: dark red, bright red, black, white.*

rock art. But this rock art is more subtle and allusive than that. By synecdoche, beliefs and experiences associated with the dance and its trans-cosmological implications permeate the art.

From this perspective, the line of dancing figures on which Diä!kwain commented and that we discussed at the beginning of this chapter is itself a

fragment of the dance (Fig. 7). There are no clapping women or other partici-
pants, but Diä!kwain nevertheless knew that it was a depiction of a dance.
Because novices are taught how to enter the spirit realm at a normal trance
dance (at least in the Kalahari today), we conclude that the painter extracted a
fragment from the larger ritual (in which all people, men, women, children,
participate) in order to highlight one particular component – the role of male
shamans. Whether Diä!kwain was right or not to go further and single out the
teaching of novices, what he and other San people had to say about the trance
dance clearly establishes its overall importance in San thought.

We have still only scratched the surface of San experience, belief and ritual.
The more obscure explanations for rock paintings that San people offered
take us deeper into what are for many Westerners mysterious realms. As we
have begun to show, the keys to those realms lie in deciphering ancient San
words and rock paintings. The words are not unproblematic explanations
that we can read like an English-language text. Rather, the words and the rock
paintings must be seen in tandem: they illuminate one another. As the next
chapters show, the 'things and deeds of sorcery' are indeed multiple and
complex.

CHAPTER 3

'These are sorcery's things'

We began to climb the thread – it was the thread of the sky![1]

When Diä!kwain commented on the line of dancers depicted in Stow's copy of a rock painting (Fig. 7), Lucy Lloyd translated his key /Xam word as 'sorcery'. As we saw in Chapter 2, this English word is misleading because of its modern connotations of 'black magic'. To build a fuller understanding of what Diä!kwain meant we now need to decipher some more of the actual /Xam San words and phrases that he used.

The /Xam phrase that Lloyd translated as 'sorcery' is *!gi:-ta didi*. Like an ancient Egyptian cartouche, it can be broken down into its constituent parts. As we saw in Chapter 2, *!gi:* is the supernatural potency that underwrites so much of San religious experience, belief and practice. The suffix *-ta* (in some instances, *-ka*) forms the possessive. As a verb, *di*, with various particles, means 'to do, act, work, make, become or happen'.[2] As a noun, *didi* is a reduplicative plural meaning 'doings, actions or deeds'.

Another of the words denoting supernatural potency that we examined in Chapter 2 is *//ke:n*. It, too, can be combined with *di* or *didi* to mean acts performed by *!gi:ten*, Lloyd's 'sorcerers'. The /Xam phrase is *//ke:n-ka didi* ('the doings of sorcery').[3] We can find no instance of an informant combining */ko:öde*, the third word meaning potency, with *di*. We are therefore unsure whether */ko:öde* had slightly different connotations from the other two words that made it impossible for it to be combined with *didi*, or whether the informants simply did not happen to use that combination in the conversations that they had with Wilhelm Bleek and Lucy Lloyd. Be that as it may, it is clear that *!gi:-ta didi* and *//ke:n-ka didi* meant the manipulation of supernatural potency by performing various deeds, what we today call rituals.

'Sorcery' also involved 'things'. These 'things' could be either material or conceptual. Material 'sorcery's things' included, and in the Kalahari still include, small bags or tortoise shells used to contain substances believed to be imbued with supernatural potency (Fig. 16). In the early 1920s, Dorothea Bleek found that Nharo San women carried small tortoise shells filled with

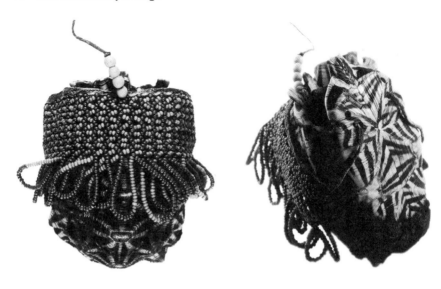

*16 A tortoise shell decorated with beads. These are used to contain potent substances.
They are carried in the trance, or healing, dance, as is shown in Figures 31 and 32.
Colours of beads: blue and orange.*

buchu; the Nharo gave the name *buchu* to a category of about a half dozen aromatic herbs.[4]

The conceptual things involved in 'sorcery' included the small, invisible 'arrows of sickness' that malevolent Kalahari shamans are still believed to shoot into people. It was the task of benevolent shamans to draw these pathogenic 'arrows' out of people, either during a trance dance or, if a person is very ill, at a 'special curing' performed by a single shaman who enters trance without the support of clapping women. Then there were what the San call 'threads of light'. In trance, shamans not only see but also engage with these iridescent lines. We will consider them in more detail in a moment.

'A sorcerer's thing'

This preamble about San words and concepts begins to throw light on somewhat enigmatic comments that Bleek and Lloyd's informants made on the two Stow copies that are the principal focus of this chapter. We deal with them one at a time.

Today what little remains of the images in Figure 17 shows that Stow captured the main elements, though he compressed them vertically so that they would fit on his sheet of cartridge paper. There are also the faint remains of various other images that he ignored; today they are so faint as to be beyond comprehensive recording. At first we suspected that the broad 'path' might in fact be a remnant of a painted snake, the rest of the image having faded before Stow visited the site. But, at least as it is today preserved, there is no sign of either a head or a tail, so we cannot be sure that it was indeed part of a snake image. We therefore take Stow's copy at face value. Overall, we can be confident that, as far as its individual images and general relationships are concerned, Stow's copy is accurate enough for our purposes. In any event, it was on Stow's copy that the informant commented, not on the actual rock painting.

Unfortunately, we do not have the original /Xam phonetic text relevant to Figure 17, as we do for that on Figure 7. The 'explanation by a Bushman' that Dorothea Bleek published seems less flowing than Diä!kwain's remarks on

17 George Stow's copy of a rock painting that a /Xam informant said was 'a sorcerer's thing'. Curiously, the central figure was said to depict 'the female Mantis'. Colours: dark red, black, white.

Figure 7 and may suggest a different informant. A more likely explanation is that the circumstances under which Lloyd obtained the comments and noted them down may well, on that occasion, have been less conducive to expansive comment than those in which she transcribed the comments on Figure 7. Either way, in the case of Stow's copy shown in Figure 17, we have what appears to be Lloyd's paraphrase or perhaps an even later, pre-publication, paraphrase by Dorothea in which she inserted a parenthetical remark:

> *A sorcerer's thing (said of the white path-like appearance). Men in the middle and two women at the bottom of the picture. The figure with animal's head said to be the female Mantis.*

Despite the problems concerning the recording of these remarks and their preparation for publication, this 'explanation' contains two key San concepts that we can elucidate with the help of other passages in the Bleek family manuscripts. They are:

– 'A sorcerer's thing'
– 'the female Mantis'

Remarkably, these two concepts appear to be the two sides of a single coin in this particular context.

First, the informant spoke of 'A sorcerer's thing'. As the parenthesis makes plain, he was referring specifically to the 'path-like' motif, the broad, undulating white band with a red line on its lower side: clearly, he did not think that it was an ordinary path through the veld. As the parenthesis implies, the notion of a path was introduced by either Lucy Lloyd or Dorothea Bleek. Nevertheless, five human figures seem to be moving along it, three towards the right and two towards the left. But they and those below the 'path' are not in the commonly depicted walking postures in which lines of unidirectional figures are often painted (Fig. 18): the figures in the copy are in postures more akin to those of dancers. We suspect that the informant's invocation of 'sorcery' was triggered, at least in part, by what he took to be a painting of dancing people. Because he situated the images in the realm of 'sorcery' – the manipulation of supernatural potency – it is there that we must look for further insights.

It seems likely that the informant thought that the 'thing' to which he was referring was one of the conceptual 'threads of light' that San shamans say they see in trance – that is, in the spirit realm that they reach by activating potency. When we listen to San people talking about things like 'threads of light', it would be easy for us to pass over what they say as fanciful or perhaps

18 A procession of striding human figures. Most wear skin cloaks; some carry quivers and bows. Colour: dark red.

merely, and vaguely, 'mythological'. There is, however, much more to it. 'Threads of light' lead us to the centre not just of San religious beliefs but to the actual generation of some of those beliefs.[5] To understand how this particular San belief was formed, we need to leave mythology for a moment and turn to another discipline altogether.

Neuropsychological laboratory research has shown that bright undulating lines, sometimes reminiscent of a spider's web, at other times less ordered, are a type of entoptic phenomenon, that is, a visual hallucination produced by the structure and functioning of the human brain when it enters certain altered states, such as trance.[6] These lines and other geometric forms (e.g., zigzags, grids and flecks) differ from religious visions (e.g., those in the Christian tradition that include, say, the Virgin Mary) in that they derive not from the cultural milieu of the visionary but from the neurological structure and electro-chemical functioning of the human brain.

An interesting aspect of entoptic phenomena is that people sometimes feel that they are blending with the geometric forms.[7] The psychologist Richard Katz asked Ju/'hoan shamans and men who had never experienced trance to draw self-portraits. The ordinary people drew stick figures while the shamans'

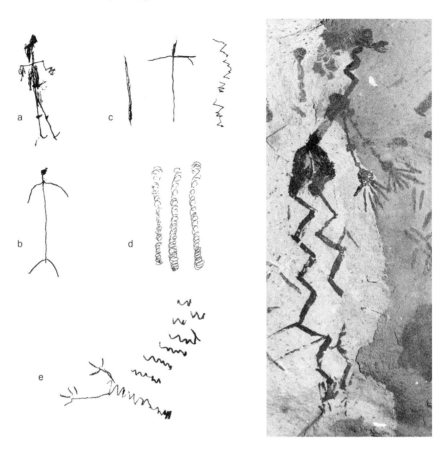

19 Richard Katz asked ordinary Kalahari San people and trance dancers to draw pictures of themselves. (a) and (b) are drawings made by ordinary people. (c), (d) and (e) are drawings made by trance dancers to show how they conceive of their bodies. The Drakensberg rock painting on the right depicts a comparable self-conception. Colour of rock painting: dark red.

drawings 'violate the ordinary rules of anatomy: as the body lines become fluid, body parts become separated' (Fig. 19).[8] This experience is seen in a San painting of a man with zigzag legs and neck (Fig. 19).

The ways in which visionaries understand zigzags, bright lines and other geometric entoptic forms is, of course, culturally controlled. They take them to be something for which their particular religious tradition has prepared them. *All* people who enter altered states of consciousness have the potential to see these iridescent lines simply because they are generated by the human brain. On the other hand, people do not *necessarily* see or value them. In some traditions people ignore the lines and other geometric forms as 'noise' that intervenes before they experience 'true' visions. That San *!gi:ten*, who strive to enter trance in medicine dances and other circumstances like special curings, report seeing these visual percepts should therefore come as no surprise. Indeed, shamans around the world report seeing iridescent geometric forms.[9] The San are no exception.

Shamans in most San groups speak about engaging with bright 'threads of light' when they are in an altered state of consciousness. Indeed, the ethnographic evidence is abundant.[10] It is reasonable to conclude that the 'threads' of which they frequently speak are the widely reported, neurologically created incandescent lines seen in some altered states. That much is straightforward and indisputable. The important question is: how do the San understand what they see?

In some instances, they speak of these 'threads' as if they were a path. Bleek and Lloyd's informant //Kabbo, himself a 19th-century /Xam San shaman,[11] spoke of 'a Bushman's path' that led to a hole in the ground: at death, people followed this path to the spirit realm.[12] A 21st-century Ju/'hoan shaman, Cgunta /kace:, similarly spoke of following one of these threads or paths to 'a big hole' leading to the spirit world: 'My teacher showed me the line to the underground hole.'[13] In the 1960s, other Ju/'hoan shamans told Katz that, having entered trance (!aia) they follow a path to an opening through which they enter the spirit realm.[14] To gain access to this 'path' they 'slip out of their skins'.[15] Trans-cosmological travel involves transformation.

Old K"xau, another Ju/'hoan shaman, told Megan Biesele what happens after shamans pass through the hole:

When we emerged, we began to climb the thread – it was the thread of the sky.... When I emerge I am already climbing, I am climbing threads that lie over in the South.... I climb one and leave it, then I go climb another one. Then I leave it and climb on another. Then I follow the thread of the wells, the one I am going to enter![16]

The experience of going down into a hole seems to transmute into the experience of rising up into the sky.

The Ju/'hoansi explain that they also walk or glide along these 'paths'. On the other hand, if they take them to be cords or ropes, they say that they climb them on their way to the supernatural realm in the sky. There they meet and entreat ≠Gao N!a, the great god. The Harvard musicologist Nicholas England learned that the great god sometimes facilitates travel to his place in the sky by letting 'down a cord to assist the soul's ascent'.[17] The lesser god //Gāuwa also 'moves from the sky to the ground and across the veld on invisible fibres which criss-cross the surface of the veld like a spider's web'.[18] The fact that different shamans speak of either holding or walking along the 'threads of light' does not imply confusion or contradiction. There is a measure of idiosyncrasy in the ways in which individual San shamans interpret the visual products of their nervous systems.

Some shamans speak of engaging with the threads of light in dreams. Sometimes a thread breaks, and a climber falls to earth: 'His body at home will just sleep.' Meanwhile the marooned shaman has to wait until it is dark again. He then makes his way back to his camp.[19] But usually the threads hold. A Ju/'hoan shaman exclaimed: 'Isn't the thread a thing of *n/om*, so it just has its own strength? You learn to work with it.'[20] The threads are, in Bleek and Lloyd's phrase, truly 'things of sorcery'.

In the rock paintings of the south-eastern mountains of South Africa and Lesotho we find depictions of long, sometimes bifurcating, thin red lines. Usually, they are fringed with white dots, but numerous variants are known (Fig. 20). The lines interact in a number of ways with other images: in addition to people being shown walking and dancing along them or holding them as if they are cords, the lines sometimes enter and leave the bodies of eland; in other instances, they enter and exit from human figures. Significantly, they frequently enter and emerge from notches or steps in the rock face on which they are painted. These inequalities in the rock become the holes to which the San say the threads lead.

There can be little doubt that the painted lines depict 'threads of light', the 'things' by which shamans entered and returned from the spirit realm.[21] They are the route to the other world, and the paintings and the ethnography combine to show that the spirit realm was believed to lie behind the walls of rock shelters. Not only the lines but also other images, such as those of animals, appear to enter or exit from cracks or steps in

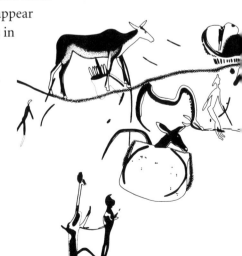

20 Part of a densely painted panel of San images now preserved in the South African Museum, Cape Town. A 'thread of light' can be seen weaving its way through the images. The large supine figure, surrounded by fish and eels, holds a fly whisk and has blood lines on its face. A buck-headed snake bleeds from the nose. Colours: dark red, black, white.

the rock walls. This feature of the paintings has led researchers to refer to the rock face itself as a 'veil' between this world and the spirit realm.[22] This point can hardly be overemphasized. The rock was highly significant, and, as an interface between realms, it became a distinct context in which the painters situated their images.

Bearing these San beliefs and rock paintings in mind, we argue that when, in 1875, the /Xam informant spoke of 'A sorcerer's thing', he was thinking of something that only a shaman can see. He said that the broad, undulating line in Figure 17 was a depiction of the hallucinated lines along which shamans move on their way to the spirit realm. That the figures appear to be dancing reinforced his view.

The informant was drawing on widespread San concepts to explain what he was told was a copy of a specific rock painting. But was he right? Here we must enter three reservations.

First, we must allow that the informant may have identified the undulating line in Figure 17 as something different from what the painter intended it to represent. If so, he was nevertheless speaking about a genuine, widely held San belief that related to the activities of shamans. What he said remains significant even if he was wrong about this particular painting. A researcher who discounts what the informant said because he may have misunderstood the copy of the rock painting misses an important source of information.

Second, painted red lines usually fringed with white dots are characteristic of the south-eastern mountains; they are not commonly found in the region where Stow made this copy, nor in the informant's homeland, about 100 km (62 miles) to the west.

Third, a researcher familiar with the lines characteristic of the south-east would not readily identify Stow's 'path-like' image in Figure 17 as one of them. It is much broader than the lines painted in the south-eastern mountains. Nevertheless, it may be another variant of the 'threads of light' concept. It may be an idiosyncratic take on the hard-wired, neurologically generated form. The feet of the figures do seem to relate to the thin red line along the lower margin of the 'path' rather than to the broad white band.

Be that as it may, the important point is that the 19th-century informant noticed a relationship between the undulating motif and the apparently dancing human figures. Confronted with copies of what Bleek and Lloyd told him were San rock paintings, he drew on San concepts to explain them as best he could and may have concluded that it must represent a 'path' to the spirit realm. The fundamental fact that he had been told that these were copies of San rock art images made him think of 'sorcery' because that was the area of San belief that he associated with rock art images. He was thus predisposed to suggest an interpretation drawn from 'the deeds of sorcery'.

The Mantis

This general understanding of the images in Figure 17 as some of 'sorcery's things' is supported by comments that Lloyd obtained on another of Stow's copies (Fig. 21). Here, too, there is another reference to the Mantis. This time we have what appears to be more like a verbatim translation than the probably summarized remarks on Figure 17, though with an insertion by Lloyd to aid identification of a figure at which the informant was presumably pointing. The informant again begins by identifying the images as 'sorcery's things':

> *These are sorcery's things. I think that one man, to the right of the spectator, having killed a hartebeest becomes like it with his companions. The Mantis going with them. The others had helped him. They become Mantises. The Mantis is not there.*

At first glance, this is one of the most puzzling of the statements that Bleek and Lloyd's informants offered on Stow's copies. The modern reader can detect little in the explanation to relate it to the copy. Yet it is a gateway to a deeper understanding of what is, for many Westerners, a strange set of beliefs.

21 George Stow's copy of a crowded panel of San rock paintings. This copy shows antelope-headed figures, a baboon, what is probably an ostrich and attenuated human figures. The largest figure is only partially preserved. Colour: dark red.

Whatever thought processes the copy triggered in the informant's mind, he brought together ideas concerning:

– 'the Mantis' and the 'female Mantis'
– hartebeest hunting
– 'sorcery's things'

Before tackling the decipherment of that tripartite nexus of belief, we dispose of what seems to be an ambiguity. The phrase 'to the right of the spectator' may be an explanatory interpolation by Lloyd or Dorothea Bleek that refers to the present-day viewer of the copy (the 'spectator'). On the other hand, the phrase may be the informant's and refer to the large figure right of centre: it may be regarded as watching the other figures and so be a 'spectator'. Again, we are not sure which words are Lloyd's or Dorothea's and which are direct transcriptions of the informant's words. The point is, however, not germane to an understanding of the overall meaning of the /Xam man's observations. We are still left confronting what he meant by 'The Mantis' and 'Mantises'.

The identity of the Mantis is fairly easily established. He is the central figure in southern San mythology.[23] He is prominent in both the Cape and Maloti collections of San myths (Chapters 7 and 8). Belief in him was widespread. In the /Xam language his name is /Kaggen. That this word also denotes the praying mantis insect led to the false colonial belief that the San were so debased as to 'worship' an insect. In fact, the /Xam San no more worshipped an insect than Christians worship a lamb. Yet, as we shall see, there are occasions when /Kaggen can get feathers (wings) and fly.[24] But, for the most part, he is what we may call a trickster-deity, as we discussed in Chapter 1. He was responsible for creating the world, but also for deceiving people; for taking hunters to antelope, but also for helping an antelope to escape. There are always two sides to the Mantis.

Importantly, it seems that /Kaggen was the first shaman. Indeed, the Mantis as the *ur*-shaman is an understanding that is key to much of /Xam San thought. In many of the tales in which he is protagonist, he behaves like an ordinary San man: he hunts, has a family, and is both wise and foolish. But he also possesses the abilities of a San shaman. He can transform himself into, for example, a hare, a puff adder, a vulture, a louse, a hartebeest, or a 'little green thing' that flies.[25] Diä!kwain tried to explain /Kaggen's protean nature to Lloyd soon after the Guy Fawkes celebrations of 5 November 1875:

The Mantis imitates what people do also, when they want us who do not know Guy Fox [sic] to be afraid. They change their faces, for they do not want us who do not know to think it is not a person. The Mantis also … cheats them that we may not know that it is he.[26]

He could 'change his face' into many things. You never knew where you were with the Mantis. In addition, the myths tell of the Mantis diving into waterholes and flying through the air, both shamanic feats. To accomplish 'miracles', such as these, he trembles (*!khauken*), as do shamans when they enter trance.[27] He also foretells the future by dreaming, as San shamans do.[28] Like a 'Lord of the Animals' in other cultures, /Kaggen was believed to possess all large antelope and so their potency: he controlled them as shamans of the game do when they seek to control the movements of antelope. Finally, in one of the /Xam tales he calms the Blue Crane by rubbing her with his sweat, a clear act of shamanic healing[29] (for more on myth see Chapters 7 and 8).

At this point, we can return to the puzzling statement that the informant gave in response to Figure 21: 'The figure with animal's head said to be the female Mantis.' Is this another of the Mantis's many manifestations?

An initial guess may be that the informant was referring, not to the Mantis himself, but to his wife. But the Mantis's wife is the Dassie (rock rabbit, or hyrax); nowhere is she said to be antelope-headed. A more likely explanation is that the informant was referring to the sexual ambivalence of the Mantis, that is, to another manifestation of his trickster status. He is said to have a digging stick fitted with a bored stone, as well as a man's bow and arrows.[30] The bored stone was associated exclusively with the digging sticks that women used to dig up edible roots.[31] Women used bored stones not merely to weight their digging sticks. They also used them to beat the ground and thereby to call up the spirits of the dead.[32] The Mantis is also left-handed,[33] another indication of femininity in San thought. Finally, he looks after children[34] and has a skin for carrying a child.[35]

Another possibility is suggested by an account that the missionary John Campbell recorded in the mid 19th century. San living near the present-day town of Taung said that the female, lesser god whom they called Ko appeared at a dance and told them where to find game:

She is a large, white figure and sheds such a brightness around, that they hardly see the fire for it; all see her as she dances with them.... They cannot ... feel what she is; but should a man be permitted to touch her, which seldom happens, she breathes hard upon his arm, and this makes him shoot better.... After Ko comes up from the ground, and dances a short time with them, she disappears, and is succeeded by her nymphs, who likewise dance a while with them.[36]

Is this the 'female Mantis'? Today San shamans in the Kalahari still speak of the bright light that they see in the dance. Here are two such accounts:

During the dance I usually see a light that comes from the people around me. This light goes straight up to the sky. I begin to see this light when I start healing during the dance. First I get filled with pain, then the light comes. It takes away all the pain. When there is no light, I feel pain. When the light arrives, the pain disappears.[37]

When you take it [medicine], it feels like all ailments are cured and then you feel a light inside you. The strength of the medicine is that it teaches you to see the light. Later you will be able to see the light without taking medicine.... When you see the light during a healing dance, it is so bright that it looks like daylight even though it is actually evening. This light brings about very special kinds of things. I become so tall that I see people as small, as if they are standing far below me. It's like I am flying over them. Although I am physically blind, I can see everything in this light.[38]

The light of which these men speak is neurologically generated but interpreted as a being from the spirit realm. The mental experience with which it is associated includes the sensation of attenuation and rising up as well as flight. It is possible, but again by no means certain, that Lloyd's informant was thinking of this light when he spoke about the 'female Mantis'.

These are our suggestions as to what the informant could have meant by 'the female Mantis'. But we remain unsure: this is indeed a puzzling statement.

The Mantis and the hartebeest

In attempting to understand what the informant meant by his remarks about hartebeest hunting and the Mantis, the essence of his comments on Figure 21, we must first ask what he thought he was looking at when he was shown Stow's copy. Did he see what we today think we see?

The context of becoming Mantises was, he quite clearly said, a hartebeest hunt. The words he used are 'having killed a hartebeest'. Yet, remarkably, there is no depiction of a hunt in Figure 21, let alone a hartebeest. The nearest thing to a hunt is the figure on the extreme right. It holds a bow and probably has arrows secured in a band or kaross around its shoulders – a commonly painted practice (Fig. 22). Significantly, this figure has a clear antelope head and long, slender horns. The horns are not those of a hartebeest (Fig. 23); they are more like eland horns, though they curve forward like a rhebok's horns rather than point straight backwards. Some decades ago, researchers would have immediately identified this figure as a hunter in an animal disguise headdress stalking his prey. As we have seen, the art was formerly widely believed to comprise hunting scenes and other representations of daily life. In Chapter 2 we considered dancing figures that do indeed seem to be wearing caps with small antelope horns, so the hunting explanation needs to be revised (Figs 12–14).

As for the rest of Stow's copy, the informant saw a group of human figures in various postures. One, in the centre, has its arms raised in a distinctive and oft-repeated clapping posture (a fragment of the dance) that may have

22 Opposite above: *A San rock painting of a baboon-like therianthrope with horns. It bleeds copiously from the nose and carries a bow and arrows (from a coloured photograph). Colours: black, dark red, white.*

23 Opposite below: *San rock paintings of hartebeest heads. The horns and ears are meticulously drawn. Colours: dark red, black.*

suggested the 'arms' of a praying mantis, but the informant's invocation of the Mantis seems to be more general than a reference to this image alone. He said: '*They* become Mantises.'

Other figures in Stow's copy have attenuations of the body or neck and antelope heads. There is also, probably, an ostrich and, more clearly, a baboon. How would the /Xam informant have responded to such a varied group of, principally, human figures? We suggest that, all in all, he thought he was looking at a depiction of a dance – but not a *procession* of dancers, as in Figure 7. In Figure 21 it was his knowledge of the shamanic dance and the transformations and mental experiences that take place in it that triggered his remarks. Such transformations are, of course, conceptual 'sorcery's things'. Indeed, the informant himself explicitly said: 'These are sorcery's things.'

'Sorcery's things', yes, but more specifically they are in some way connected with both hartebeest hunting and the Mantis. The underlying conceptual framework that brings those two apparently disparate elements together is discernible in other parts of the Bleek and Lloyd Collection. We consider the elements one at a time.

Hunting is not merely an economic practice. It is in fact a part of the San conceptual milieu that is related to 'sorcery'. Even a common activity like hunting is hedged around with beliefs and rituals. In the first place, the 19th-century /Xam San spoke of an empathetic, supernatural bond that they believed existed between a hunter and the antelope that he is tracking, after having wounded it with a poisoned arrow.[39] To ensure success, the hunter must behave as he wishes the antelope to behave. He limps and keeps his eyes downcast. If he runs fast, the antelope will run fast and escape. He also refrains from urinating, lest the wounded animal also urinates and so loses the poison. If he has to return to camp before having found the wounded antelope, he must spend a restless night so that the antelope too will not sleep and regain its strength. While in the camp, the man must not smell the scent of a cooking pot: 'The hartebeest will also smell what the man has smelt, and the poison which the man has shot into the hartebeest will become cool.'[40]

Elizabeth Marshall Thomas[41] describes watching a Ju/'hoan hunter unconsciously imitating a hunted antelope:

Witabe, too, was completely absorbed. Although he did not run after the wildebeest, he got to his feet and gazed after them, unconsciously making a gesture with his hand representing the head and horns of a wildebeest. He moved his hand in time with their running, saying softly: 'Huh, huh, boo. Huh, huh, boo', the sound of their breath and grunting as they ran.[42]

In a sense, the hunter becomes the antelope. He thinks himself into the animal.

These beliefs about hunting go only some way to contextualizing the informant's comments on Figure 21. In order to have made these observations about the images he must have had a pre-existing notion that, in some way, linked the Mantis to hartebeest. What was this link? A /Xam man said: 'Our parents used to ask us, Did we not see that the hartebeest's head resembled the Mantis's head? It feels that it belongs to the Mantis: that is why its head resembles his head.'[43] The way in which a hartebeest's horns bend backwards does resemble the antennae of a mantis. What people in one culture take to be a resemblance may not be apparent to people in a different culture. In this case, a visual relationship between hartebeest, praying mantises and the Mantis himself, though not obvious to Westerners, was a traditional /Xam San belief.

But there is more to the relationship than mere resemblance. The hartebeest was also one of the Mantis's many manifestations: 'The Mantis is one who cheated the children, by becoming a hartebeest, by resembling a dead hartebeest.'[44] He could transform himself fully into a hartebeest to the extent that people could not be sure whether they were looking at an antelope or their trickster-deity.

An easily missed implication in what the /Xam man said in response to Stow's copy (Fig. 21) is that this transformation of people into Mantises happened *after the death of a hunted hartebeest*. Here we encounter another connection in the closely woven fabric of San ideas and beliefs. After killing a large antelope, the San almost invariably hold a trance dance: there is meat and potency in abundance. The transformation may therefore have been a result of people dancing hartebeest potency. Lorna Marshall was told that, when a man dances the Giraffe Dance, he 'becomes giraffe'; the same is true of the Honey Dance: he 'becomes honey'.[45] This point explains why the informant said the hunter 'becomes like it [a hartebeest]' – and then, in what may appear to be a contradiction, 'They become Mantises.' Dancing and hunting are closely related in San thought in another way. The Ju/'hoan respect word for eland, the most potency-filled animal, is *tcheni*, which means 'dance'.[46] When hunters are tracking an eland, a man may whisper '*Tcheni* is hiding behind that tree.' They are hunting 'dance'.

In what sense, then, was '[T]he Mantis going with them', that is, with the hunters? Although he protects hartebeest, the Mantis sometimes leads hunters to animals. As we have pointed out, his unpredictability was at the heart of

/Xam San beliefs about him. To secure his assistance, people prayed to him. In the first half of the 19th century, Arbousset and Daumas recorded such a San prayer. The missionaries considered it 'material and gross' and indicative of 'an idolatrous people', though today it may not, in essence, sound markedly different from many Christian prayers: 'Give us this day our daily bread.' After all, the man was praying with his children, not just himself, in mind:

> Lord, is it that thou dost not like me?
> Lord, lead to me a male gnu.
> I like much having my belly filled;
> My oldest son, my oldest daughter,
> Like much to have their bellies filled.
> Lord, bring a male gnu under my darts.[47]

The word that Arbousset and Daumas translated as 'Lord' was 'kaank. It is clearly a form of /Kaggen, the apostrophe at the beginning being the then-common way of indicating a click. Similar prayers addressed to the /Xam trickster-deity /Kaggen were not recorded, but in the Kalahari the Ju/'hoansi call upon their great god //Gāuwa and the (usually malevolent) spirits of the dead to assist them in hunting. Sometimes they do this during a medicine dance: '//Gāuwa help us [to get game]; we are dying of hunger.'[48] Lorna Marshall writes of a Ju/'hoan man who composed a song that hunters sometimes sing when they are out looking for animals:

> //Gāuwa must help us that we kill an animal.
> //Gāuwa, help us. We are dying of hunger.
> //Gāuwa does not give us help.
> He is cheating. He is bluffing.
> //Gāuwa will bring something for us to kill next day
> After he himself hunts and has eaten meat,
> When he is full and is feeling well.[49]

Although //Gāuwa (also known as ≠Gao!Na) is the great god of the Ju/'hoansi, we can detect elements of the trickster in his supposed behaviour: 'cheating' and 'bluffing' are prominent characteristics of /Kaggen.

Again, there is a measure of ambivalence. The Mantis loved the hartebeest and the eland. One /Xam man expressed this belief memorably: '[H]e made his heart of the Eland and the Hartebeest.'[50] The Mantis therefore sometimes tried to frustrate the hunter of a hartebeest. Describing the ways in which the Mantis worked to save a hunted hartebeest and how a hunter may nevertheless be successful, a /Xam man said that the Mantis would come to the hunter's hut. If the man's wife chased him (in his insect form?) away, and thus did not properly respect him, he would enable the hartebeest to escape.[51]

This relationship between /Kaggen and the hartebeest may explain a 19th-century /Xam statement that Sigrid Schmidt, the German folklorist who has catalogued Khoisan myths and folktales, and indeed many other researchers find puzzling:[52] 'My father-in-law [//Kabbo] had Mantises, he was a Mantis's man.'[53] The word Lloyd translated as 'had' is /ki. It means 'to have' or 'to possess'.[54] /Xam ɵpwaiten-ka !gi:ten, or game shamans, were said to 'possess' creatures as varied as springbok and locusts. At first glance it appears that //Kabbo possessed praying mantises in this way. The puzzling statement, therefore, may simply mean that //Kabbo was a !gi:xa who 'possessed', not only mantises, but hartebeests themselves. In discussing the concept of possessed animals and potency, Richard Katz and Megan Biesele make the important point that it does not imply any sort of exclusivity; they suggest that 'stewardship' gives a better idea of how the San think of this sort of possession. The shaman conserves potency and sees to its proper use for the benefit of the whole community.[55]

Another link between hartebeests and /Kaggen is that they shared a nickname. The /Xam called the hartebeest 'old man Tinderbox owner',[56] and the Mantis was also called 'Tinderbox', the /Xam word being '//Kandoro'. This word can be broken down into its constituents: //kan means 'to possess', while doro is a 'tinderbox' or the fire-sticks that the San twirl to light a fire.[57] As we saw in Chapter 2, fire activates supernatural potency as shamans dance around it; fire causes potency to 'boil' in the shamans, rise up their spines and 'explode' in their heads.[58] As we have seen, /Kaggen was himself a shaman, probably the first shaman. In this, he parallels the Ju/'hoan great god ≠Gao!Na who provided the people with fire-sticks.[59] Many beliefs are pan-San.

We can now begin to fathom what the informant meant when he commented on the Stow copy (Fig. 21). When, in Lloyd's translation, he said, 'They become Mantises', he was probably substituting 'mantises' for 'hartebeests'. The people who had killed a hartebeest became hartebeest-Mantises. Lloyd, mistaking his meaning, seems to have enquired where the Mantis himself was in the picture. The informant replied, logically enough, 'The Mantis is not there.' The Mantis was invisible. //Kabbo said that /Kaggen 'can be by you, without your seeing him',[60] and Arbousset and Daumas learned that 'one does not see him with the eyes, but knows him with the heart'.[61] This may be why no convincing depictions of mantises have been found in San rock art.[62]

/Kaggen was an invisible, pervasive, omnipresent, protean presence inhabiting crucial areas of San life, especially those of doubtful outcome, such as hunting.[63] If he is not visibly there in the hunt, where is he? This a question that Joseph Orpen put to Qing. He replied:

We don't know, but the elands do. Have you not hunted and heard his cry, when the elands suddenly start and run to his call? Where he is, elands are in droves like cattle.[64]

There is a mystical region of plenty where /Kaggen lives. We consider it in more detail in Chapters 7 and 8.

In sum, we make the following points to clarify the /Xam man's puzzling comments on Stow's copy (Fig. 21):

1 *'Having killed a hartebeest, [the hunter] becomes like it with his companions.'* As /Kaggen can change into a hartebeest, so too can a man, especially a shaman, who has hunted a hartebeest and appropriated its potency.

2 *'The Mantis going with them.'* The hunters had implored /Kaggen to assist them in killing an antelope.

3 *'The others had helped him. They become Mantises.'* Either the hunters become hartebeests by behaving as if they were wounded, or, more likely, they are subsequently transformed at the ensuing dance.

4 *'The Mantis is not there.'* The informant says that the painter did not depict /Kaggen himself. /Kaggen was an unseen presence, even though he was 'with them' in the dance.

Our decipherment of the informant's comment may at first seem to be a number of confused contradictions, but his words can be understood by setting them in the overall context of San thought. A single San remark cannot be understood in isolation. Even if we cannot formulate a precise, consistent explanation in the English language, we can begin to sense the mercurial nature of San beliefs about supernatural things and the way that they infiltrate the activity of hunting.

'Sorcery's things'

When asked to comment on Stow's copy of San rock paintings (Fig. 21), the 19th-century /Xam San man began with a general remark: 'These are sorcery's things.' Certain aspects of the copy, perhaps ones not immediately apparent to a modern Western viewer, made him think of 'sorcery' rather than mundane daily life. It is unclear whether he meant that the individual images *depicted* 'sorcery's things' (like arrows of sickness and threads of light) or whether he was referring to the paintings themselves. Were rock paintings themselves 'sorcery's things', as were the tortoise-shell boxes used to contain powerful substances? Were they made as *things to be used* in shamans' attempts to reach the spirit realm? If images went in and out of the rock face, as they most certainly do, were they merely 'pictures' or were they actual 'things' that led through the 'veil' into the spirit realm? If paintings of eland were reservoirs of potency on which shamans, and perhaps other people as well, could draw, the images themselves were indeed 'sorcery's things'.

'Sorcery' was a complex concept with many manifestations. One of its principal contexts was, as we see in the next chapter, discovered through San people's comments on some otherwise inexplicable rock paintings of strange creatures.

CHAPTER 4

Discovering Rain

*The dark and sombre majesty of scene was increased by the heavy masses
of clouds overhanging the mountain-top and occasionally emitting
brilliant streams of lightning, followed by the low, hoarse growl
of the passing storm.[1]*

The San comments that we have so far deciphered are fairly straightforward compared with those that we discuss in this and the next chapter. In cases where more than one informant gave independent explanations for a specific rock painting, we clearly enter a more complex terrain of potential disagreement and confusion. At the same time, it is not surprising that the area of San belief and ritual which elicited these multiple comments is one that has long gripped the attention of Western travellers and scholars.

In the early years of the 20th century, the Irish Presbyterian missionary Reverend Samuel Shaw Dornan (1871–1941) found himself fascinated by the Kalahari San. Like so many other Western travellers, he marvelled at the way in which they were able to live in the unforgiving environment of the desert. Among the San's accomplishments that amazed him were the men's hunting strategies and weapons – especially their deadly poisoned arrows – and the skill with which women were able to spot, by the merest wisp of dead leaves, a nourishing and water-providing bulb beneath the desert sand.

When it came to religion, Dornan was more sympathetic towards the San than some of his predecessors. He at least acknowledged that they held beliefs about God, life after death and even some notions of resurrection, but he was dismayed by their general vagueness concerning these matters. Understandably, given his biblical background, he was especially interested in San mythology. He found that San life depended much on the changing seasons, especially the coming of the spectacular first thunderstorms of summer, and he was therefore surprised that they did not more clearly entertain the sort of beliefs that he called 'sidereal worship' and that they did not ascribe to the heavenly bodies' control of the seasons. After all, rain was supremely important to them. If the rains failed, 'the game disappeared or migrated, and the Bushmen had to follow or starve. At such times they were very hard pushed to live, and the old and the infirm must have died off.'[2]

Dornan noticed that the coming of the summer rains triggered a chain reaction: 'The first thunderstorm that heralds the rainy season is the cause of much rejoicing, because rain means grass, and grass means game and plenty of food.'[3] A century earlier, another missionary, John Campbell, thought that the rainy season could be called 'the Bushman's harvest, for the ground being softened by the rain, they can easily pull up roots'.[4] Dornan and Campbell were not alone in noticing a link between rain and joyful celebration. The linguist Clement M. Doke observed dances that he thought were 'in honour of the new grass',[5] and the 17th-century traveller Sir John Barrow noted that the San danced for several nights at the first rain.[6]

In the southern African interior, rain usually comes in the form of localized thunderstorms, though softer, more general rains are known. The San speak of male and female rain, respectively the thunderstorm and the gentle rains. Sometimes, with clear skies above them, people see rain falling from cumulus clouds far away, and they long for the storm to move in their direction. If it does not, they may strike camp and move to the place where rain has fallen. There they await the transformation of the veld: the bushes sprout and the bulbs that have lain hidden beneath the sand for the long, dry winter send up shoots that alert San women to their presence.

Given the colonial interest in the contribution of rain to survival in harsh southern African environments, it was inevitable that, sooner or later, the Bleek family would have enquired about their /Xam informants' beliefs concerning rain. But the way in which Wilhelm Bleek and Lucy Lloyd managed to elicit some truly remarkable accounts of /Xam rain-making resulted from a series of fortunate events.

It all began with what became a widely reproduced and much discussed rock painting. The ways in which this painting has been variously interpreted illustrate the necessity of constantly moving back and forth between the three registers of our 'Rosetta Stone' (Preface). Researchers who remain with only one register court disaster.

First encounters

In 1835 the Scottish soldier and traveller Sir James Alexander explored a valley known as the Langkloof. It is in what is now the south-eastern part of the Western Cape Province. He wished to see 'drawings executed by the former occupiers of the country'.[7] Like some other early travellers, he was surprised to find that 'these rude attempts of uncivilized artists are not utterly devoid of merit'. For the most part he aligned himself with the colonial view that the paintings were simple records of daily life. His colonial perspective is clear in what he had to say about a group of human figures (Fig. 24): imaginatively, he concluded that it depicted 'an embassy of females suing for peace'. He added: 'No one can deny that their reception is a gracious one, to judge by the polite attitudes of the male figures, perhaps chiefs.'[8] Although the sex of none of the figures is shown, Alexander thought that one group depicted women, the other men; in accordance with the spirit of the times, the women were subservient, whereas the men were gracious, polite chiefs.

Alexander ran out of ideas when he was confronted by a painting that defied a naturalistic explanation (Fig. 25). It is in a site now known as Ezeljagdspoort. Strikingly, it seems to show apparently fishtailed figures. Alexander wrote: 'We are unable to assist the reader, even by a conjecture, in elucidating the meaning of that which he here sees represented.'[9] Nevertheless, he turned to racist colonial lore and suggested that the painting may refer to 'the amphibious nature attributed to the whites by the natives in the olden day'. The supposed 'amphibious nature' of the images took hold on the public imagination. Alexander's copyist, Major C. Michell, concentrated on getting the 'amphibious' features right, but he omitted other details such as the fingers at the ends of the elongated figure's arms and the two straight lines at this figure's shoulder. He also misrepresented the undulating lines.

When writers who see the art as principally narrative have to deal with patently non-real images like the Ezeljagdspoort group, they frequently identify them as a 'scene' from a myth rather than from daily life. In this way they preserve their position, albeit in a broader sense. As we shall see in subsequent chapters, myth has remained an alluring explanation for many researchers;

24 *An 1830s copy of a San rock painting that was interpreted as 'an embassy of females suing for peace'. The copy suggests that the images were only partially preserved at that time. Colour: unknown.*

25 A modern copy of the San rock painting that in the 19th century was erroneously interpreted as depicting mermaids. Colour: dark red.

the position is perhaps understandable, especially for those who do not know San ethnography in any detail. But once we delve more deeply into San beliefs and rituals, we encounter more persuasive explanations. That turned out to be the case with the Ezeljagdspoort images.

Some decades after Alexander visited the site, the paintings were copied by H. C. Schunke. He submitted his copy and other copies of rock paintings to Wilhelm Bleek. In his 1875 *Second Report Concerning Bushman Researches*, Bleek referred to Schunke's copy but unfortunately added an ambiguous comment that misled numerous subsequent researchers: 'The subject of it (the watermaidens), was explained in a fine old legend to Mr D. Ballot (who kindly copied it for Mr Schunke), by a very old Bushman still surviving in those parts.'[10] The old San man's Dutch name was Afrikaander. For one, Alex Willcox, a well-known writer on San rock art, 'The story behind the paintings … was, according to Dr Bleek, told to a Mr Ballot by an old Bushman then still living in the district'.[11] Later, Jeff Leeuwenburg, another rock art researcher, similarly accepted that the legend was a direct explanation of the painting.[12] Others followed.

The legend does indeed seem to fit the images. It tells of a young girl who was dragged into a dark pool by watermaidens. When the girl's mother found what had happened to her, she collected herbs and ground them to a powder. She then scattered the powder on the surface of the water. As a result, the girl came out of the pool unharmed, though the watermaidens had licked her cheeks white because they loved her so much.[13]

Maidens and water pools feature in various San tales. In one that Diä!kwain recounted to Lucy Lloyd, young girls carried off by the rain are transformed into flowers that grow in the water.[14] It is important to notice that in none of the tales about watermaidens are the beings said to have fishtails: on the contrary, they have human-like bodies and they walk on the ground. The fishtail idea derives from Western notions of mermaids.

Nevertheless there is much in Afrikaander's tale that is consonant with San beliefs, but whether these beliefs can be related to the Ezeljagdspoort 'fishtail' painting is open to question. Close reading of the historical record and an account of the painting given by one of Bleek and Lloyd's /Xam informants, casts a different light on the matter and shows how important it is to be critical of the ethno-historical record. We begin with Afrikaander's legend.

Fortunately, the pieces of lined blue writing paper on which Ballot recorded the legend have been preserved in the Jagger Library, University of Cape Town. The title and opening paragraph are crucial:

A story told to me by an old Bushman who appears to be between 70 or 80 years of age. On asking old Afrikaander: 'Do you believe in Watermeide?' he lit his pipe, took off his hat, sat on the ground, and then commenced: …

Immediately, one can see that Afrikaander was responding to Ballot's question about watermaidens, not to the painting itself. Ballot asked him a leading question based on his own misinterpretation of the forked-tailed figures and then linked the old San man's answer to the painting. Indeed, there is no evidence that the man had seen the painting in reality or even in the form of a copy. Certainly, he did not refer to any of the details of the painting, the curious elongated central figure or even the famous 'fishtails'. Nor did he refer to the actions being performed by the people, although these obviously call for explanation. Indeed, the legend cannot be said to be an explanation of the rock painting. Perhaps realizing that the man had not seen the painting, Bleek subsequently wrote in his report that what he took to be 'the *subject* of it' was explained by the legend (emphasis added).

There is therefore no compelling reason to link the old San man's watermaiden legend to the Ezeljagdspoort painting. A quite different and more persuasive explanation was, however, soon to emerge.

/Han≠kasso and Lloyd

Three years after Bleek's death in 1875, Lucy Lloyd showed a copy of the Ezeljagdspoort painting to the /Xam San man /Han≠kasso. It was the year before he returned to his /Xam homeland. He gave a complex explanation that, unlike Afrikaander's, refers to specific features of the images and unashamedly admits puzzlement at certain points. /Han≠kasso's statement is clearly a valuable document, even though he admits to a degree of ignorance. Like the comments we discussed in the previous chapter, his explanation again refers to 'sorcery'. The parentheses are Lloyd's:

> I think that the rain's navel is that which goes (along here). I think that these people, they address the rain that the rain's navel may not kill them, that the rain's navel may be favourable towards them. That the rain's navel may not kill them. That the rain's navel may keep favourable towards them. This man he has hold of a thing which resembles a stick. I think that they are rain's people. I do not know them, for I behold that they are people. For they have their arms: they resemble people. They feel that they are sorcerers, the rain's sorcerers they are: for this man is holding a thing which resembles **/khoe** (a curved stick used in making a Bushman house). I do not know whether it is a **/khoe**, for I see the thing resembles a **/khoe**. These people (i.e. those on the lower side of the line in the picture) I do not know whether the rain's navel divides them from the other people. People (they) are, sorcerers, rain's sorcerers. They make the rain to fall and the rain's clouds come out on account of them. Hence the rain falls, … and the place becomes green on account of it. This thing (i.e. what we should have called the right arm of the rain figure), it is the one which resembles a caterpillar, the rain's caterpillar.[15]

The first point to notice is that /Han≠kasso was not particularly interested in the ichthyoid tails of the figures, even though, in view of the Ballot legend, it is highly probable that Lloyd directed his attention to their fishlike appearance. Indeed, his observation 'I behold that they are people. For, they have their arms' may have been given in response to an unrecorded question about the 'fishtails' that Lloyd put to him. Nor did /Han≠kasso find the curious depiction of what he took to be the legs of the figures unusual; he was more inclined to identify the figures as human beings because of their arms. His repeated insistence that 'they resemble people' may have been prompted by further questions that Lloyd put to him. Importantly, he mentioned neither fishtails nor watermaidens nor half-fish, half-human creatures.

Instead /Han≠kasso said that the painting had something to do with weather control and that the figures were 'rain's sorcerers'. As we briefly saw in Chapter 2, there were different kinds of *!gi:ten*, Lloyd's 'sorcerers'. One of these types comprised *!khwa-ka !gi:ten*, who were believed to be able to make rain and to protect people from violent thunderstorms.[16] In the /Xam language *!khwa* means both water and rain. The principal manner in which *!khwa-ka !gi:ten* made rain is the topic of our next chapter. Here we try to decipher some of the details of /Han≠kasso's statement about the enigmatic Ezeljagdspoort images.

In the first remark that Lloyd recorded, probably a response to a question from her, /Han≠kasso identified what we see as a greatly attenuated human figure as 'the rain's navel', saying 'that which goes (along here)'. His use of 'goes' and Lloyd's parenthesis suggest he was actually pointing to the long, curving line; he did not use the words 'man' or 'person' ('people') as he did when he referred to the other figures in the group. Furthermore, at the end of his statement he said, 'This thing (i.e. what we should have called the right arm of the rain figure), it is the one which resembles a caterpillar, the rain's caterpillar' (Lloyd's parenthesis). A few manuscript pages later /Han≠kasso explained more about the 'rain's caterpillar'. Again, the parenthesis is Lloyd's:

> The rain's //*kerri-ssi-!kau* (caterpillar) are large. They dwell in the water; they are those which are large. They do not have hair on their backs. They are going into the water … they run out of the water…. Their back's things, they are red. The Bushmen do not eat them; for they are poisonous. If they bite a Bushman, the Bushman dies on account of it.[17]

If /Han≠kasso thought that an arm of the elongated figure was a caterpillar, he apparently did not perceive the image as in any way human. When he used the phrase 'the rain's navel', he was thus referring to only the line, without realizing it was an attenuated human figure. If the figures are indeed shamans of the rain, as /Han≠kasso claimed, the attenuation of the principal figure is explicable. Attenuation and rising up are sensations experienced by people in certain altered states. As we saw in the last chapter, a Kalahari San shaman said that the light he experienced in trance 'brings about very special kinds of things. I become so tall that I see people as small, as if they are standing far below me. It's like I am flying over them.'[18] Again and again, the painted images, San ethnography and neuropsychology complement one another in highly persuasive ways.

Still, it could be argued that the linear form of the elongated image suggests that 'umbilical cord' may be a better if not exact phrase. Lloyd, however, gives all the few recorded uses of the /Xam word *!Λhain* as 'navel'. 'The rain's navel' is in fact one of a set of anatomical metaphors that included 'the rain's legs', 'the rain's hair', 'the rain's breath' and 'the rain's blood', all of which we discuss in later chapters. !Λhain, however, poses its own intriguing problems. We need to examine as many uses of the /Xam word as possible. In doing so, we find an association between the human navel and the work of rain !gi:ten. In a statement given independently of the Ezeljagdspoort painting, Diä!kwain said that people do three things when they wish to protect their camp from an 'angry' thunderstorm that could blow down their fragile huts.

First, Diä!kwain told Lloyd that they stand in front of their dwellings, facing in the direction from which storms come, and 'strike their (?navels) with their fists' and 'press their hand in their ?navel' (Lloyd's parenthesis).[19] Lloyd placed a question mark before 'navel' here, but the manuscript shows it is the same /Xam word that /Han≠kasso used. Almost certainly, Diä!kwain would have assisted with the translation by a gesture; the word must have something to do with the general area of the stomach. But Lloyd's question mark suggests that 'navel' is not an exact equivalent of the /Xam word. If the word meant no more than 'navel', it would have been easy enough for Diä!kwain to indicate this by pointing. One possible explanation is that !Λhain meant the stomach and diaphragm, not just the navel itself, because this is the part of the body where a shaman's potency starts to 'boil' when he enters trance.[20] As the 'boiling' increases, the stomach muscles contract painfully and the man bends forward (Fig. 26). It is therefore significant that the large, central figure in the Ezeljagdspoort painting that appears to be holding a short stick is bending forward (Fig. 25). Numerous rock paintings of trance dances depict this posture.[21] The striking of the !Λhain and the pressing of a hand into the stomach may thus have been a ritual dramatization of some of the physical effects of trance: whether they themselves were shamans of the rain or not, people performed these actions to invoke the power of trance experiences as they tried to control a dangerous storm. Although no figures in the Ezeljagdspoort painting are shown striking their stomachs, that ritual may have relevance to the general theme of the painting as proposed by Diä!kwain.

Second, Diä!kwain said that the shamans of the rain 'snap their fingers at the rain' while they are facing the threatening storm and pressing 'their hand in their ?navel'.[22] Snapping fingers, or simply pointing (Pl. 6), was a way of shooting potency into a person or animal.[23] Finger-snapping was therefore related to the striking of the navel in that both gestures were implicated in ritual protection from violent storms.

26 A San rock painting depicting a trance dance. The dancers bend forward as their stomach muscles contract. They are surrounded by flecks of supernatural potency that can be seen only by shamans. Four of the dancers bleed from the nose. Colours: dark red, white, black.

Third, Diä!kwain said that people apostrophized the rain when they wished to disperse a thunderstorm: 'Thou shall falling turn back … for thou dost not a little lighten, for it seems as if thou are very angry'.[24] This is similar to what /Han≠kasso said when he commented on the figures in the Ezeljagdspoort painting: 'they address the rain that the rain's navel may not kill them, that the rain's navel may be favourable towards them'.[25] Intriguingly, rock art researcher Jeremy Hollmann goes further and suggests that the Ezeljagdspoort imagery itself may have had a prophylactic function in that it too 'apostrophized', or 'addressed', the rain.[26]

All in all, it seems that the 'navel' was associated in ways that we do not fully understand, with supernatural potency and the activities of shamans of the rain. Given such /Xam phrases as 'the rain's legs' (columns of falling rain beneath a thundercloud), and the rain's 'breath' (mist), we wonder whether *!Λhain* in this context meant 'umbilical cord' and was perhaps a San way of speaking about a tornado, a long funnel reaching down from a cloud. It may be that the figures in the painting are 'shepherding' the rain in this form to keep it from harming people and their dwellings. Either way, it is clear that, even if he noticed them, /Han≠kasso did not think that the human attributes of the line in Figure 25 (its head, arms and fingers) warranted comment.

The most controversial feature of the painting – the forked tails – remains unexplained. The image of a mermaid is so strong in Western thought that researchers have found it difficult to think beyond it. What we believe to be the real answer to the Ezeljagdspoort puzzle lies not in mermaids but in the sort of 'sorcery' that we encountered in Chapters 2 and 3.

Generalities and particulars

Why was /Han≠kasso unable to explain the painted 'forked tails'? In what ways, or in what particulars, is his testimony to be trusted? To answer those questions we recall that there were, and still are, fundamental beliefs and associated rituals that, with local variations, are pan-San. The ethnographies from widely separated San groups have much in common.[27] Wilhelm Bleek himself commented that the information he and Lucy Lloyd were collecting from their Cape /Xam informants had many parallels with what Qing had told Joseph Orpen in the south-eastern mountains.[28] As we have seen, the principal mythological figure /Kaggen (Cagn), the San trickster-deity, appears in both regions, though the tales themselves are not common to both.

Rain-making beliefs and rituals, too, were common to both regions. Yet, the specific ways in which those beliefs and rituals were expressed in the rock art of the two regions varied. So it is with the forked-tailed figures. They are concentrated in a comparatively small area in the south-eastern Cape (Fig. 27): as far as we know, they are not found in the region where /Han≠kasso lived or, for that matter, where Qing lived. This tension between widely held beliefs and their localized expressions of them explains why, though he had the necessary pan-San background knowledge, /Han≠kasso was unfamiliar with painted 'forked-tailed' figures.

A key point here is that neither he nor the Bleek family, nor indeed Alexander, Schunke or Ballot, knew that the Ezeljagdspoort figures represented a theme that is repeated at many rock shelters in the south-eastern Cape. This broader sweep of evidence was brought to light by Hollmann, who surveyed the region in which the figures are found: there are far more of them and they are more complex than the few known from Ezeljagdspoort had led us to expect.[29] In the same way that we examine multiple contexts in which puzzling San words are used, so when we collate many examples of 'forked-tailed' figures from a range of sites do we begin to see similarities that answer at least some of our questions about them.[30]

Many of these figures have their arms in a swept-back position that suggest wings (Fig. 28a). Then, too, their orientations suggest swooping flight, a point we take up in the next section. One of the forked-tailed figures at another site is wearing an eared cap (Fig. 28c). As we saw in Chapter 2, shamans who were believed to control the movements of game wore caps sewn with antelope ears standing up. Indeed, shamans are often depicted wearing them. Trance dances do not have just one function. At a single dance various aims are achieved: shamans try to ward off 'arrows of sickness', draw sickness out of people, go on out-of-body journeys and make rain.

As his survey progressed, Hollmann discovered further diagnostic features of forked-tailed figures. He found instances of them bleeding from the nose at two sites, while other figures in the distinctive clapping posture are sometimes associated with forked-tailed figures. These are two indications of the trance dance (Fig. 28b).[31] As Hollmann points out, the nasal bleeding and clapping of some forked-tailed figures link them and, by implication, the Ezeljagdspoort painting, to the experiences that San *!gi:ten* have when they enter an altered state of consciousness (Chapters 2 and 3). The nasal blood that Hollmann found depicted is especially strong evidence to confirm /Han≠kasso's view

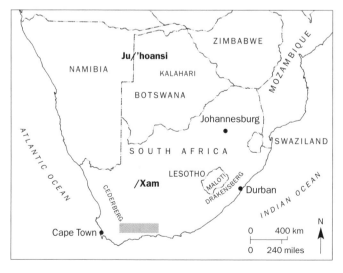

27 *Map of southern Africa. The grey shading shows the area in which depictions of forked-tailed figures ('swift-people') are found.*

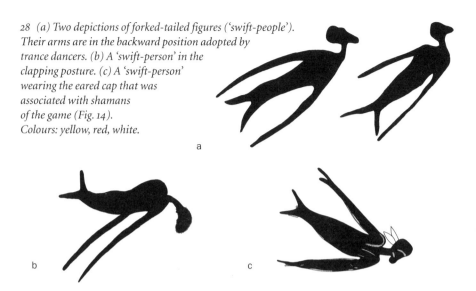

28 *(a) Two depictions of forked-tailed figures ('swift-people').*
Their arms are in the backward position adopted by
trance dancers. (b) A 'swift-person' in the
clapping posture. (c) A 'swift-person'
wearing the eared cap that was
associated with shamans
of the game (Fig. 14).
Colours: yellow, red, white.

that the Ezeljagdspoort images depict shamans – whatever else he may have had to guess about them. Indeed, any initial doubt we may have felt regarding /Han≠kasso's competence to identify the Ezeljagdspoort figures as shamans is assuaged by Hollmann's new evidence: it confirms an association with 'sorcery'.

To follow up the linkage between the 'forked-tailed' images and shamans, we need to examine neuropsychological research into certain experiences generated by altered states of consciousness. Then we need to consider some of the other paintings that Hollmann found in the region of Ezeljagdspoort and, moreover, a range of San beliefs about birds.

Taking flight

Neuropsychological research and ethnographic evidence both show that flight is a common, indeed worldwide, way of describing the sensations of weightlessness, dissociation from one's body, journeys to distant places and changes in perspective that include looking down on one's surroundings.[32] Today neurological research is being done on just what electrochemical events in the brain cause this sensation, but there is no dispute that flight is a common, perhaps the most common, experience that people have in deeply altered states. Certainly, San shamans all over southern Africa spoke and still speak about flying. One of the oldest statements came from Diä!kwain. Speaking about a shaman, he told Lloyd:

At some other time, when we are liable to forget him, he turns into a little bird, he comes to see us where we live and flies about our heads. Sometimes he sits on our heads, he sits peeping at us to see if we are still as we were when we left him....
As he flies away he chirps, just as a little bird does when it flies away.[33]

Diä!kwain did not say what species he meant by 'little bird'. But in another statement he was more specific and said that the swallow was the 'rain's thing'.[34] The word that Lloyd translated as 'swallow' was *!kwerri-/nan*. Again, we need to analyse the San word. The second part of it is obscure, but the first part means 'to thunder' or 'to strike with lightning'. In /Xam thought, it was the rain (*!khwa*) that was said to strike (*!kwerriten*).[35] Another word for 'swallow' was */kabbi-ta-!khwa*;[36] *ta* forms the possessive case and explicitly links the bird to *!khwa*, rain. Thus whatever */kabbi* and */nan* may have meant, both of the words translated as 'swallow' point to a close association between those birds and rain. Diä!kwain clearly expressed this association when he said that swallows 'come when the rain clouds are in the sky'.[37] Such beliefs were not restricted to the 19th-century southern San. Still today in the northern Kalahari Desert, the Ju/'hoan San call swallows *glace'mhsi*, 'children of the rain'.[38]

The association goes further. Diä!kwain said that people should not throw stones (a sign of disrespect) at swallows because 'the swallow is with the things which the sorcerers take out [*/ki*, which means "to possess", as a shaman possesses potency], which they send about. Those are the things which the swallow resembles.'[39] A man who did not heed this injunction was said to have fallen unconscious because 'the swallow had entered into him'.[40] For the San, a shaman could embody a swallow. The relevance of these beliefs to the Ezeljagdspoort painting becomes inescapable when we recall that /Han≠kasso explicitly identified the figures with forked tails as 'the rain's sorcerers' and added that they 'make the rain to fall and the rain's clouds come out on account of them'.[41]

The close links between rain-making shamans, swallows and clouds should be seen together with statements about shamans turning into birds. Each contributing in its own way, the ethnographic, neuropsychological and painted data combine to suggest very strongly that the Ezeljagdspoort images in Figure 25 depict not fish-people, as has been widely supposed, but rather rain-making shamans in the form of birds.

But were they, specifically, swallows? Working from a number of perspectives, Hollmann, who (as noted) has intensively investigated the region where these paintings are found, has persuasively argued that they depict

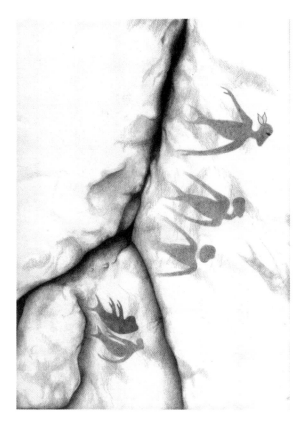

29 Six forked-tailed figures ('swift-people') depicted as if they are emerging from a crack in the rock face. Colours: yellow, red.

swift-people rather than swallow-people. Swallows (*Hirundinidae*) are, for many people, indistinguishable from swifts (*Apodidae*), and may have been so for Bleek and Lloyd. Both species have forked tails, though their wing shapes differ: swift wings are slender and scimitar-like, whereas swallow wings are somewhat wider.[42] To support his conclusion, Hollmann cites two types of swift behaviour that recall San people at a trance dance. First, swifts wheel around in the sky and utter loud screaming sounds. Ornithologists call this behaviour 'circusing' or 'screaming party/display';[43] it frequently takes place before migratory flights. This behaviour recalls the frenzied dancing and screaming that takes place at a San trance dance. Secondly, swifts flap their wings so that they meet above and below the bird's body and thus make a clapping sound.

Another feature of swift behaviour is that certain kinds of swifts commonly take over the igloo-shaped mud nests that swallows construct on the walls of rock shelters. Swifts' own nests are usually made in rock crevices or attached to the angle between the back wall of a rock shelter and a rock overhang. When the birds arrive at the nests they do so at high speed and appear to crash into the rock face. Strikingly, rock paintings of forked-tailed figures often appear to exit from or enter into inequalities in the rock face (Fig. 29).[44] As we have seen, the San thought of the rock face as a 'veil' between this world and the spirit world. The rock was as important as the images themselves.

All in all, we can go beneath the surface of /Han≠kasso's puzzling explanation of the Ezeljagdspoort painting. Despite his professed ignorance on a number of points, we can be sure that the images have to do with events and beings in the spirit realm, that they express San beliefs about birds (in particular swallows and swifts), and that these birds, together with /Han≠kasso's remarks, link the painted groups to rain-control.

A step forward

The most important point that we have established in this chapter is that none of the three registers of our 'Rosetta Stone' can be taken in isolation and at face value. None is a direct, straightforward expression of San ideas that we can 'read' with ease. All three registers have to be interrelated and deciphered. Summing up and taking our three San registers in turn, we can say:

- *San rock paintings*, the most enigmatic of the registers, cannot be unproblematically understood by modern Westerners. If we take them at face value, we read our own Western concepts into them. We end up unquestioningly accepting that the San believed in fishtailed mermaids and that they painted them at Ezeljagdspoort. Specific paintings have to be seen in the context of all the art in a given region. Researchers must therefore be familiar with the art at first hand: they need to examine large numbers of rock shelters to see how the images are placed on the rock face, how they relate one to another and in what ways many are subtle variations on common themes.

- *San language statements* given in response to copies of rock paintings must be similarly contextualized. Not only must the actual San words be minutely examined; they must also be seen in as many contexts as possible so that nuances of meaning can be extracted from them. Further, no informant is omniscient. (This is, of course, true of any religious context: no priest knows everything about Christianity, though some know a lot more than others.) San statements about beliefs and rituals must therefore be seen in context every bit as much as San rock art images. It is by moving back and forth between many statements that we are able to discern continuities and differences and thus construct flexible understandings of San beliefs to fit local circumstances.

– Lastly, and most obviously, *English (or other Western) language transla-tions of San texts* must be carefully scrutinized. Ideally, they should be compared with the original San language texts. Where that is not possi-ble, English language translations of specific but now lost San statements must be seen in the light of translations of texts for which we do have the original language versions.

It has become clear that the three registers of our 'Rosetta Stone' are parallel texts: they are not three stages in a developing sequence of understanding. We must move back and forth between them. As we do so, we need to bring in other sources of information. These include knowledge of animal behav-iour that the San would have known intimately and neuropsychology that tells us what human beings experience when they engage in activities such as the trance dance. Explanations of San rock art that favour broad, rather abstract interpretations without thoroughly exploring all three registers should be treated with suspicion. Those explanations have no safeguards against thoroughgoing Western biases and hidden assumptions about what art is and what it does.

These principles of interpretation set us up to tackle an extension of the San beliefs that we have discussed in this chapter. That extension is a category of rock art images that points to a conceptualization and painted manifesta-tion of San beliefs about natural phenomena. We now move away from the south-eastern Cape and its images of flight to examine another type of image altogether.

CHAPTER 5

Capturing Rain

That animal which the men are catching is a *snake* (!).[1]

In her 1889 report to the Cape of Good Hope Parliament entitled *A Short Account of Further Bushman Material Collected*, Lucy Lloyd wrote that it was:

impossible adequately to acknowledge the enormous help in the Bushman researches which has been afforded by the copies of Bushman drawings and paintings, particularly by the very large collection made by the late Mr. G. W. Stow: for which it is hoped that means of publication may eventually be found.

She went on to say that:

some very curious ideas, possessed by the Bushmen, which would probably otherwise not have come to light at all, have become known to us in the course of their endeavours to explain some of the pictures submitted to them.[2]

Chief among these 'very curious ideas' was the whole complex area of rain-making. San beliefs about capturing *!khwa*, the rain, first came to light in 1873 when Joseph Orpen listened to his San guide, Qing, talking about rock paintings in the Sehonghong rock shelter in what is now southern Lesotho. This young man lived in the area of the Sehonghong shelter and indeed guided Orpen to the paintings. Orpen's 1874 copy of these images is now one of the most famous San rock paintings (Pl. 14, Fig. 30).

Sehonghong is a large, approximately 100-m (328-ft) long rock shelter on the southern bank of the Sehonghong river, a tributary of the Senqu river in southern Lesotho. It is named after a legendary San man of that name who, in the turbulent years of the 19th century, assumed the status of a chief. According to present-day residents living nearby, the last San people of this area, led by Soai, another San chief, were killed in this shelter. Soai is said to have taken refuge by submerging himself in a deep pool in the Senqu river, with only his nose above the surface. But to no avail: he was shot while hiding in the pool. Patricia Vinnicombe describes the event: 'His body, adorned with bracelets of elephant ivory and a belt of beautifully worked beads, was subsequently dragged from the river and cut up for "medicine".'[3]

30 Above: *Joseph Millerd Orpen's 1874 copy of the Sehonghong rain-animal scene. Its position on his full, fold-out colour plate in the* Cape Monthly Magazine *is shown in Plate 14. Colours: bright red, black, white.*

31 Below: *Patricia Vinnicombe's 1960s copy of the Sehonghong rain-animal scene. This copy gives the true proportions of the images and shows the flecks scattered among them. Colours: bright red, black, white.*

The paintings on which Qing commented are not clearly visible in the Sehonghong shelter today (Fig. 31). They are now very faded and take some time to locate.[4] They are painted in an orange-red pigment similar to that used in 19th-century paintings in the region that include colonial imagery, such as horses and rifles.

Although it is not seriously misleading, Orpen's copy is not very accurate. A tracing that Vinnicombe made of the images in the 1960s gives a much better idea of what was actually painted on the rock (Fig. 31).[5] The imbalance in prominence between the two sub-groups of images in Orpen's copy (the smaller painted group is the larger in his copy) is so different from that of the original rock painting that we wonder whether Orpen fashioned his final copy from two separate rough sketches, the relative sizes of which he had by that time forgotten. It seems unlikely that he could have made the error in the presence of the actual paintings, especially when he was so careful with small details, such as the human figures' caps. Another detail that Orpen did not miss is a number of flecks scattered among the figures.[6] Unfortunately, these were omitted for technical reasons when the copy was first published in 1874 as a 'chromo-lithograph'.[7] When, about 90 years later, Vinnicombe came to trace the images, fewer flecks were visible. Today, some 50 years after Vinnicombe's work, the flecks are even more faded, though some can still be detected, especially with image-enhancing techniques.[8]

Orpen sent his copy, together with three other copies, all done on a single sheet of cardboard, to the editor of the *Cape Monthly Magazine* in Cape Town. As it happened, Orpen's copies arrived in Cape Town before his accompanying article, 'A glimpse into the mythology of the Maluti Bushmen'. Realizing the copies' importance, the editor at once took them to Wilhelm Bleek's residence in the suburb still known as Mowbray. There, Bleek showed them to Diä!kwain. This seems to have happened before Bleek had seen the article, so he could not have asked leading questions or put possible interpretations into his informant's heads. In any event, the differences between Qing's and Diä!kwain's observations are, as we shall see, sufficient to guarantee independence.

A transcription of Diä!kwain's explanation began on 21 July 1874. Subsequently, on 14 January 1875, Lucy Lloyd obtained from Diä!kwain further details of the 'very curious ideas' that so intrigued her and Wilhelm Bleek.[9] As she discovered, rain and rain-making were a rich area of /Xam belief and ritual, and, when Dorothea Bleek came to publish parts of her father's and her aunt's texts in the 1930s, she was easily able to compile two substantial collations in the journal *Bantu Studies* (now *African Studies*).[10] In one of these, she included a text and translation entitled 'Leading out the rain-animal', but she omitted to say that it was obtained in response to Orpen's copy.[11]

We thus have independent San explanations of the Sehonghong painting from two informants, Qing and Diä!kwain, who lived far apart and did not know one another. It is important to disentangle the accounts that these two men gave and to distinguish between the circumstances in which they were recorded. Then the key question is: Did the informants fundamentally confirm or contradict one another's explanations?

Speaking of the rain

Qing's explanation of the Sehonghong images was the first San comment on a rock painting ever to be recorded. It is of particular interest for the way in which he segues from an account of rain-making (with a very puzzling identification of the animal) to a description of the trance dance and healing practices (Chapter 2). Unlike the Bleek and Lloyd material, we do not have a phonetic transcript of Qing's remarks. In Orpen's transcription, the following is what he said (original parentheses and emphasis underlined):

> That animal which the men are catching is a _snake_ (!). They are holding out charms to it, and catching it with a long reim – (see picture). They are all under water, and those strokes are things growing under water. They are people spoilt by the – dance, because their noses bleed. Cagn gave us the song of this dance, and told us to dance it, and people would die from it, and he would give charms to raise them again. It is a circular dance of men and women, following each other, and it is danced all night. Some fall down; some become as if mad and sick; blood runs from the noses of others whose charms are weak, and they eat charm medicine, in which there is burnt snake powder. When a man is sick, this dance is danced round him, and the dancers put both hands under their arm-pits, and press their hands on him, and when he coughs the initiated put out their hands and receive what has injured him – secret things. The initiated who know secret things are Qognqé; the sick person is hang cäi.[12]

Apart from Qing's curious identification of the four-legged animal as a snake, this explanation of the images is explicit enough, but we need to examine our other source of insight into these images. This second source comprises two parts. First, it seems that Bleek and Lloyd initially obtained comments on Orpen's copies in an informal, untranscribed discussion with Diä!kwain, and, second, in the course of a longer phonetic transcription that was intended to clarify some of the points that Diä!kwain had made in the initial conversation. Bleek published a summary of his untranscribed discussion in the 'Remarks' that the editor of the _Cape Monthly Magazine_ asked him to append to Orpen's article. Interestingly, this published summary touches on important points that do not recur in the subsequent, more formal, verbatim account. Whereas Orpen purported to give a translation of Qing's actual words, in this summary we hear Bleek's voice to some extent ('Mangolong' is present-day Sehonghong) (original parentheses):

> *The paintings from the cave Mangolong represent rainmaking. We see here a water thing, or water cow, which, in the lower part, is discovered by a Bushman, behind whom a Bushwoman stands. This Bushman beckons to others to come and help him. They then charm the animal, and attach a rope to its nose, – and in the upper part of the picture it is shown as led by the Bushmen, who desire to lead it over as large a tract of country as they can, in order that the rain should extend as far as possible, – their superstition being that wherever this animal goes rain will fall. The strokes indicate rain. Of the Bushmen who drag the water cow, two are men (sorcerers), of whom the chief one is nearest to the animal. In their hands are boxes made of tortoise (!khu) shell (containing charmed boochoo) from which strings, perhaps ornamented with beads, are dangling down. They are said to be of Kafir manufacture. The two men are preceded by two Bushman women, of whom one wears a cap on her head.*[13]

That is Wilhelm Bleek's short, hastily prepared summary for the *Cape Monthly Magazine*. Later, in his 1875 report to the Cape Colony Government, he mentioned Diä!kwain's subsequent 68-page-long explanation. He wrote that he had, by that time, translated only the first two pages of it.[14] He completed the report in February 1875, and it was published in May of that year. He died three months later on 17 August. The handwriting in the manuscript suggests that Lucy Lloyd returned to the text and, taking it up on notebook page 2,542, continued the translation, though she left a number of pages at the end untranslated.

In 1930, when Dorothea Bleek was preparing Stow's copies for publication, she eliminated some repetition from her father's translation of Diä!kwain's longer comment and her aunt's completion of it. Comparison with the manuscript shows that she did not change it in any substantial way, nor did she omit anything significant. She then placed her recension alongside Stow's Plate 34 in *Rock Paintings in South Africa*, our Plate 16. Although this is not an inappropriate juxtaposition, we should remember that this account of rainmaking derived initially from Diä!kwain's response to Orpen's, not Stow's, copy. It is also important to notice that, in this longer account, Diä!kwain did not refer directly to any of the images in Orpen's copy. Instead, he started by saying that he was now telling Bleek and Lloyd what his mother had taught him about rain-making. It seems that, although his long account was initially triggered by Orpen's copy, he was giving a more general description of San rain-making, possibly without even having Orpen's copy before him.

We give Dorothea Bleek's 1930 version here in full with key /Xam words from the manuscript added in brackets; we have standardized the spelling of these /Xam words:[15]

> *My mother told me that people pull out the water cow [!khwa-ka xoro] and lead her over their place, that the rain may fall at their place, in order that the wild-onion leaves may sprout there. If the rain [!khwa] does not fall they will die. Therefore the medicine men [!gi:ten] shall go and kill the water cow [!khwa-ka xoro] at the place to which they go to stay near the wild-onion leaves, so that they can dig out and eat the wild onions. If the rain did not fall, they would not see the wild-onion leaves, for these are bulbs which they dig out and eat; they are the Bushman's food. Therefore they beg the rain medicine men [!khwa-ka !gi:ten] to make rain fall for them. This is the reason why the medicine man works magic [≠xamma] for them. The water's people [!khwa-ka !é] walk about, they charm [≠xamma; Bleek: conjure] the water, they make it rain, so that the mothers may dig and feed their children, and that the children may dig and feed themselves. They sling a thong over the water cow's [!khwa-ka xoro] horns, they lead her out and make her walk, they kill her on the way. They cut her up so that the rain may fall where they have killed her. The rain does fall; they bring the rain by means of the water cow's flesh. The rain falls behind them as they go home, it follows them; the people who asked for the rain really see the rain clouds.*

The value of all these comments by Qing and Diä!kwain cannot be over-estimated. Together, they establish another clear link between San beliefs, rituals and rock paintings. But there are some curious contradictions and mis-understandings that need to be cleared up.

Contradictions?

The most striking anomaly is Qing's identification of the rain-animal in Orpen's Sehonghong copy as a snake. Orpen's insertion of a parenthetical exclamation mark suggests that he challenged Qing about this apparent misidentification but that the San man remained adamant. Is this the whole story of what happened? Various explanations for Qing's (apparent) insis-tence are possible.[16]

First, a number of creatures, such as snakes, tortoises, fish, swallows and frogs, were said to be the 'rain's things'.[17] The identification of the creature as a snake might therefore have arisen through some confusion created by the difficulties of translation with which Orpen had to contend. At the beginning of his article, he admitted that he may have failed to understand Qing

'accurately when speaking through different translators'.[18] More than one translator and possibly more than two languages were involved: Qing's San language, the interpreter's SeSotho and Orpen's own English. During the back-and-forth discussion that must have taken place either Qing himself or one of the interpreters might have substituted prominent SeSotho beliefs about a large serpent dwelling in rivers and pools. There are in fact numerous paintings of large serpents that may well depict widely held southern African beliefs about subaquatic snakes; some of them may be rain-snakes rather than rain-animals.[19] We should, however, not overestimate the potentially debilitating effect of multiple interpreters. Qing spoke his own San language but in this conversation he was probably speaking SePhuti, which is partly SeSotho, the interpreter's language. Orpen himself could probably speak some SeSotho.

The next two explanations are not necessarily mutually exclusive. One of us (SC) tends to favour the first; the other (DLW) leans towards the second.

The first is that Qing was using his word for snake in a generic rather than a specific sense. For him, all rain creatures, be they quadrupeds or serpents, were called 'snakes'. The folklorist Sigrid Schmidt emphasizes the blending of rain-snakes and rain-animals: the rain could take on different forms.[20]

The second allows that it is not clear whether Orpen wrote down Qing's comments about the 'snake' while they were in the actual shelter or – as seems more likely – whether he did so later when, as he put it, they were 'happy and at ease smoking over camp-fires'.[21] Indeed, Orpen admits that he wrote down some of Qing's 'fragmentary stories ... then *and since*'[22] (emphasis added).

32 *A scene showing the capture of a rain-snake found near the Sehonghong shelter. Human figures bleed from the nose, clap, bend forward, lie prone and drag the rain-snake by a rope that appears to be attached to its nose. They are surrounded by flecks. Colours: bright red.*

He may therefore have noted down Qing's remark about the men catching a 'snake' sometime after having been in the Sehonghong shelter.

Given this rather disjointed sequence of events, it seems likely that Orpen misremembered the location of Qing's statement about the snake. Close by, on the other side of the Senqu river, is a site that contains a painting of a snake with what appears to be a thong attached to its nose (Fig. 32).[23] Two human figures are holding the thong and apparently pulling on it. As in the Sehonghong shelter, there are flecks painted around the figures. The *action* depicted – a creature being apprehended by people holding a thong and surrounded by flecks – is identical to the one in the Sehonghong shelter. In addition, the 'snake' shelter painting has women clapping and men bleeding from the nose. These clear indications of the trance dance explain why Qing led from the snake-catching element directly into a description of a trance dance and explicitly mentioned nasal bleeding.

This nearby painting leads us to argue that Qing and Orpen were talking at cross purposes. Sitting around the campfire, Qing was thinking of the snake being drawn along and the people clapping and bleeding from the nose, while Orpen was thinking of the quadruped being similarly controlled in the

Sehonghong shelter, where these are no clapping and bleeding figures. At the time, the Senqu river was in flood,[24] so it seems unlikely that Orpen was able to visit the snake shelter. But Qing could very well have pointed across the river to the shelter, which is easily visible from the south bank where Orpen's party was. Qing guided Orpen to a number of painted rock shelters, so it is likely that he would have pointed to and described the rain-snake painting, even if they could not cross the river to reach it. Some researchers have concluded that Qing's identification of the 'snake' shows that his testimony is thoroughly untrustworthy. However, the discovery of a nearby painting depicting the capture of a rain-snake surrounded by clapping and bleeding figures confirms that he *did* know what he was talking about.

Orpen's account requires further decipherment. Having given a number of the myths that Qing recounted and that constitute the bulk of his article, Orpen turns to the rock paintings that he copied and gives Qing's comments on them. Orpen introduces this new section about the 'snake' with the following words:

> The men with rhebok's heads, Haqwé and Canaté, and the tailed men, Qweqweté, live mostly under water; they tame elands and snakes. The animal which the men are catching …

The fairly extensive remarks that Qing gave about 'catching [the] snake (!)' immediately follow, without any break.

The fundamental issue here is whether Qing's sentence about the men with rhebok heads refers to specific images that Orpen copied or to a general class of rock art images. One way of looking at the problem starts by recalling that, near the beginning of the article, Orpen says that he 'commenced by asking him what the pictures of men with rhebok's heads meant'.[25] Qing replied: 'They were men who had died and now lived in rivers, and *were spoilt at the same time as the elands* and by the dances of which you have seen paintings' (original italics). This comment requires explanation before we address Qing's later remark about Haqwé and Canaté.

Researchers have debated whether Qing's remark about dying and living in rivers is a single statement or an abbreviation of a myth.[26] The point is, however, not germane to understanding the essence of what he said. What is important is that dying, being under water and spoiling are three San ways of talking about being in the spirit realm, that is, in an altered state of consciousness. When a shaman falls down in deep trance, people say that he has died. In that state, a sense of weightlessness, affected vision, inhibited movement and sounds in the ears all come together to suggest the experience of being under water. This reading of Qing's words is confirmed beyond dispute by his statement that they were '*spoilt at the same time as the elands* and by the dances'. He said quite explicitly that it was the trance dance that effected the 'spoiling'.

The key, if puzzling, word here is 'spoilt'. Researchers have suggested various readings. The answer is, however, to be found in the Kalahari. The Ju/'hoansi still use their word for 'spoil' (*kxwia*) to mean 'to fall in deep trance'.[27] And, as if that were not clear enough, Qing added that they were spoilt 'by the dances of which you have seen paintings'.

Thereafter, Orpen gives a series of myths, largely about /Kaggen (Cagn in his orthography). We return to some of them in Chapters 7 and 8. For the present, we note that, after giving the myths, Orpen reverts to rock paintings by again referring to 'men with rhebok's heads'. His first question to Qing about these paintings seems to have been about a class of images rather than specific images. Perhaps it was a general question that Orpen posed one evening as they were sitting around a campfire.

It appears to us that Orpen's second use of the phrase was also general: he was asking about therianthropic images in general. Our evidence for this con-clusion is that Qing referred to two personages by name (Haqwé and Canaté) and to 'the tailed men' (Fig. 33). The copy that has only two human figures is the one Orpen labelled 'From cave at source of Kraai River, District Wood-house'. The 'tailed men' are five in number *and* come from what Orpen calls the 'upper cave at Mangolong in the Maluti' (today 'Mangolong' is known as Sehonghong or Pitsaneng). The first point to notice is that the Kraai river is nowhere near the section of the Senqu and its tributaries that Orpen visited with Qing. Orpen must have made this copy on another journey without

33 J. M. Orpen's copy of the 'tailed men' that he found in a site he called 'upper cave at Mangolong in the Maluti'. The site has not been rediscovered. Colours: black, white.

Qing, or, more probably, on his rather circuitous return journey after his failure to arrest Langalibalele, the chief whom he was trying to apprehend. Second, the phrase 'upper cave at Mangalong' is ambiguous. It is not clear whether he meant a cave farther upstream in the same valley as Sehonghong or whether he meant higher up the slope. The set of five tailed figures has not been re-found.

There are two clues as to what Qing meant, at least in general terms. First, he said that all of the painted men – Haqwé, Canaté, the five 'tailed men' and Qweqweté – 'live mostly under water'. This repeats Orpen's version of Qing's remark from the beginning of the article ('now lived in rivers'). Importantly, *all* the therianthropic figures about which he was talking lived, not always but rather 'mostly', in the subaquatic and subterranean spirit realm that shamans visit in their altered states of consciousness.

Second, Qing went on to say that these men with rhebok's heads 'tame eland and snakes'. They were not just 'ordinary' spirit beings, perhaps ordinary spirits of the dead. They had special powers. But in exactly what sense did they 'tame' eland and snakes? We suggest that 'tame' is Orpen's translation of a San word that Qing used, one that may also be given as 'control' or 'possess'. It is probable that Qing said that these men *possessed* rhebok rather than eland potency, which enabled them to control game and the rain.[28] In the /Xam language the word we translate as 'possess' was /ki. This suggestion is confirmed by a comment that Diä!kwain made on the Sehonghong rain-animal painting. Referring to the people who are leading the creature as *!gi:ten*, he explained:

> For these are sorcerers [*!gi:ten*] who have [/ki] things whose bodies they own [/ki]. These things enable them to appear to see. So it happens that when these things have seen anything which the sorcerer does not know, he perceives by his magic [*/xutten/xutten*] what is happening.[29]

They possessed (/ki) eland and rain-snakes, a concept that Orpen understood as 'taming'.

The names Haqwé, Canaté and Qweqweté remain mysterious. It should, however, be noted that none of the Sehonghong rain-animal scene figures has an antelope head. Rather, two of them are wearing the sort of eared cap that one of Wilhelm Bleek's informants said are worn by shamans of the game (Fig. 14).[30]

Qing's citing of two names, Haqwé and Canaté, has suggested to some researchers that they were mythological personages who featured in tales now lost.[31] That restricted explanation is untenable. We must remember that mythology comprises narratives that took place in the distant past, whereas rain-making is not a myth but rather a ritual that is also repeatedly performed in the present. Qing made it clear that these personages were involved in rituals, not myths.

A more easily explained discrepancy is between Qing's statement that the flecks among the images 'are things growing under water' and Diä!kwain's view that 'The strokes indicate rain.' As will soon become apparent, the two men were thinking of different stages in a rain-making sequence. Qing thought that the painting depicted something happening in a pool or river and therefore interpreted the strokes as some sort of aquatic plants. Diä!kwain, on the other hand, imagined a later phase in the ritual when the people are leading the animal across the country, the rain falling as they go.

These problems aside, Bleek seems to have been baffled by what Diä!kwain was telling him. He was, after all, standing on the threshold of unsuspected expanses of the San supernatural realm. What could all this about attaching a rope to a 'water cow' possibly mean? Perhaps he broke off writing down his translation on the second page so that he and Lloyd could discuss the meaning of what they were hearing. Be that as it may, at the point where he suspended his translation he entered a note saying that the events that Diä!kwain was describing appeared to him not to be 'literal': 'the sense is apparently the reverse'[32] – though he did not know exactly what 'the reverse' was.

To understand 'the reverse', we list four principal points on which Qing and Diä!kwain agreed. They are:

1 The images depicted a rain-making activity, though Qing does not explicitly mention rain-making.
2 This activity was taking place at least partially under water.
3 The people were attaching a rope (reim: leather thong) to the creature, a 'rain-animal'.
4 The activity was being performed by 'sorcerers'.

In his longer response, the one that Dorothea Bleek placed next to Stow's copy, Diä!kwain explained that people led the rain-animal over the veld and killed it so that its 'flesh' would become precipitation. As they returned home the rain seemed to follow them to where they wanted it to fall: it was as if they had led the rain (the storm cloud) by means of a rope.

With these points established, we can now look more closely at the actual words that the informants used and at other details that fill out our understanding of this activity.

Mercurial *!khwa*

We begin by recalling that the /Xam word *!khwa* could mean both 'rain' and 'water' (Chapter 4). Whether it was falling from the sky or standing in a pool was a secondary consideration. In both contexts, *!khwa* had what Lucy Lloyd translated as 'magic power'. We know this because she was told that a girl at puberty 'has the rain's magic power'. The /Xam word that the informant used here was */koö-dde*.[33] As we have seen (Chapter 2), this word is one of three that denote the supernatural potency that San shamans harness. A link between power and puberty was suggested in another way. Girls experiencing their first menstruation were called 'new maidens', *!kwi /a //ka:n*. The word meaning 'new', *//ka:n*, could also be applied to recently fallen rain (in the /Xam language the adjective follows the noun that it qualifies). Its use in a variety of contexts shows that *//ka:n* has the connotation of 'especially potent'. In sum, we conclude that *!khwa* was imbued with potency.

More complexity awaits the researcher. *!Khwa* had three manifestations. It could be perceived as precipitation; it could be a creature (the rain-animal); and it could be a being who, in a myth about the Early Race, courts and abducts a young girl.[34] In some contexts it is difficult to be sure whether the informant is talking about precipitation or about a 'rain-animal' or about the rather indistinct mythological personage. This elusiveness is characteristic of San thought: it is Westerners who desire precision and, if they achieve it, they do so at the expense of some of the power of San thought.

Let us now look in more detail at one of *!khwa*'s manifestations, the one that most clearly establishes a connection between beliefs and rock paintings (Pls 16–19; Fig. 34; see Fig. 31). The /Xam word that denotes a rain-animal is *!khwa:-ka xoro*. Like the other /Xam phrases we have analysed, we can break this compound noun down into its constituent parts. The second syllable (*-ka*) forms the possessive case. *Xoro* means a large animal and may be used to refer to an ox. In the rock art, a rain-animal is usually a chunky quadruped of no recognizable species, though, understandably, some resemble hippopotami. The eland, too, can be a rain-animal. In a /Xam myth, hunters of the Early Race who had killed an eland placed its meat on a fire only to find that it immediately turned into 'rain' and evaporated. Unwittingly, they had killed the rain, which, in revenge, then turned them into frogs.[35]

Like the rain itself, a rain-animal may be male or female – a thunderstorm (a rain-bull) or a gentle rain (a rain-cow). A she-rain could be 'milked', its milk becoming rain.[36] An angry thunderstorm could be difficult to control.

34 *Two variations on rain-animals. The upper painting shows a man holding out what appears to be a fly whisk to the creature's nose. See Plate 19 for the full scene. The lower photograph shows a large rain-animal issuing forth from a crack in the rock face.*
Colours: (above) see Plate 19; (below) white, dark red.

Part of Diä!kwain's long account of rain-making deals with an occasion on which the thong that had been attached to a rain-animal broke; the creature escaped and the rain-makers had to return to camp without success.[37] A taut rope to a rain-animal made a ringing sound reminiscent of a musical bow as people tried to 'lead out' the creature. A rain-maker told how he used to feel the pleasant vibrations of the rope when he lay asleep, but no longer because the rain-maker !Nuin-/kúïten had died: 'For things continue to be unpleasant to me; I do not hear the ringing sound (in the sky) which I used to hear.'[38]

Capturing rain-animals in the art

The Bleek family informants identified a number of rain-animals in Stow's copies. Rain-animals are a prominent feature in the art of the region where he worked; it is now part of the eastern Free State, the Eastern Cape and southern Lesotho. Speaking of Orpen's Sehonghong copy, Diä!kwain told Bleek and Lloyd: 'Of the Bushmen who drag the water cow, two are men (sorcerers), of whom the chief one is nearest to the animal' (original parenthesis).[39] In his longer account he used the word *!khwa-ka !gi:ten*. In Chapter 2 we found that the second word, the one that Lloyd translated as 'sorcerer', means a shaman filled with *!gi:*, potency. In Chapter 1 we saw that there were specialist shamans: some were 'shamans of the rain'.

Qing enlarged on this idea. He said that the people leading the rain-animal were 'spoilt by the — dance, because their noses bleed'. In fact, none of Orpen's copies shows people bleeding from the nose; as we have seen, Qing was probably referring to the rain-snake painting (Fig. 32), which is accompanied by bleeding and clapping people. With these words about blood, Qing quite naturally segued to the trance dance itself. He described the dancers following one another, becoming frenzied in trance, bleeding from the nose and healing the sick. Evidently, rain-making and healing could both be accomplished at trance dances, though some *!khwa-ka !gi:ten* made rain in other circumstances, such as dreams.[40]

/Xam informants repeatedly confirmed the connection that Qing made between rain-making and 'sorcery'. To describe the 'leading out' of a rain-animal, Diä!kwain used the word ≠*xamma*. At first Lloyd translated it as 'work magic' and 'conjure'.[41] Elsewhere she gave it simply as 'fetch' or 'seek'.[42] In another account, Diä!kwain used the word //*kāï* in connection with capturing a rain-animal; Lloyd translated it as 'lead out'[43] and, perhaps with the advice of the informant, added a gloss: 'To lead out *by magic*'.[44]

There is an interesting painted detail in the Sehonghong rain-animal scene on which Diä!kwain commented. It is one of the 'things of sorcery' (Chapter 3). He told Bleek that the objects the people were carrying were tortoise-shell containers (Fig. 16): 'In their hands are boxes made of tortoise (!khu) shell (containing charmed boochoo) from which strings, perhaps ornamented with beads, are dangling down' (original parentheses).[45] Although Qing did not specifically mention tortoise-shell containers, he did speak of 'charms' being held out to the rain-animal: he had the same general understanding of what was depicted. As Diä!kwain made clear, at least some of these 'charms' were the aromatic herbs known as *buchu* (here given as 'boochoo'), though Qing mentions 'burnt snake powder'. After all, in his understanding, the men are catching a rain-*snake*.

Buchu as a 'charm' takes us back again to the nexus of girls at puberty and *!khwa*.[46] Because a young girl could easily anger *!khwa*, she resorted to the use of *buchu*:

> When a young girl approaches the water and it is raining gently, she grinds buchu. Then as she approaches the pond, she scoops out the buchu and strews it on the water. When she has strewn the water with buchu, she comes and darkens the parts of the water which float on top with red haematite because the rain loves buchu very much, for buchu is what it smells.[47]

This passage helps us to understand why, on an occasion when a rain-bull escaped, the rain-makers were told, 'You should have put *buchu* on the things; you should have given the men who crept up with you *buchu*, so that they smelt of *buchu*.'[48]

Buchu calms the rain, but it has other uses as well. Qing went on to describe the use of *buchu* in the trance dance. Men in the throes of violent trance ('their noses bleed ... people would die from it') were, he said, given 'charms'. The 'charms' calmed them and helped 'to raise them again'. Diä!kwain similarly explained that *buchu* should be given to a man in deep trance to prevent him from turning into a lion.[49] He also said that, when a shaman had 'snored' (sniffed) a 'lion' out of an ailing person, he was given *buchu* to smell because it induced sneezing and he would be able to sneeze out the sickness, probably itself in the form of a 'lion'.[50] As we have seen (Chapter 2), deep trance is spoken of as death and is the key feature of the dance, its ultimate purpose. This is why Qing said that Cagn had told the people to dance the trance dance, that they would 'die from it' and that 'he would give charms to raise them again'.

Second thoughts: further insights

Diä!kwain gave Lucy Lloyd another explanation of the Sehonghong painting (Fig. 30) as late as 20 February 1876. In it, he enlarged on his earlier explanation of the things carried by the people leading the rain-animal and added information that increases our understanding of 'sorcerers' and how other people regarded them. Dorothea Bleek published his further explanation with adjustments to Lloyd's translation of it. Unfortunately, she omitted an important point that Lloyd added as a note.

The following is Dorothea's 1935 recension of Lloyd's translation with key /Xam words added from the manuscript. Diä!kwain begins by insisting that the people leading the rain-animal are 'sorcerers':

> *The thing (held by the first man on the right) is like the thing which people take when they are practising sorcery, for they mean to let other people, who are dying of sorcery, smell it, those (learners) who are not strong enough yet. This will help them to practise sorcery [di //ke:n], for these things are in the things with which they strengthen their senses [/xutten-/xutten].*
>
> *For these are not people who are like ordinary Bushmen. For they are sorcerers [!gi:ten], and if we who are not like them go to them, though we always walk behind their backs, it seems as if something bewitches [//ke:n te] us, for these sorcerers [!gi:ten] bewitch [//ke:n te] us. We die without feeling ill.*
>
> *For these are sorcerers who have things whose bodies they own. These things enable them to appear to see. So it happens that when these things have seen anything which the sorcerer does not know, he perceives by his magic [/xutten/xutten] what is happening.*[51]

Lloyd's omitted note says explicitly that the 'thing' held by the man leading the rain-animal (Lloyd's parenthesis indicates which image is meant) is a tortoise shell 'in which *buchu* is'.[52] As we have seen, tortoise-shell containers of *buchu* are important 'things of sorcery'.

Today, the Kalahari Ju/'hoansi still use tortoise shells to produce medicine smoke in trance rituals (Fig. 16). They say that the tortoise shell contains, among other special substances such as *buchu*, the urine of a mystical giraffe, one of the principal animals whose potency they activate and harness in the trance dance. They drop a glowing piece of wood from the dance fire into the shell to cause its contents to smoulder. They then waft the smoke over a man to prepare him for hunting. They say that both the tortoise, in the sense of a mystical creature, and the medicine box made from its shell, 'sends you to the animals'.[53] Again we have an instance of 'sorcery' being linked to hunting.

One of Diä!kwain's /Xam phrases gives us further insight into how the San thought of 'sorcery'. The phrase that Lloyd translated as 'bewitch' is //ke:n te. The first word is one of the three words for supernatural potency that we have already encountered. The second word, te, means 'to fly, spring, get up, throw'.[54] Thus, sorcerers could harm other people by 'throwing' potency at them.

Diä!kwain's explanation also introduces another concept related to the 'deeds of sorcery': /xutten/xutten. This word is a reduplicative plural and, literally, means 'arteries'. At first Lloyd translated the phrase at the end of the first paragraph in which it appears as 'with which they work magic'.[55] She then deleted this and rephrased the words as 'with which they strengthen their senses'. What are 'their senses'? In /Xam thought, the !gi: that enabled people to be !gi:ten was, at least partially, in their arteries. For instance, Diä!kwain elsewhere spoke of the !kháuä, a word that Lloyd translated as 'vertebral artery', though there is really no such anatomical feature.[56] He said that, when a man returns from an out-of-body journey, he is given buchu to smell because his !kháuä 'has risen up'.[57] In addition, people would sing in order to make his 'vertebral artery lie down'; the songs would be 'medicine songs' that contained and activated !gi:. If they did not do these things, he could suffer an internal haemorrhage and turn into a lion[58] (see Chapter 6 for more on lions). If there is no 'vertebral artery', what did Diä!kwain mean?

One way of understanding these beliefs about !kháuä is to note that the word can be used as a verb to mean 'to boil'.[59] As we have seen, boiling was probably a /Xam metaphor for the rising sensation that a person in trance experiences moving up the spine. The 'boiling' metaphor is still used by the Ju/'hoansi to describe this component of trance experience.[60]

The last paragraph of Diä!kwain's 'second thoughts' may actually refer to the three figures with antelope heads who are bending forward and, in Orpen's copy, are to the left of the rain-animal group (see Pl. 14). Below these figures, Orpen wrote, 'From the cave of Medikane in the Maluti'. Diä!kwain was now speaking of another shamanic accomplishment: knowing what is happening far away. San shamans obtained such knowledge by turning into a various creatures. These are the 'things whose bodies they own'. The word that Lloyd translated as 'things' is t/wen. It means not only 'things' but also 'game animals'[61] and was frequently so used. (The word translated 'thing' in the first line of the explanation is tsa.) The phrase fits the Medikane therianthropic figures better than it does the rain-animal group. Apart from antelope, other creatures into which San shamans transformed themselves in order to ascertain what is happening afar include jackals[62] and birds.[63]

Diä!kwain's second comment on Orpen's copies brought to light new ideas. He was not alone. Researchers today find that returning to complex panels of San images seems always to lead to new insights. The art seems inexhaustible.

Another use of 'threads of light'

Both Qing and Diä!kwain mention a thong, or rope, being used to lead the rain-animal. At first, this may seem to be an ordinary material object, like the tortoise shells of which Diä!kwain spoke. But there is another possibility. As we saw in Chapter 3, people in trance worldwide see bright, sinuous and sometimes bifurcating filaments, or lines, that are one of the non-real visual percepts known as entoptic phenomena. These are the 'threads of light' that San shamans say they climb or along which they float on their way to God's house in the sky.[64] But in the 1920s Viktor Lebzelter found that the Kalahari Ju/'hoansi also climbed these 'threads of light' and what was almost certainly *buchu* for another specific purpose – to seek rain:

Finally the great captain in the sky hears the lamentation. The magician goes outside the camp and sees a thin cord being let down from the sky. He climbs a certain way up this, but the great captain comes down to meet him half-way. As soon as the magician sees the great captain, he throws a powder up to him; whereupon the great captain lifts him up high and takes him into his house. There the magician prays to him: 'Lord, help us, the children are dying, we thirst and hunger.' So long does he pray and plead that at last the captain says: 'It is well, I shall send water, that the children may have water and veldkos.' Then he again accompanies the magician half-way down the cord. As soon as the latter has reached the ground, he releases his hold upon the cord, which is at once drawn up again. The rain follows immediately.[65]

35 *A shaman wearing an eared cap holds a 'thread of light' that leads to an eland's nose and hoofs. Both the man and the eland stand on the line. Colours: dark red, white.*

36 A highly complex scene of rain-animals, fish, cattle and shamans. They are integrated with 'threads of light' that surround and emerge from the smaller, central rain-animal. A shaman with an antelope head holds the 'thread of light' to control the rain. In the 19th century the San made rain for cattle-herding, Bantu-speaking farmers. Colours: shades of red, white, black.

As we have seen, these threads are frequently painted in the south-eastern mountains and surrounding areas, where they are usually red and fringed with small white dots. In some paintings the dot-fringed lines connect with animals, often the heads of eland (Fig. 35). If we bear in mind what Lebzelter found and the /Xam belief that the rain could take the form of an eland, it may be that these painted eland are the rain, and the lines, though not fringed with white dots, are being used by people to capture it. It therefore seems likely that the 'ropes' depicted in the Sehonghong painting and elsewhere,[66] apparently attached to the nose of a rain-animal, derive from the entoptic form. The association of 'threads of light' with rain-animals is especially clear in a highly complex scene that brings together two rain-animals, fish, cattle and an antelope-headed shaman who holds a section of the multiple lines (Fig. 36). The whole experience of capturing and leading a rain-animal thus included hallucinations of rain-animals and also the hard-wired geometric percepts.

Stow's copies of rain-animals

We have now considered the accounts that San people gave in response to Orpen's copy of a rain-making scene showing shamans of the rain capturing a rain-animal in the spirit world. The informants' statements that Dorothea Bleek set next to Stow's copies of rain-animals are much shorter and often more enigmatic.

As we have pointed out, Dorothea placed Diä!kwain's longer account next to a copy made by Stow (Pl. 16). When, 50 years before, Lucy Lloyd showed this copy to an informant, he offered a short comment that she paraphrased:

She-rain with rainbow over her. (She-rains said to have rainbows over them.)

We now know what he meant by a 'she-rain', but his mention of a rainbow requires some explanation. The /Xam believed the rainbow to be /Kaggen's dwelling in the sky. Though no informant said so explicitly, it was the place to which at least some 'threads of light' led. Bleek and Lloyd's informant /Han≠kasso explained: 'The Rainbow is yellow in that part which lies above; the piece which seems red lies below. For the Mantis, who is also yellow, lies above, and Kwammang-a lies below.... Men call it Kwammang-a....Then people say: "The rainbow stands yonder and the rain will break."'[67] /Kwammang-a (the name has an initial click) was /Kaggen's son-in-law.

In response to Stow's copy shown in Plate 17, the /Xam informant said:

The rain with white quartz which has hail.

This is one of those statements that seem to allude – all too elliptically – to complex beliefs. To uncover some of those beliefs we turn to information that Lorna Marshall obtained from the Kalahari Ju/'hoansi. They spoke of 'lightning teeth' and 'rain teeth', which, Marshall found, was fulgurite, the crystalline substance that is produced by the fusion of sand or rock caused by lightning.[68] They use it by placing it in their rain-making horn. This horn, which Marshall calls 'a vestige of rainmaking ... from the distant past', contained other rain 'medicine' – certain roots and the heartwood of the /ana tree to provide redness and water. The idea of the rain having teeth is an extension of the concept of a rain-animal: as we have seen, this 'creature' was said to have legs (columns of rain falling from a thunderstorm), breath (mist) and hair (wisps of cloud below a thunderstorm).

The mention of quartz is particularly interesting because, worldwide, quartz is believed to have supernatural properties and is associated with altered states of consciousness.[69] Shamans perceive in quartz the light that they experience inwardly. Speaking of this light, a San shaman said, 'The light knocks me out.'[70] In a child burial in the Oakhurst cave on the southern Cape coast a large, broken quartz crystal was wedged in the left eye socket.[71] Though the evidence is slight, it seems that quartz was associated in some unspecified way with rain-making and with 'seeing'. That hailstones are similar in appearance to quartz is clear.

But we can go further. The informant said that white quartz 'has' hail. Here again it seems that the informant was referring to the notion of /ki, 'to have', 'to possess', or 'to control'. As we have seen, shamans were said to /ki certain animals in that they could derive potency from them or control their movements. Does the statement we are now examining suggest that quartz itself had comparable powers over hail and thunderstorms? Further, did shamans who owned quartz crystals thereby possess power over hail and rain? We can only speculate.

We can now see that the rain had many manifestations, and many things – animals, objects and girls at puberty – were associated with it. Once we are able to recognize a category of belief and the images used to signify it, we can start to decipher a range of rock paintings and iron out mistakes made in past interpretations. As we see in the next chapter, even major errors can lead to insights.

CHAPTER 6

Truth Hidden in Error

The lion on the other side belongs to the other lot of people.[1]

In the list of illustrations at the beginning of George William Stow's *The Native Races of South Africa* (1905), Plate 10 is mistakenly described as 'Bushman Painting of Elands and Lions'.[2] In the original rock painting there are no lions. The erroneous description was probably written by Lucy Lloyd, who selected some of Stow's copies for inclusion in his posthumously published book. Some 30 years before, Stow had himself fallen into the same trap when he commented on what eventually became Plate 12 of *Rock Paintings in South Africa* (1930),[3] the focus of this chapter (Pl. 20). In this instance, he believed that he could detect not just depictions of lions but, in addition, accoutrements of a lion hunt. His comment differs from those of a Cape /Xam San informant on the same copy in a way that illustrates the chasm between a Western predilection to discern rather crude narratives in the arts of small-scale societies and the subtlety and elusiveness of those cultures' thought.

Today, we know that, as in many of his copies, Stow rearranged the images in Plate 20 and, in doing so, created false groupings. A far more accurate copy made by the German ethnographer and explorer Leo Frobenius[4] in the 1920s and our own tracing of the images made in 2009 (Fig. 37) both show that the elongated ovals are not arranged in such uniform lines, nor are they as regularly shaped as Stow has them. More significantly, he completely rearranged the right-hand side of the panel. Of the many images that he did not include, we point to the head and neck of a serpent that appear to issue from a crack in the rock face just to the left of his copy (compare Pls 20 and 21 with Fig. 37). As we show in this chapter, it is key to understanding the panel as a whole.

37 A recent tracing of the panel of images shown in Stow's copy (Pl. 20) and in the photograph in Plate 21. In the centre, a serpent with tusks emerges from the rock face. Colours: see Plate 21.

Believing that San rock art in general was a literal representation, or 'history',[5] Stow began his personal explanation of Plate 20[6] by saying that he detected a lion hunt and that the rows of oval shapes depicted shields that the San made from eland hide and used:

especially in attacking the lion, when this piece of defensive armour was fastened on to their backs, so that should the brute spring upon them they threw themselves on the ground and drew themselves up under it after the manner of the tortoise, and thus afforded their companions an opportunity of rescuing them.[7]

Stow's essentially literal approach to the art led him astray. In the first place, there is no evidence that the San hunted lions. Generally, they gave them a wide berth and even left meat for them after a kill so that they would not pursue the departing hunters.[8]

Stow's lion-hunting explanation receives a more fundamental blow. The two supposed 'lions' are in fact the remains of partially faded eland paintings.[9] His mistaken understandings of them are at centre left and right of Plate 20. The white paint that the San used to depict the neck, dewlap, head and lower legs of an eland fades more swiftly than the red used for the rest of the body.

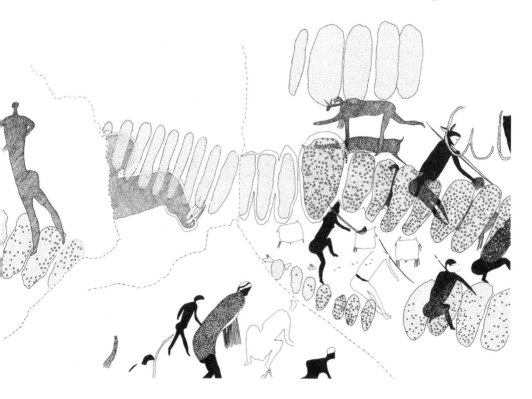

38 An etching of a lion hunt in colonial times, published by Sir James Alexander in the 1830s. The large mane of the lion, especially noted by early travellers, was sometimes thought to be suggested by the hump of partially preserved San rock paintings of eland antelope.

As a result, the bulky hump of the eland that remains after the white paint has disappeared has sometimes been mistaken for a lion's head and mane. To emphasize this interpretation, Stow added lines at the neck to separate it from the mane: there are no such lines in the image itself; he deliberately doctored his copy to suit his perception that they were lions. Sometimes, though not here, the red line along an eland's neck projects from the hump and confirms the species depicted. Figure 38[10] shows how early travellers pictured a lion with a large mane; parallels between this illustration and partially preserved San paintings of eland are clear. Indisputably, the images in question do not depict lions. Just as there are so few scenes that can be identified as 'antelope hunts',[11] so another supposed painted 'record' of the San's way of life falls away. Moreover, why did the San painter depict so many finely detailed 'shields' in three rows (there are over 50)? Stow offers no explanation. (We label the 'shields' as 'scutiforms' because their general shape may be said to resemble shields.)

Not surprisingly, Lucy Lloyd's /Xam informant did not confirm Stow's view, but he did follow the copyist's mistaken identification of lions. Probably Lloyd (who, it will be remembered, had never seen any rock paintings) was influenced by Stow's interpretation of these partially preserved images and consequently told her informant that they depicted lions. Then we must also recall that the informant himself was unfamiliar with the conventions of rock paintings in the region where Stow worked. He was therefore not in a position to contradict Lloyd. He simply accepted that two of the images in Plate 20 depicted lions. Now, in retrospect, we may add 'fortunately', because his error led to some fascinating insights.

A brief remark

Fifty years after Lloyd recorded the San comments, her niece, Dorothea Bleek, was puzzled when she came to prepare Stow's copies for publication. Understandably, she described the informant's observation on Plate 20 as a 'rather incomprehensible interpretation':

> Lion to the right. His daughter in white close to it. The lion on the other side belongs to the other lot of people.

At first glance, this puzzling statement may seem to be a prosaic identification of a species (lions), as is the case with San comments on other copies of rock paintings.[12] But it differs from those explanations because, in this instance, the informant went on to point to baffling relationships between the supposed lions and the people depicted adjacent to them. Fundamentally, whatever he may have meant by 'daughter' and 'belongs to', he did not see the images as simply reflecting daily life. Though brief, the statement is pregnant with meaning.

The informant's comments are thus paradoxically both incorrect and correct. He was incorrect in that the two images in question do not depict lions: they are eland. He was, however, correct in the sense that his initially puzzling statement expresses genuine San beliefs about lions. We are therefore left asking: How can a lion be said to have a 'daughter'? In what sense can a lion 'belong' to a group of people? The answers to these questions lead us to a set of San beliefs that illuminate other rock paintings in which lions are indisputably depicted. We consider one of them towards the end of this chapter. But now we need to examine how the informant's error opened up a far-reaching line of inquiry.

The San and lions

For the San, the lion was much more than a dangerous predator. It was fearfully associated with the spirit realm.[13] Megan Biesele[14] says that, for the Ju/'hoan San, lions are 'the ancient dark enemies of human beings', and Elizabeth Marshall Thomas found that the Ju/'hoansi 'treated the lions and the gods in somewhat the same way'. If the Ju/'hoansi chanced upon a lion, they addressed it as *n!a* ('big' or 'old'), a term that they use when speaking of the gods.[15] As is the case in numerous societies, the San employed avoidance, or respect, words when referring to powerful things or beings.

Nineteenth-century /Xam children, for instance, were taught to avoid the word for lion, //khā, and use instead /kuken, which means 'hair'.[16] The hair around a lion's paw, unlike, say, a dog's, makes small diagnostic prick marks in the sand; as //Kabbo put it, 'a lion's feet are hairy; a dog's feet are not hairy'.[17] For the San, spoor (tracks) are important; they believe that there is a close association between an animal and its spoor. For instance, when hunting an eland, they take care not to cross the antelope's spoor in case they frighten the animal in some mystical way (Chapter 9).[18]

Another /Xam avoidance word for lion was /kerre-/e. Lloyd translated it as 'lighting in'.[19] The exact meaning of /kerre-/e is unclear, but her translation suggests, we believe rightly, something intangible, ethereal. The /Xam also used the phrase tsá a: /na: /hoken e. Literally, taken word by word, it means 'thing whose head black/dark is identical with'. The /Xam used /hoken to denote any dark colour, but, generally, the word has connotations of danger and inimical influences. Lloyd translated the whole phrase as 'thing whose head's darkness it is'. In both this phrase and /kerre-/e light is played off against darkness. /Han≠kasso explained why his people used these two complementary phrases: 'for we feel that it walks at night after lying asleep while the sun was up'.[20] Moreover, the nocturnal lion was believed to have the supernatural ability to cause the sun to set and thus to bring darkness in which it could conceal itself.[21] Being both nocturnal and diurnal, such lions bridged the opposition night/day.

Perhaps the bright shining of a lion's eyes in the darkness beyond the light of a campfire suggests why it was called 'lighting-in' (Fig. 39). As one /Xam man put it: 'Dost thou not think (that) our fathers also said to me, that the lion's eye can also sometimes resemble a fire at night?'[22] (original parenthesis). According to the /Xam, failure to use either /kerre-/e or the phrase tsá a: /na /hoken e as an avoidance word could cause the flies, who overheard everything, to tell the lion that he had been disrespected (owls and crows performed a similar function).[23] He would then come in the night and snatch the miscreant from his hut.[24] Moreover, offended lions knew where to go to find the man with whom they were angry because they had the ability to acquire knowledge through dreams, as, too, did San shamans.[25] Lions were believed to be sentient creatures with supernatural abilities.

The /Xam also believed the lion to have another mystical ability that is difficult to understand, but that may be related to both /kerre-/e and the longer phrase tsá a: /na /hoken e. /Han≠kasso told Lloyd: 'When the lion is still coming, his head's reflection comes in sight before him, it looks like a real

lion. His head's reflection (it is) with which he deceives us'[26] (original parenthesis). The word /Han≠kasso used was /hu/hunta. Dorothea Bleek's *Bushman
Dictionary* gives /hu/hunta tentatively as 'image (?), shadow (?), reflection (?)'
and exemplifies it with only the passage I have quoted;[27] it was not a common
word. Even though we may not fully understand the meaning of /hu/hunta,
we can see that the lion was believed to adopt a supernatural form, a mystical
simulacrum, in order to deceive people.

That 'mirage' is only part of the lion's transformative powers. It shared with
shamans an ability to transform itself in other ways. For instance, it could
turn itself into a hartebeest in order to trick hunters to follow it; then, when
they came close to it, the animal turned back into a lion, causing much
terror.[28] It also turned itself into a person by putting 'its tail over its head: then
it trots (along) like a man'[29] (original parenthesis). The /Xam believed that
lions had a supernatural ability to become like people.

*39 'The lion's eye can
sometimes resemble a fire
at night.' A lion, its eyes
burning in the dark, stalks
towards a campfire.*

Lions and shamans

The other side of the coin is people, more precisely shamans, turning into lions. The San believed that any lion encountered in the veld could be a transformed shaman, especially if it behaved in a strange way. For instance, in a story about a young man who was carried off by a lion, we learn that a lion that does not die after being wounded is actually a 'sorcerer' (*!gi:xa*) in his leonine incarnation.[30] This sort of transformation was sometimes evident when a shaman healed people by sniffing ('snoring') sickness out of them: he made a noise like a lion.[31] A lion, or perhaps a shaman in that form, could enter into a man and cause sickness. Another shaman, who was healing a sick man, 'snored' the lion out of him. When this happened, the healer himself became like a lion and tried to bite people: 'Then people give him *buchu* to smell, and he sneezes the lion out.'[32] Moreover, it was said that lion's hair grew on the back of a shaman in violent trance; people rubbed fat on him to remove the hair and sang protective songs to calm him.[33] If people did not take care of a trancing shaman in this way, he would turn into a lion.[34] There was thus a dangerous transferral of leonine qualities from the sickness to the shaman.

Indeed, one shaman, !Nuin-/kúïten, killed a settler's ox while on a nocturnal */xāun*, a word that Lloyd translated as 'magical expedition' – one of what she called the 'deeds of sorcery' (Chapter 3).[35] The farmer pursued him and fatally wounded him. Before all this happened, !Nuin-/kúïten tried to avoid strife in his camp by concealing his lion's body from other people.[36] But he was not entirely successful. Diä!kwain recalled: 'My father used to tell me what !Nuin-/kúïten used to do when he became a lion, he walked treading upon hair (lion's hair).... For it looks as if someone big has gone along here.... [W]e see his spoor'[37] (original parenthesis). Shamans were so much like lions that they, too, were believed to 'walk on hair'.

Present-day Kalahari San retain the belief that a shaman can transform into a lion. One man told Richard Katz: 'These great healers went hunting as lions, searching for people to kill.... When a healer changes into a lion, only other healers can see him. To ordinary people he is invisible.'[38] Another man said: 'When I turn into a lion, I can feel my lion-hair growing and my lion-teeth forming. I'm inside that lion, no longer a person. Others to whom I appear see me just as another lion.'[39] Mathias Guenther also found that, among the San, 'the lion was a trance dancer's most common spirit incarnation'.[40] Conversely, lions are unable to distinguish between themselves and shamans in leonine form; a man who can turn into a lion is able to go out and mix with a pride of lions.[41] These are the experiences of benign shamans. The moment of incarnation is, however, so complete and intense that onlookers feel it as much as the shaman himself.[42]

Lorna Marshall learned that malevolent shamans too 'can take the form of lions and fly through the air'[43] – the /xāun, or out-of-body journeys, of which the /Xam spoke. The Ju/'hoansi use the word jom to mean a pawed creature and, as a verb, to travel abroad in the form of a lion and perhaps kill people.[44] The Nharo San take this idea further. They use the phrase xam.ti.≠xíí to denote a shaman; it means 'lion's eye' and refers to a shaman's 'supposed ability to travel across the sky as a shooting star'[45] – another reference to light and lions' eyes.

When a nocturnal trance dance is taking place, lions are often heard roaring in the darkness beyond the firelight. Guenther caught the essence of these unnerving moments: 'Their roars add to the sense of awe and dread that hangs over people at this moment [of transformation] in the dancer's experience, as it complements mystical peril from spirit beings with potential real danger from actual animals.'[46] In the Kalahari today, when San people refer to 'an eerie or strange time', such as an eclipse, they use the expression, 'Lions are walking.'[47]

Lions and human communities

These beliefs about lions and shamans are central to San thought. Indeed, the Ju/'hoan have a concept that they call !kui g!oq; it deals with dangerous relations between people and carnivores and involves notions of 'bad luck'. It is much discussed around campfires.[48] Taking note of !kui g!oq and the other beliefs, we can begin to understand what Lucy Lloyd's informant meant when he said that one of the supposed lions in Stow's copy had a daughter and that the other 'belonged to' a group of human figures. In a long account of lions and some of their habits, //Kabbo said that '[t]hey talk, they also are people', but 'people who are different'.[49] Like people, they have brothers, wives, daughters and sons: they live in family groups. The informant's remark that the lion's daughter is depicted is therefore understandable.

Moreover, leonine shamans can be associated with – 'belong to', in the informant's phrase – groups of people. In the Kalahari today, people speak about malevolent leonine shamans who 'belong to' a distant camp coming to a trance dance to harm members of that group. In response, one or more of their own shamans enter trance so that they can fight off the marauders in the spirit realm. The next day, after the excitement of the dance has subsided, people gather to hear about spiritual experiences of this kind. They feel reassured that their shamans were able to protect them. At this time, the malevolent shamans who come during the night are explicitly said to belong to a distant, often only vaguely identified, group. As a result, the source of sickness and social discord is located outside the small, tightly knit band. Destructive friction that would be caused by identifying the source within the small social group is thus avoided. The informant's suggestion that two groups of people are depicted in Plate 20, each with its own 'lion', fits in with these beliefs.

It is now clear that, overall, the informant was saying something that parallels the other San comments on rock paintings that we have discussed. Though he did not use the word, he interpreted the images in terms of what Lloyd called 'sorcery'. No other interpretation makes sense of lions 'belonging' to groups of people and having relatives. Ironically, we know that the painter of the images had no such ideas in mind. He or she depicted eland, not lions, and it was probably the relationship between the human figures and eland as sources of potency that mattered to him or her. This conclusion fits well with other images in Stow's copy on which the informant did not comment.

Other 'things of sorcery'

In the top left corner of Plate 20 there are two figures with antelope heads and one that appears to have ears or short horns. As we pointed out in Chapter 2, transformation into antelope is a common feature of San religious beliefs and rock art.

Centre right are two figures with lines emanating from their armpits. One has an arm raised in a commonly painted gesture. Similar lines are associated with two lower figures and with one centre left. Patricia Vinnicombe argues that such lines probably do not represent decorative tassels made of leather thongs, as some researchers have thought, but rather perspiration.[50] As she points out, perspiration was associated with supernatural potency; it could be good or bad. These contrasting manifestations of sweat potency are seen in two /Xam myths. In a tale about the Mantis and a troop of baboons, the trickster-deity 'anointed the child's eye with (the perspiration of) his armpits' as part of a long process of healing'[51] (original parenthesis). The bad aspect of sweat is seen in a myth of a female hyena who poisons 'Bushman rice' (termite eggs) with the 'blackened perspiration of her armpits' and gives it to the wife of the Dawn's-Heart Star (Jupiter); it turns her into a lioness or lynx.[52]

Sweat played a prominent role in the San trance dance. As we saw in Chapter 2, Qing told Orpen that 'the dancers put both hands under their armpits, and press their hands on' the sick person.[53] Among the /Xam, a sick or injured man was rubbed with sweat from a man's armpit, sweat mixed with a protective medicinal plant.[54] Richard Lee reports that the sweat worked up by a vigorous Ju/'hoan trance dance is the visible expression of potency on the body.[55] He describes it as 'a most important phenomenon in healing': 'Sweat is rubbed onto and into the body of the person being healed.'[56] The potency is in the smell of the sweat. That is why a shaman in trance is rubbed with the sweat from another shaman's armpits to protect him while his spirit is away on out-of-body travel.[57] Further, Lorna Marshall suspected that people threw their legs over a shaman who has fallen in trance 'to get sweat on to the man directly from the backs of their knees, a sweaty place'.[58] Lines, generally shorter than those from a figure's armpits, are sometimes painted at its knees. These lines, like the armpit lines, may represent sweat.

A dramatic lion panel

Occasionally, researchers find exceptionally complex panels of images that show us the experiential reality of transformation into a lion in unequivocal detail. These panels can be used to contextualize and illuminate less detailed groups of images. An effective test of any interpretation of rock art images is to see to what extent it dovetails with diverse details in a range of rock paintings. The more features of a panel of images that an explanation clarifies in terms of authentic San beliefs and practices, the more confidence we shall have in it. Repeated links between images and beliefs show that a connection is not accidental. It is to such a panel in the Eastern Cape Province that we now turn.

This panel shows a running lion with whiskers and teeth; it is pursuing ten human figures (Fig. 40). Any impression that this is a depiction of a real lion chasing real hunters in a real incident is soon dispelled. The whole scene is filled with indications as to the supernatural context of the event.[59]

Even at first glance, the unnaturally long feline tail suggests that we are not looking at a realistic depiction of a lion. But there is much more in the panel. Two of the fleeing figures bleed from the nose and are therefore clearly in trance.[60] They look back over their shoulders at the lion. The long lines that emanate from the tops of their heads almost certainly represent their spirits leaving their bodies via what the San believe is a hole in the top of the head

40 A San rock painting showing a mystical lion pursuing 10 fleeing human figures, some of whom have hooves and bleed from the nose. Above them 16 figures appear to take to the air, their legs tucked beneath them in a kneeling posture. Some have antelope heads and some bleed from the nose. Lines probably depicting their spirits leaving from the tops of their heads lead to a hollow in the rock.

(Chapter 2).[61] Trancers report a peculiar sensation in this part of the body: 'When the top of your head and the inside of your neck go "za-za", that is the arrival of num [potency].'[62]

Above the fleeing human figures are 16 transformed figures that have been called 'trance buck' or 'flying buck'. With antelope heads, they are part-human, part-antelope and depict a benign transformation of a shaman into an antelope coupled with the experience of flight in trance.[63] Like the running human figures, they too have long lines leading from the tops of their heads. The lines lead to a hollow in the rock. At least three of these 'trance buck' bleed from the nose. Some are in the kneeling posture into which a trancing shaman often falls; others, more comprehensively transformed, have no legs. A number have their arms in the backward position that some shamans adopt when potency, as a Ju/'hoan man put it, 'is going into your body, when you are asking god for power'.[64] Both the fleeing men and the trance buck are hirsute and thus recall the growth of hair on a shaman in violent trance.[65] On the far left an isolated figure, not shown in figure 40, bends forward in the posture that trancers assume when their potency boils painfully in their stomachs; a spirit line leaves from the top of its head. All these features indisputably situate the panel in the context of the trance dance and its mystical experiences.

The enigmatic rectangular forms at some of the figures' chests may depict the small 'medicine bags' in which shamans carry various substances. These bags are often slung around the neck so that they hang down onto the chest. In addition to containing potency-imbued substances, bags have transformative powers. In a /Xam myth, /Kaggen transforms himself into a 'flying thing' (a praying mantis) by getting into a bag.[66] Elsewhere he describes himself: 'I shall have wings, I shall fly when I am green, I shall be a little green thing.'[67] Getting into a leather bag was like 'getting into an animal' – like diving into a deep, dark pool of potency. The trance buck also have lines coming from their chests. It is possible that these lines depict sweat, but their position suggests that they more probably (or in addition) represent the tingling or pricking sensation that San shamans feel in the sternum and which they associate with the 'boiling' of their potency. A Ju/'hoan shaman explained: 'Then your front spine and your back spine are pricked with these thorns.'[68]

Near and just above the head of the lion is a uniquely elaborated figure with outstretched arms and complex emanations from its head and chest. Its head is turned towards the viewer of the panel. Because it differs from all the other figures, and because of its position above the first of the fleeing figures, we suggest that it may represent a specific shaman who is attempting to control the charging feline and thus protect the people it is pursuing.

In summary, we can say that, in Figure 40, we have a vivid representation of a spiritual encounter between a lion that may have 'belonged' to one group of people and the terrified, fleeing shamans of another group. There is little doubt that the painter of this panel spelled out what more laconic painters implied by their depictions of solitary lions. As San shamans often say, the spirit realm can be a fearful place, not something with which ordinary people should meddle.

Rare depictions

Two groups of people, each associated with a lion, set the stage for the sort of supernatural conflict of which the /Xam San spoke and of which the Kalahari San still speak. However, the San seem to have been reluctant to make images of such threatening creatures.[69] It is therefore not surprising that rock paintings of lions are comparatively rare. For example, Harald Pager found only 45 depictions of felines among the 12,762 images in his Drakensberg research area.[70] Nevertheless, as Vinnicombe pointed out, such images are 'consistently repeated'.[71]

The rock art with which Bleek and Lloyd's informants were personally familiar consisted of the engravings on the central and more western parts of the interior of South Africa. Here, too, depictions of lions are rare.[72] Generally though, rock engravings tend to be one or two images on a stone: 'scenic groups', though sometimes found, are uncommon. Yet some lion engravings are meticulous and, to our eyes, beautiful.

What would the engravings with which the /Xam informants have been familiar have looked like? At a site some 150 km (93 miles) to the east of the place where Diä!kwain lived there are engravings of grotesque creatures made by scraping the patina from the rock to leave a lighter colour image. Their tufted tails suggest that they depict lions. Often they have an exaggerated mouth that is wide open (Fig. 41). These images seem to emphasize the fearful killing and maiming ability of lions – their /hoken, or 'dangerous darkness'. Whatever conclusion we come to, we should see these grotesque images, not from a Western perspective, but within the framework of San beliefs about lions. Perhaps they depict prowling leonine shamans, just the sort of creature that roars in the darkness beyond the firelight. If not the Devil himself, they probably represent a shaman who, 'as a roaring lion, walketh about, seeking whom he may devour'.

41 A San rock engraving of two mystical lions with large open jaws.

Why did the San depict lions?

What, then, can we say about the comparatively few paintings of felines that do exist? Vinnicombe summed up her discussion of depictions of felines in terms of general, one could say abstract, symbolism:

These records of Xam Bushman attitudes towards the larger carnivores suggest that lions and leopards were associated with harm as opposed to benefit, with disease as opposed to health, insecurity not security, malevolence rather than benevolence, with death as opposed to life. The essence symbolised by carnivores – the large biting animals – was the opposite of the essence symbolised by herbivores – the large non-biting animals. Antelope were regarded as a constructive force in Bushman symbolism. Lions and leopards were destructive.[73]

She was right in broad terms. The San do think of felines as negatively opposed to the positive taxon of herbivores.[74] But we do not believe that they painted disembodied symbols of abstract concepts that floated contextless on the rock face. Rather, they placed their painted images in contexts that gave them a specificity and experiential reality. In coming to this conclusion, we need to distinguish between, on the one hand, the 'philosophical' system of San thought that we ourselves construct by inferring meanings and associations from a variety of statements given by San people, and, on the other hand, the actual social and cognitive contexts in which the San painted their images. But what was this context?

The act of painting was part of a complex, multi-stage ritual. For the San, the rock face was not a *tabula rasa*, a blank slate, on which 'artists' could paint whatever they wished.[75] On the contrary, it was an 'interface' between this world and the spirit realm, and therefore a meaningful context that semantically 'framed' images placed on it.[76] A painting of a lion, situated on this interface, may have triggered, in San viewers, associations of darkness, fear and the supernatural simply by being, in the first instance, a manifestation of a malevolent shaman, but the San themselves probably did not think of the image as a symbol consciously painted to convey such abstract qualities and states. Rather, they reified feelings of fear and impending doom (the Ju/'hoan concept of *!kui g!oq*) in material – concrete – images of malevolent, leonine shamans whom they had experienced in the spirit world. San manipulation of painted symbols was not so much abstract as experiential and specific.

But why did the San sometimes depict solitary lions in amongst other images? A clue may be found in what we already know about the relationship between San image-makers and their images. We know that San images were more than 'pictures': they were powerful things in themselves, objects that influenced people's beliefs and behaviour. Some depictions of eland, for instance, were reservoirs of potency to which dancing shamans could turn when they felt that they needed more potency.[77] In this way, images continued to function long after they were made.

Something similar, though in some sense in reverse, may have existed between image-makers and their depictions of lions.[78] Taking into account San beliefs about the very nature of images and the transitional rock face on which they were placed, we argue that the act of depicting a lion gave the image-maker some control over what the image depicted – that is, over a malevolent shaman who, if not confronted and defeated, would cause havoc in the painter's band. The image reified otherwise abstract and, for ordinary people, benevolent shamans' rather nebulous visionary experiences of conflicts with malevolent leonine shamans in the spirit realm.

Depictions of lions thus achieved two complementary things. First, because everyone knew that painted and engraved images were more than simple pictures, those of lions confirmed the existence of dangerous leonine shamans; they materialized otherwise vague threats. Second, though at the same time, the images reassured people of the image-maker's *control* over malevolent shamans: the image-makers had, after all, made the images and thereby 'nailed down' the leonine spirit beings that endangered their community. In doing so, the image-makers, who were probably in many cases themselves shamans, entrenched their respected position in the community as protectors against supernatural influences; image-making and subsequent engagement with images was embedded in the social matrix and had social consequences.[79]

'Formlings' and the spirit realm

We have left until last the most puzzling feature of Stow's copy (Plate 20), the one that he thought depicted shields used in lion hunts. Can some truth be hidden in his error?

Today, the overall shape and packed nature of Stow's scutiforms will remind most southern African rock art researchers of a class of images known as 'formlings'. This word is a hybrid English-German neologism that the German explorer and ethnographer Leo Frobenius concocted in the 1930s to denote a type of rock art image that is common in Zimbabwe[80] but that is also found, though less frequently, in the northern parts of South Africa,[81] and

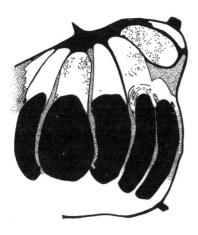

42 Left: 'Formlings'
painted in Zimbabwe.
Right: A section of a
termite mound from
which the 'formling'
images may derive.

occasionally elsewhere as well.[82] The word itself is neutral: it means little more than 'shapes'. Broadly described, formlings are cigar-shaped ovals, often with lighter-coloured caps, that may be found individually but that are more often stacked together in groups ranging from 2 to more than 20.

By and large, there have been two approaches to finding out what form-lings mean. One way is to see them as grain bins,[83] stockaded villages,[84] quivers, mats, xylophones,[85] beehives[86] and clouds.[87] Another perspective is to accept them as pure, abstract symbols. Peter Garlake, for instance, argues that form-lings symbolize the *gebesi*, the general area between the diaphragm and the waist that painfully contracts when a San shaman enters trance.[88]

More recently, archaeologist Siyakha Mguni has convincingly argued that at least some formlings in Zimbabwe depict the internal structure of termite mounds and, in some instances, the mounds' relationship with entities in the environment, such as trees (Fig. 42). Termites were an important source of nutrition for the San, and their nests were probably seen as the foci of potency;[89] some of the features of termite nests, he suggests, are exaggerated in accordance with San beliefs about supernatural potency.

Can the same be said of the Eastern Cape images that Stow copied? Termites were certainly a valued food.[90] The Bleek and Lloyd Collection tells how the /Xam dug 'Bushman rice' (termite larvae) out of the ground:[91] 'They eat the flying ants, when the ant's rain has fallen.'[92] Termite chrysalises were a nutritious food for the /Xam San. But they were also implicated in supernat-ural events. Lloyd learned that the /kitten-/kitten, a little black bird, 'bewitches the ants' chrysalides, when it feels summer is there, and they fly out'.[93] The chrysalises were not simply a prosaic food: they were supernaturally controlled. Depictions of termite mounds may therefore have pointed to openings into the nether realm over which shamans had control. In the piles of earth raised by these insects we see the nether world breaking through into the realm of daily life. As the rock paintings themselves proclaim, the sphere of the spirits was never far away.

While we acknowledge that some formlings in Zimbabwe probably represent termite mounds, we have come to another conclusion, one that takes us back to an older idea and one that Mguni also suggested: at least some may depict honeycombs. Figure 43 shows a set of honeycombs in a vertical crack in the rock face of a shelter about 12 km (7.45 miles) from the site of the painting in question. The stacked nature of the combs and their oval shapes certainly recall the painted scutiforms in Plate 20. The dots painted on the scutiforms may represent either bees themselves or the cells that are clearly visible in Figure 43. Numerous comparable paintings in the Drakensberg have been persuasively interpreted as honeycombs.[94]

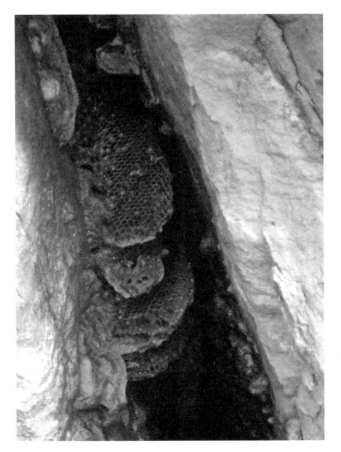

43 Natural honeycombs occur in stacks in the cracks of rock faces. The individual cells and the bees themselves can be seen here.

Bees and honey were important to the San throughout southern Africa in interrelated ways. The Cape San called /Kaggen's wife the 'Dassie' (hyrax, rock rabbit), a small mammal that lives in cliffs[95] where bees have their hives, while among the Ju/'hoansi the wife of the principal deity, though not a dassie (there are few cliffs and consequently few dassies in the Kalahari Desert), is said to be the 'Mother of the Bees'.[96] This association seems to have been widespread. Wilhelm Bleek noticed that, in Orpen's transcription, the name of Cagn's wife was Coti. This name he thought 'may be identical' with the first syllable of /Huntu!katt!katten (Orpen's initial 'C' being the dental click, /), which means a dassie, but he cautiously added that 'this is not certain'.[97]

The Cape San used a bull-roarer (*!goin !goin*) to cause the bees to swarm and leave their hives so that people could collect honey in safety.[98] The San bull-roarer was a flat piece of wood some 32 cm (12.5 in) long and 3 cm (1.18 in) wide that was attached to a length of string about 40 cm (15.7 in) long and thereby to a stick that could be used to twirl the flat wood and produce a roaring sound.[99] In one account, the people are said to 'beat the *goin !goin*'.[100] The word that Lloyd translated as 'beat' is *!kauken*; in addition to the obvious meaning, it was used to mean to tremble as a man's spirit leaves his body in trance.[101] In the /Xam text, the men took the honey home to the hungry women and a dance ensued: the women clapped, while the men danced. The dance lasted through the night until dawn.

There is no explicit reference to this being a trance dance (as we have pointed out, no /Xam word meaning 'trance' was recorded), but a part of the narrative suggests that the /Xam were performing a trance dance after eating honey. The informant who spoke about the bull-roarer described a significant moment: 'Therefore, the sun shines upon the backs of their heads.' In an added note he explained: 'The men are those, on the backs of whose heads the sun shines', and Lloyd explained: '*literally*, the holes above the nape of their neck'.[102] What did the informant mean? The Kalahari Ju/'hoansi consider dawn to be an especially potent time in a trance dance that lasted all night. Lorna Marshall saw what happens at this transitional time: 'Always at dawn comes a high moment, and sunrise is often the highest of all. As the sun rises, the people sing the Sun song. They feel that the *n/um* is very strong then.'[103] The Ju/'hoansi call the area at the back of the neck the *n//au*: it is the spot from which their shamans expel sickness that they have drawn out of people.[104] We have found nothing in the Bleek and Lloyd collection to suggest that the /Xam expelled sickness through this spot, but it was clearly important to them – the parallel with the Ju/'hoansi is striking.[105]

44 A group of men dance along a 'thread of light' while bees swarm above them. On the right one of the dancers bleeds from the nose and bends forward towards a strange creature that holds decorated dancing sticks. Colours: shades of red, white.

In the Kalahari today, honey is believed to have much potency, and the Ju/'hoansi have a medicine dance named 'Honey'.[106] Moreover, they like to dance when the bees are swarming – not, of course, actually in a swarm (Fig. 44). They believe that the bees are messengers of the Great God.[107] Writing about trance dances, Marshall says that when a man dances the Giraffe Dance he 'becomes giraffe'; the same is true of the Honey Dance: he 'becomes honey … Bees and honey both have n/um.'[108] Like other 'strong' things, honey transforms people.

For the /Xam, honey was also a creative substance. /Kaggen used it in his creation of the first eland: 'The Mantis put the honey in the water; he called the Eland, it was a big Eland. Then the Eland came leaping out of the reeds…. The Eland came up and stood; the Mantis moistened its hair and smoothed it with the honey-water.'[109]

The discovery of oval, stacked honeycombs near the site on which Stow based his copy (Pl. 20), and the rich beliefs about bees, potency and the trance dance, seem to us highly significant. Further, the position of the combs in a crack in the rock face may have suggested to the San an interconnection between this world and the spirit realm behind the rock face. It is therefore significant that just next to some of the scutiforms there is a marked crack and angle in the rock. Out of this opening to the underworld emerges a rearing serpent with strange tusks (Fig. 37). Another discovery at this site throws light on this serpent.

Music and transition

As one of us (SC) was working on this panel, he found, hidden among the faded images, at least seven men playing musical bows; four of them are shown in Figure 37. Still today, the San rest one end of a bow on their shoulder and then tap the string with a stick – as the figures in the paintings are doing. The lower end of the bow is placed on a resonator, usually a gourd or melon (Fig. 45). Among the /Xam, /Han≠kasso told of /Kāunu, a rain-maker who was able to call up the rain by striking his bow string: 'he sat and took up the bow, while we were asleep … we heard the bow-string as he was striking it

45 *A Kalahari San man playing a musical bow. He rests the lower end of the bow on a melon to act as a resonator.*

there'. He was a 'real medicine man' with great power: 'the clouds came up …
it rained there, poured down until the sun set'.[110] The tusked serpent emerging
from a crack in the rock face is therefore probably a rain-snake (Chapter 5)
summoned by the bow players, who were, in turn, empowered by the potency
of honey. In a comparable painting, a bow player seems to summon a bulky,
spotted rain-animal from an angle in the rock (Fig. 49).

There is in Plate 21 a remarkable coming together of San beliefs and rituals
– all of which Stow missed. Although there are neither lions nor shields
depicted, we have nevertheless learned a great deal about San beliefs concerning lions and shamans. We also find that potency is represented by painted
honeycombs and that shamans play musical bows to activate potency and call
up the rain-snake. The permeability of the rock face is implied by the honeycombs that lodge in clefts and by the emerging serpent. All in all, the panel is a
portal to a spiritual dimension. Yet it was built up over time, probably by a
series of painters. Each participated in the panel and developed ideas implicit
in the work of his or her predecessors. Carefully deciphered, this panel gives
us a good idea of how San rock art 'works' – very differently from traditional
Western art. But there are still unfathomed depths of meaning.

As we see in the following two chapters, honey and bees play a role in San
mythology. We therefore ask: does San mythology hold any clues that can
help us to decipher the meanings of the art? In answering this often-asked
question, we are led to an understanding of how the San perceived the landscapes in which they lived. Again, an important truth is brought home to us:
San thought, religious experience and ritual formed a closely interrelated
network.

CHAPTER 7

The Imagistic Web of Myth

And Qwanciqutshaa killed an eland and purified himself and his wife.[1]

Modestly, Joseph Millerd Orpen entitled his 1874 article 'A glimpse into the mythology of the Maluti Bushmen'. It is much more than a glimpse. Without his pioneering work we would know nothing about the mythology of the San people who made the rock paintings of the south-eastern mountains, some of which we discussed in previous chapters. His article is an astonishingly rich source for all students of mythology, whether they work in southern Africa or elsewhere. Its global importance was recognized early on, and it was reprinted in the journal *Folklore* in 1919. In more recent times, Orpen's article has become foundational for southern African rock art researchers, but the myths that it contains have received little independent attention.

Orpen found that recording San mythology was a frustrating task. What he was hearing seemed muddled and fragmentary. Perhaps because he was familiar with the myths of ancient Greece and Rome, tales that have a beginning, a middle and an end, as well as a purpose, be it moral or explanatory, he expected something more coherent and more intelligible. Then, too, the biblical mythology with which he was familiar suggested specific types of narrative myth. Perhaps with Genesis in mind, Orpen seems to have been especially interested in creation myths. But, overall, he ascribed the apparent confusion that he encountered in part to the use of several interpreters. He also thought that Qing, the young San man who was his guide, did not know the tales properly: 'Qing is a young man, and the stories seem in part imperfect, perhaps owing to his not having learnt them well.'[2]

A more persuasive reason why Qing did not know certain things became evident when Orpen asked what he thought was a straightforward, specifically mythological question concerning origins and creation: 'Where did Coti [Cagn's wife] come from?' Qing replied that he did not know 'secrets that are not spoken of'. These 'secrets', he said, were known by only 'the initiated men of that dance'.[3] He himself was not an 'initiated man' of that dance.

The rest of Orpen's article shows that the dance of which Qing spoke was the shamans' trance dance in which, as the young San man himself put it, 'some become as if made and sick' and 'blood runs from the noses of others whose charms are weak'.[4] In Chapter 2 we explained how people were 'initiated' into this dance. It was not by an 'initiation ceremony', such as many societies hold to mark entry into adulthood. Rather, novices repeatedly danced behind an experienced, older shaman, thus learning by protracted participation how to dance themselves into an altered state of consciousness and thereby visit the spirit realm.

Was Qing correct in thinking that San shamans had the answers to mythological questions such as the creation of Coti? We are inclined to think that many shamans were not as well informed as Qing supposed them to be. The point is that Qing *believed* shamans to have insights into the origin of mythological beings. He, and no doubt others, thought that shamans possessed knowledge about spirit beings because they frequently visited the realm in which those beings lived. Knowledge obtained via these experiences did not constitute a canon of 'secrets' jealously guarded by shamans, such as one associates with 'secret societies' in other cultures. As we have seen, San shamans speak freely about what they experience in the spirit realm. The so-called 'secrets' were merely matters about which people did not bother to think. That is probably what Qing meant by 'secrets that are not spoken of'.

Orpen missed this link between mythology and the knowledge that shamans acquired by means of the dance and their trans-cosmological journeys – as have many researchers up to the present day who think of mythology as an autonomous component of San thought and belief. Yet the dance is an essential part of our understanding of San thought: indeed, Qing stated explicitly that it was San shamans who held the key to fundamental aspects of San mythology. How can we turn that key?

The surface and the depths of myths

Since the time when Orpen was writing in the 1870s, folklorists, psychologists, historians of religion, literary scholars and social anthropologists have done an immense amount of work on world mythology. Names like Claude Lévi-Strauss and Joseph Campbell immediately spring to mind. They and many others have asked fundamental questions: What is a myth? Do myths differ from, perhaps simpler, folk tales? How can we extract the 'meaning' of a myth from its narrative? In any event, in what sense can a myth be said to have 'a meaning'? Why do groups of people identify themselves by their allegiance to certain myths and reject the myths of other communities and religions? In what circumstances do people recount myths? Are at least some myths closely related to rituals?

In answer to these questions, two fundamental, though not exclusive, approaches to myth have emerged. One is to see the narrative of a myth as paramount.[5] This meta-linguistic approach leans heavily towards aetiological tales (e.g., how certain landscape features came about) and also towards the dramatization of moral precepts (breaches of moral codes lead to punishment). The other approach to myth plays down narrative and emphasizes internal features and the structures of the tales. The structuralist position is that, within the mythology of a community, there are fundamental elements, or building blocks, and it is the essence (their inner, often hidden, meaning) of these repeated building blocks and the ways in which they relate to one another that create the real power behind the narrative.[6] Building blocks may include, among others, symbolic items of material culture, mental and corporeal experiences, repeated movements through the landscape, or, in strict structuralist terms, binary oppositions, such as day/night and life/death, and their multiple permutations. Once the narrative is seen as of comparatively minor importance, it becomes clear that individual narrators in pre-literate societies, like that of the San, can arrange and elaborate episodes and key building blocks according to what they think is appropriate at any given time.[7] Always, whatever approach we pursue, myth can be understood only in its own cultural setting, no matter what cross-cultural parallels we may be able to detect.

Without in any way diminishing the importance of narrative, it is principally the 'building-block' approach to San myths that we take up in this chapter. But we do not follow a strict structuralist approach.[8] The building blocks that we identify are not binary oppositions. Rather, they are 'happenings' that derive from San trance experiences. These 'happenings' give a flavour to narratives and obliquely refer to the status of shamans in San society: they cannot be said to 'structure' the narratives in a Lévi-Straussian sense.

At the outset, we need to emphasize that what we have to say does not apply to *all* San tales. Some scholars distinguish between folk tales and myths, though they acknowledge that the distinction is often hard to draw. It is easy to declare the tale of Little Red Riding Hood to be a folk tale and the Exodus of the Israelites from Egypt to be a sacred narrative, but there are often in-between tales that seem to have a bit of both categories. Acknowledging that there are no hard-and-fast definitions, we take narratives that involve origins and transformations to be myths. These transformations include, for instance, people turning into spirit beings, animals changing into other animals, people turning into animals and vice versa, and transformations effected by the movement of people or animals from one cosmological plane to another. These are the narratives that we discuss. But it is not always easy for people from another culture to detect evidence for transformation. As a result, researchers have sometimes discarded narratives as simple cautionary tales for children when, in fact, they are constructed on a foundation that implies, rather than explicitly describes, transformations.

In this chapter we do not attempt to analyse a single San myth in great detail.[9] Instead we explore a relationship that is implied by the three registers of our Rosetta Stone (see Preface, pp. 8–9). We begin this task by highlighting some aspects of painted panels of rock art images. We then show that principles detectable in those panels help us to uncover parallels between San rock paintings and what we argue are the imagistic, rather than narrative, patterns of myths.[10] The anthropologist Harvey Whitehouse uses 'imagistic' to denote religions that do not have written scriptures;[11] accepting that meaning, we extend its use to cover the deployment of an open-ended set of images in religious experience, myth and art.

Spiritual panoramas

Westerners who confront complex panels of San rock art images, some of which stretch for some metres, do not know where to start looking (see Pls 5, 21). How can they decipher them? Should they start at the left and move towards the right? Or should they do it the other way around? Can the panels be seen as comic-strips? Soon they conclude that a panel of many images does not have a beginning and an end in that sense. Frustrated, they then seek to break the panel up into clusters of images that seem to have been made by one painter at a single time and that appear, possibly by the actions performed by human figures, to constitute a unit – so-called 'activity groups'.[12] Homing in on these units, some of which appear to be narrative whereas others are less easy to categorize, modern viewers isolate images that they think were made by different painters and so miss intentional interrelationships between earlier paintings and those that were added by subsequent painters. In the end, researchers lose sight of the whole panel and what *its entirety* may have meant to San people.

The first thing to realize is that large, complex panels of rock paintings were cumulatively constructed over many years. They were not planned with a 'completed' form in mind. Rather, they were open-ended and invited the participation of generations of independent painters. Many panels are in their present state not because the painters considered them complete, but, more tragically, because the traditional San way of life in the region came to a catastrophic end. Consequently, we need to study the ways in which painters added to panels and related their contributions to already-existing images. This is an ongoing line of research.[13] This simple and really rather obvious point already begins to undermine an exclusively narrative approach to rock art panels, the approach that sees them as conglomerations of petty narratives of daily life with a light seasoning of 'mythology'.

One feature of San rock art panels that especially moves from narrative to essence needs to be emphasized when we approach the relationship between rock paintings and mythology. We mentioned it in Chapter 2, and called it synecdoche – a part stands for a whole.[14] We can now introduce a new distinction. 'Fragments of the dance' (Chapter 2) are of two kinds: those that can be seen by anybody at a dance and those that cannot be seen by everyone. In speaking of the first kind we may use the word 'realistic', as we would when referring to a painting of, say, a dance rattle that minutely shows the individual cocoons or antelope ears from which its segments were made. Realistic fragments of the dance include:

- people bleeding from the nose
- people bending forward at the waist
- people with their arms held in a backward or outward position
- women clapping
- a fly whisk
- dance rattles

The other kind of 'fragment of the dance' comprises conceptual entities, things that can be 'seen' only by shamans in trance. They include:

- the 'threads of light' to which we return in the next chapter
- lines from the top of the head that depict the spirit leaving the body
- transformations of people into animals
- entry into the spirit realm through holes in the ground or the rock face

All these painted fragments of the dance probably operated on at least three levels: First, they implied the significance of the whole dance. It was through the trance dance that people were healed and society was protected from malign influences. Second, the fragments drew attention to key moments in shamans' spiritual journeys from this world to the spirit realm. As the Kalahari San still say, the 'breakthrough' into the spirit realm is terrifying but also immensely beneficial for the community. Third, by their very nature, each fragment focused on an individual. The dance was certainly a communal ritual, but, notwithstanding the combined activity of a community, it is the individual shaman who achieves breakthrough into the spirit realm. Each time an individual danced and entered the spirit world, it was a new, valued and specific instance of one person's journey. As Megan Biesele writes, 'Ju/'hoansi themselves treat these experiences as unique messages from the beyond, accessible in no other way save through trance, and they regard narratives of the experiences as documents valuable to share.'[15] Similarly, in rock art panels individual revelations are embedded in the commonwealth of knowledge. A particular kind of relationship between certain individuals and their communities is thus implied by San rock art.

Often panels that at first glance appear to be assemblages of beautiful depictions of animals turn out to be peppered with fragments of the dance. Even within a single activity group, one may find, say, six men walking in a line. Only one of them bleeds from the nose, but that figure clearly implicates the others in the religious activity of reaching out to the spirit realm. At the level of the whole panel, such figures implicate those around them. The same is true of the dance itself. Biesele found that 'all who come to the dance experience an uplifting energy which they feel to be a necessary part of their lives'.[16]

Then we must recall that the rock face is a contextualizing 'veil' between this world and the spirit realm: sometimes, as we saw in Chapters 4 and 5, images appear to issue forth from (or enter into) the spirit world through steps and cracks in the rock on which they are painted.[17] Fragments of the dance thus combine with the liminal nature of the rock face on which they were painted to unite the whole panel in a mosaic of spiritual experiences. In some ways, San rock art panels are like stained-glass windows in medieval cathedrals: the 'light' from the spiritual domain shines through them and animates them so that they become manifestations of spiritual things rather than mere 'pictures'. Both San paintings and ecclesiastical stained glass induce enveloping mental states of awe, fear and comfort.

How do these thoughts about painted panels and mythology help us to approach specific San myths?

The San cosmos

Everything that the San did, thought and experienced, be it what we would (not altogether appropriately) call secular or sacred, happened within a specific cosmological framework. Herein lies the key to understanding both San myth and art. Once we understand the levels that made up the totality of the San cosmos, the nature of the movements from place to place that occur in myths and the ways in which the images are painted on the rock combine to make overall sense.

Clues to the structure of the 19th-century San cosmos are scattered throughout the texts that Wilhelm Bleek and Lucy Lloyd collected and those that Orpen obtained from Qing.[18] These beliefs persist among San groups in the present-day Kalahari. We now outline the San cosmos and then move on to see how an appreciation of the levels of that cosmos help us to understand otherwise obscure myths.

Briefly, the San recognized three cosmological levels. In the middle was the level on which they lived their daily lives, hunted animals and gathered plant foods. Above was a level of spiritual things. Here were god and other spirit beings, all of whom lived alongside god's vast herds of animals. As Qing put it when Orpen asked him where Cagn was, 'Where he is, elands are in droves like cattle.'[19] Below the level of daily life was a subterranean spiritual realm, accessible by means of holes in the ground and waterholes. Here, under water, dwelt the rain-animal and other spirit beings.

This summary may be misleading because it implies more rigidity in San cosmology than the people themselves would have recognized. Again, we must distinguish between the rather philosophical 'systems' that we construct from a collection of indigenous statements and the less formalized, day-to-day thinking of people. The San spirit realms overflowed into the level of daily life, and shamans had the ability to travel with some frequency between the three levels. An out-of-body journey, beginning on the level of daily life, could proceed by entering a hole in the ground or a waterhole and then, after subterranean travel, rise up to the realm above. The three levels thus interacted, and the fundamental San religious experience was movement between cosmological levels.

The purposes for these journeys were multiple. Some shamans went to the spirit realm to plead for the sick; others fought off malevolent shamans who tried to infect people with sickness; others sought information about the location of animals; still others were more concerned with capturing a subaquatic rain-animal in the lowest level and then leading it through the sky so that its blood and milk could fall as rain. But shamans were not the only people who could experience the spirit realms. Ordinary people could address god and ask for blessings of food. They could also encounter spirit beings, such as shamans in the form of lions (Chapter 6). Everyone was continuously aware of the proximity of spiritual things.

!Khwa, girls and frogs

As we pointed out in Chapter 1, it is significant that San informants seldom referred directly to myths when they commented on copies of rock paintings. The art cannot be said to be in any general, overall sense illustrative of mythology. More frequently, the images reminded informants of 'sorcery', the 'things and deeds of sorcery' and rain-making. There were, however, two occasions when the San commentators seem to have referred to a tale of people being transformed into frogs. It was recorded in a number of versions. Lucy Lloyd entitled one of these 'The girl's story; the frogs' story'.[20]

Before considering this tale, we need to note that the site at which Stow claimed one of the relevant paintings (Fig. 46) existed has not been relocated. Dorothea Bleek 'hunted in some of the many kloofs [Dutch for 'narrow valleys'] and under several waterfalls' when, in the late 1920s, she was prepar-

46 George Stow's copy of a San rock painting that purports to depict a line of frogs.
It reminded a /Xam informant of a tale in which the rain turned people into frogs because
a girl at puberty had misbehaved. Colours: white, black, dark red.

ing Stow's copies for publication, but she was unsuccessful. Subsequent researchers and our own efforts have fared no better, but one of us (SC) did find a collapsed rock shelter next to a waterfall on the farm that Stow mentions as being the location of the paintings. Perhaps the lost images are now buried under the fallen rock. Nevertheless, some researchers privately express doubts as to the authenticity of Stow's copy, and we are inclined to agree that reservations may well be in order. For one thing, paintings of frogs are extremely rare, and, for another, the putative frog images in Stow's copy are stylistically unusual. Still, the myth to which the 19th-century informant referred interests us in its own right because of the elements it combines.

Two of Bleek and Lloyd's informants commented on Stow's Plate 45 (see Fig. 46). We do not have a phonetic transcription of the comments of either, only Lloyd's summary and her interpolated remarks. One of the informants said:

> The water is destroying these people, changing them into frogs, because a girl had been eating touken, a ground food.

The second informant said:

> They become frogs. The girl whose fault it is in the brown dress (the sixth figure from the right), the Rain being angry with her. The third said to be her father, fourth her mother. The figure to the extreme left was hunting and is blown by the wind into the water.

We give our own brief summary of the myth to which Dorothea Bleek believed the informants were referring. In dramatized performance and as transcribed by Lloyd it was much longer:

A girl who was ill lay in a hut. The other people went out to seek chrysalides [Chapter 6]. A young child remained at home and observed what happened. The ill girl went to the waterhole and killed a Water-child. As a result, !khwa turned her and the other people as well into frogs. !Khwa was as large as a bull, and his children were the size of calves.[21]

This is the kind of San tale that appears trivial if the significances of its elements are unknown to the modern reader. It could easily be dismissed as a simple folk tale seemingly featuring the 'watermeide' that we encountered in Chapter 4. Indeed, for the informants who cited the narrative in response to Stow's copy, it seems to have been taken as a cautionary tale for young girls to behave themselves. But we need to dig deeper. As fragments of the dance are scattered through panels of rock art images, so too are certain pivotal concepts – building blocks – scattered through myths. They give the whole myth significance and coherence, and, moreover, link myths one to another conceptually rather than narratively. We therefore need to know something about San understandings of the ill girl, waterholes and frogs.

As in some comparable /Xam accounts of rituals, the girl is at puberty (what, in Lloyd's translation, the /Xam called 'a new maiden') and is consequently secluded in a hut.[22] At this time of life, she possess supernatural powers. Diä!kwain explained that if a 'new maiden' curses a man, the rain will strike him dead with lightning: 'For, she when she is a maiden, she has the rain's magic power [*!khwa ka /ko:öde*].' Here, as in some other tales, *!khwa* is personified and must be treated with respect. Girls ambivalently poised at puberty can command the supernatural potency of the rain.

The transformation into frogs takes place at a waterhole. The narrator spoke of 'descending' into a 'spring'. As we have seen, the /Xam word *!khwa* was used to mean both water and rain: *!khwa* wells up in waterholes and falls from the sky. It will be recalled that shamans of the rain claimed to dive into waterholes to capture a *!khwa-ka xoro*, a rain-animal (Chapter 5). Both water and waterholes are mediators between levels of the San cosmos, between material and spiritual realms. As such, they are powerful places of transformation.[23]

The third element is frogs. They, too, are mediators between levels of the cosmos: they live in water and on dry land.[24] Qing gave a comparable explanation of the tailed figures shown in one of Orpen's copies (Fig. 33). He said that they 'live mostly under water; they tame elands and snakes'.[25] That they 'live *mostly* under water' implies that they are amphibious. The concept of amphibiousness intrigued some painters, and they expressed it by depicting creatures that could live both on land and under water. There is, for instance, a single (as far as we know) painting of a pair of crabs (Fig. 47).[26] One may suppose that it is the quirky sport of an imaginative painter, but crabs' associations of transition between land and water are implied by the close juxtaposition of depictions of leather bags (not shown in Figure 47). As we saw in Chapter 6, getting into a bag was, for the /Xam, a mode of transformation and transition. The painting goes further in that it shows that the smaller of the two crabs lacks pincers. Why? Crabs are territorial and may attack other crabs if they trespass on their territory. In such fights, a vanquished crab may lose its pincers (in time, they will grow again). If the amphibious crabs are shamans who have passed through the transformation

47 The theme of being under water as a way of conveying the sensations of altered states of consciousness is uniquely expressed in a painting of two crabs in what may be a pool of water. The small crab has lost its pincers, probably in combat with the larger one. Colour: black.

48 Below: Figures, one of whom bleeds from the nose, rise up out of a deep cleft in the rock that has been smeared with black paint. The large figure has an antelope head. The under-water theme is expressed by the presence of fish, eels and turtles. A cluster of about 12 fly whisks point to the trance dance. Colours: shades of red, black, white.

of water, they probably represent a battle in the spiritual (subaquatic) realm, such as shamans often report.[27]

Another painting shows antelope-headed figures rising from a deep crack in the rock (one bleeds from the nose): around them are not only fish and eels, underwater creatures, but also what we take to be amphibious turtles (Fig. 48).[28] /Han≠kasso told Lloyd that both the tortoise and the 'water tortoise' were 'things that the rain puts aside as its meat. Therefore Bushmen fear them

greatly.'[29] Seen in the context of other paintings of amphibious creatures, the line of frogs in Figure 46 implies hazardous transition between realms, the foundation of the myth to which the informant referred.

The point we make here is that, though this tale of frogs may seem trivial as a narrative, its elements are rich in cosmological and 'sorcery' connotations. Still, we doubt that the tale was indeed the subject of the rock painting in Figure 46 and that the images were merely illustrative of it. It seems more likely to us that the significance of the paintings for those who made and viewed them lay in the rarely depicted frog-like creatures. The principal subject of the painting, if it can be said to have one, is the cosmological mediation that frogs imply. And, as we have seen in previous chapters, transition is a concept that suffuses San rock art.

Honey and transition

The way in which cosmological levels were projected onto the specific natural environment in which a community of San people lived is more clearly evident in two myths that Qing related to Orpen.[30] Neither appears in our other 19th-century source, the Bleek and Lloyd Collection. Although they come from markedly different climatic and physical environments some 600 km (373 miles) apart, there are nevertheless notable parallels between the collections.[31] Exactly what constitutes those parallels is, we argue, what we are now discussing: the 'building blocks' of the San cosmos and trans-cosmological travel.

The first of the two myths that we examine features Cogaz, who, in Orpen's collection, was Cagn's elder son:

> Cagn found an eagle getting honey from a precipice, and said, 'My friend, give me some too;' and it said 'Wait a bit,' and it took a comb and put it down, and went back and took more, and told Cagn to take the rest, and he climbed up and licked what remained on the rock, and when he tried to come down he found he could not. Presently, he thought of his charms, and took some from his belt, and caused them to go to Cogaz to ask advice; and Cogaz sent word back by means of the charms that he was to make water to run down the rock, and he would find himself able to come down: he did so, and when he got down, he descended into the ground and came up again, and he did this three times, and the third time he came up near the eagle, in the form of a large bull eland; and the eagle said, 'What a big eland,' and went to kill it, and it threw an assegai, which passed it on the right side, and then another, which missed it, to the left, and a third, which passed between its legs, and the eagle trampled on it, and immediately hail fell and stunned the eagle, and Cagn killed it,

and took some of the honey home to Cogaz, and told him he had killed the eagle
which had acted treacherously to him, and Cogaz said 'You will get harm some day
by all these fightings.'[32]

If we adopt the narrative approach to this myth, we can perhaps say that it is a cautionary tale: it is unwise to try to take other people's honey. Indeed, it ends with Cogaz's admonition: 'You will get harm some day by all these fightings.' But, if we look beneath the narrative surface, we find the levels of the San cosmos, a desire for potency, and the supernatural abilities of shamans who possess 'charms' and who can control the rain. This, we argue, is the real impact of the tale, however subliminal: the myth is an affirmation of the tiered cosmos *and* the powers of shamans to transcend it in their endeavours to maintain social harmony and the health of the community.

In broad terms, then, the tale concerns honey and trans-cosmological travel, together with a mixture of reality and supernatural events. But there are also mythical equivalents to the 'fragments of the dance' that are scattered through painted panels. To decipher the myth we need to look beneath the narrative surface to these less obvious elements.

We begin by noting that honey was not only a valued food for the San, their gods and the spirits of the dead:[33] it also appears in numerous myths from all San groups, not just the /Xam and Maloti people. Along with fat, another greatly desired food, the Ju/'hoan San of the Kalahari Desert consider honey anomalous because it can be both eaten and drunk. As the 19th-century /Xam man //Kabbo put it, 'They will eat the honey's liquid fat.'[34] The idioms 'to eat fat' and 'to eat honey' can mean to have sexual intercourse; they also refer to the collaborative interaction of men and women in the trance dance.[35] Importantly, honey has much potency and is the name of one of the Ju/'hoan medicine songs that are sung at trance dances. As Lorna Marshall put it: 'These dances are named for these things because the things are vital, life-and-death things and they are strong, as the curing medicine in the music is strong.'[36] As we have seen, when a man dances the Giraffe Dance he 'becomes giraffe'; the same is true of the Honey Dance: he 'becomes honey'.[37] One Ju/'hoan shaman, /Gao, told how he received his Honey Song: 'It was daytime, and he was awake when //Gāuwa appeared to him and bid him follow to a tree that had a beehive in it. //Gāuwa pushed /Gao in the hole in the tree where the baby bees and the honey were. Bees and honey both have n/um.'[38]

Even as a man may possess honey potency, so too may he own a beehive and mark it as his property. Anyone who stole another man's honey ran the risk of being killed.[39] Stow reported that the San of the south-eastern mountains owned hives that were lodged in the cliffs; these hives could be inherited.[40] To reach them, the San hammered wooden pegs into the rock to act as footholds.[41] People returned to their hives seasonally each year.[42] In the more open, treeless /Xam San country, the people exploited underground hives; honey may also be found in old termite mounds that bees have taken over.[43] In a /Xam myth, /Kaggen digs out honey for the little springbok.[44] As we saw in Chapter 6, these underground honey hives were closed by a large stone,[45] as were the locust holes that shamans controlled.

In the Drakensberg there are rock paintings of people apparently climbing ladders to hives from which swarms of bees emerge.[46] As we saw in the previous chapter, there are also paintings that show the nested catenary curve form that honeycombs assume in the wild; many such images have minutely painted bees.[47] Why would the San have painted honeycombs? A probable answer is that honey and the activity of obtaining it was, like hunting eland, indicative of the acquisition of potency. Confirmation of this suggestion comes from paintings that show hives and bees explicitly associated with dancing shamans, a number of whom bleed from the nose and wear dancing rattles (Fig. 44). The close association between bees, honey, potency and trance dancing is indisputable.

The background to the myth is now becoming plainer. The surface narrative is that the eagle probably owned a hive high on a cliff, and Cagn tried to obtain some of his honey. But honey also represents potency: Cagn, himself a shaman, tried to obtain the eagle's potency. The theme of combat between shamans is taken up in other myths and rock paintings. But, as often happens in /Xam myths, Cagn was tricked and, in this instance, left hanging on the rock face. Eventually, after using his 'charms' (probably *buchu*), he was able to climb down by means of water. It is not clear whether 'to make water' means to urinate or simply to wet the rock. Either way, water is, as we saw in Chapter 4, a mediator between cosmological levels.

Passing between cosmological levels is still more clearly evident in what followed. Cagn 'descended into the ground and came up again, and he did this three times'. This is a common form of San (and other) shamanic travel. For instance, Kxao Giraffe, an old Ju/'hoan shaman, told how his 'protector', the giraffe, told him that he would enter the earth: 'That I would travel far through the earth and then emerge at another place.' Then he rose to the upper level of the cosmos: 'When we emerged, we began to climb the thread – it was the thread of the sky.'[48] Prior to that, water had facilitated his underground travel: 'We travelled until we came to a wide body of water. It was a river. He took me to the river. The two halves of the river lay to either side of us, one to the left and one to the right.'[49] In that manner, Kxao Giraffe reached the place where the spirits were dancing. There he learned how to trance dance.

When Cagn emerged from his third passage underground, he transformed himself into a large bull eland, the most potent and the fattest of all animals. Then, in an episode that recalls a /Xam myth about a fight that /Kaggen had with the meerkats (his affines) who had killed his eland and acquired its potency,[50] Cagn is able, by the potency of the eland, to deflect the eagle's assegais (spears). Finally, !khwa again comes to Cagn's rescue, and hail (Chapter 5) kills the eagle.

Eland and precipices

In another of Qing's myths we encounter a similar cosmological structure along with some highly evocative imagery.[51] It concerns Qwanciqutshaa, a mythical 'chief [who] used to live alone', who had 'great power' and through whom Cagn 'gave orders':[52]

And Qwanciqutshaa killed an eland and purified himself and his wife, and told her to grind canna-, and she did so, and he sprinkled it on the ground, and all the elands that had died became alive again, and some came in with assegais sticking in them, which had been stuck by these people who had wanted to kill him. And he took out the assegais, a whole bundle, and they remained in his place; and it was a place enclosed with hills and precipices, and there was one pass, and it was constantly filled with a freezingly cold mist, so that none could pass through it, and those men all remained outside, and they ate sticks at last, and died of hunger. But his brother (or her brother), in chasing an eland he had wounded, pursued it closely through that mist, and Qwanciqutshaa saw the elands running about, frightened at that wounded eland and the assegai that was sticking in it, and he came out and saw his brother, and he said, 'Oh! my brother, I have been injured; you see now where I am.' And the next morning he killed an eland for his brother, and he told him to go back and call his mother and his friends, and he did so, and when they came they told him how the other people had died of hunger outside; and they stayed with him, and the place smelt of meat.

At the heart of this myth is the death of eland, a pivotal San image in both myth and rock art. Like Cagn, Qwanciqutshaa himself had a herd of eland.[53] They were a kind of alarm system for him: when he saw them running wildly

49   A large spotted rain-animal emerges from a step in the rock.
A man plays a musical bow, while others dance and clap. A dead
eland above is probably the source of the potency they are
activating. Colours: shades of red, white, black.

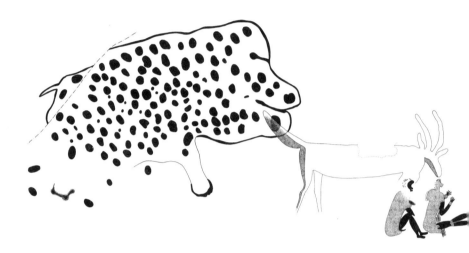

about, he knew that trouble was brewing. These mystical herds were all concentrations of potency in the upper level of the tiered San cosmos.

Redolent with connotations, the myth links the registers of our Rosetta
Stone and opens up a way into the complexity of San thought patterns.
Neither San myth nor art can be deciphered without an appreciation of the
dying eland's unifying role: it is at the centre of the web of San thought, ritual
and rock art.[54]

The eland was /Kaggen's favourite creature, though the trickster-deity is
not mentioned in this story. A series of /Xam myths tells how he created the
eland in a waterhole, an opening between the levels of San cosmology, and
fed it on honey, that cherished food imbued with potency. As the eland grew
in size, he anointed its flanks with honey and water.[55] To /Kaggen's great dis-
tress, the eland was killed: 'Then he wept; tears fell from his eyes, because he
did not see the Eland.'[56] Diä!kwain explained /Kaggen's continuing affection
for the eland:

The Mantis does not love us, if we kill an Eland … the Hartebeest was the one whom he
made after the death of his Eland. That is why he did not love the Eland and the Hartebeest a little, he loved them dearly, for he made his heart of the Eland and the
Hartebeest.[57]

Understandably, /Kaggen was constantly with the eland. The /Xam said that he sat 'between the Eland's horns' and, by various ruses, tried to trick hunters so that the eland could escape from them.[58]

The eland was and still is believed to have more potency than any other animal. Understandably, the Ju/'hoan San like to perform a trance dance next to the carcass of an eland so that they can harness its released potency (Fig. 49). As they pull back the skin of a dead eland, a sweet odour arises: it is taken to be evidence of the eland's potency. Here we have an explanation of Qing's opening statement: 'And Qwanciqutshaa killed an eland and purified himself and his wife.' Those who killed an eland ran the risk of offending Cagn and had to observe certain customs to avoid the suffering that could follow. Paradoxically, the killing of an eland was a transgression and also a prelude to the 'purification' that was subsequently needed.

In San thought, 'purification' is an inappropriate word. This is another translation problem. What Qing meant was that Qwanciqutshaa performed a trance dance and, during it, he was able to combat any evil influences that may have come upon him and his household as a result of the killing. The role of the trance dance in what Orpen called 'purification' is clear: during the dance, all the people present are 'cured' by the laying on of hands. The shamans draw sickness from them and then cast it back into the darkness from which it came; they also travel to Cagn and plead for the sick. It was thus through a trance dance that Cagn's anger could be assuaged and people could be 'purified'. The ambivalence of an eland kill lies in the death of a highly potent animal and then the using of its potency to protect the killer.

The first killing of an eland in the myth about Qwanciqutshaa was followed by 'purification'. The second had a similar sequel. Qwanciqutshaa's brother wounded, apparently mortally, an eland, which then frightened Qwanciqutshaa's eland herd. Moreover, Qwanciqutshaa himself claimed to be 'injured'. The next day he killed an eland 'for his brother' so that his brother could be 'purified' by the dance that would follow. The second killing ends with evocative words: 'and they stayed with him, and the place smelt of meat.' The brother and his family moved up through the freezing mist, known to the San as 'the rain's breath',[59] to transcend the tiered cosmos and participate in what Orpen thought of as an act of 'purification'.

Three points are of interest here. First, the wounding of the eland facilitated access to the upper reaches beyond the mist (Qwanciqutshaa 'pursued it closely through the mist') and, by implication, simultaneously angered Cagn ('The Mantis does not love us, if we kill an Eland'). Second, a result of the brother's killing the eland and Qwanciqutshaa's subsequent 'purification' was that 'his mother and his friends' stayed with Qwanciqutshaa. When the San kill a large animal, such as an eland, people gather from scattered camps to share the abundance of meat and to enjoy the relaxed social relations and healing dance that ensue. Third, smell is, in San thought, a vehicle for potency: if 'the place smelt of meat', it was filled with protective eland potency that can deflect assegais and arrows of sickness (Chapter 2) and protect people from sickness. The other people who had to remain outside, and were thus not able to participate in the dance, 'died of hunger'.

A performance of the whole myth was probably much enjoyed by those listening. The San are not solemn about their mythology: still today, there is much dramatization, interruption and hilarity. But on such occasions there is also more than entertainment. A performance of the Qwanciqutshaa myth subtly reinforced the status of shamans as key figures in the nexus of eland, dancing, the banishment of sickness and movement between levels of the cosmos.[60] Each performance of the myth, *even if there are variations in the narrative*, reinforced fundamental cosmological and religious beliefs.

'There's magic in the web of it'

Myth and art come together in a striking way in numerous rock shelters hidden in secluded kloofs, or as Qing put it, 'enclosed by hills and precipices'. In these shelters, painted panels often contain abundant images of eland – old bulls, cows, foals and yearlings, sometimes painted one on top of another (Pls 5, 25). Why did the San keep on painting eland after eland? In addition to being reservoirs of potency, the ever-growing painted herds may have created an ambience in which it was easy to sense the presence of Cagn. As Qing said, 'Where he is, elands are in droves like cattle.'[61] People could turn to the paintings for spiritual sustenance and reassurance.

Although eland feature in San myths, it is now clear that San rock paintings did not 'illustrate' myths in the way that pictures illustrate a child's book. Nor is there any evidence that that 'mythology' can be put forward as anything but a superficial and vague explanation for the complexity of San rock art. Once we break away from the restricting fetters of a narrative approach to mythology, we can begin to enquire about the significance of the repetitive elements in so many tales. Immediately, we find ourselves in the realm of cosmology and the 'sorcery' that transcends cosmological levels and thereby brings not only social viability but also personal happiness to human communities. If we can speak of fragments of the dance, we can also speak of 'myth elements' or 'building blocks', pregnant nuggets of significance that, in many but not all San myths, together provide a foundation on which narratives may be variously deployed.

While material fragments of the dance repeatedly crop up in San myths (for example, people bleed from the nose), it is the conceptual ones that most subtly give the narrative its deeper significance (for example, people entering holes in the ground or passing through a barrier of mist). Both rock art and myths are thus tightly woven webs of reality and purely conceptual elements. Both straddle the divide between the material world and the spirit realm. Both wrestle with and try to clarify elusive relationships between these two supposed spheres of existence and the emotions that they elicit in people.

In the next chapter, we discuss the cosmological *mise en scène* of Qing's myths. We also show that elements of the process of reconciling conceptual and material worlds can be seen in the beliefs of other cultures.

CHAPTER 8

Into the Unknown

[T]hen they churned and produced multitudes of elands, and the earth was covered with them.[1]

When we were deciphering San myths in the previous chapter, we were also learning about the mountains and valleys in which Qing, Qwanciqutshaa and the other mythical people of whom Qing spoke lived (Pls 1, 26, 27). We made our way beneath towering cliffs and through 'one pass [that] was constantly filled with a freezingly cold mist'. In Qing's myth, this mist was a barrier 'that none could pass through'.[2] It was 'the rain's breath'. Above the mist, modern climbers emerge from the narrow passes and come out onto the high, capping basalt rock of the Drakensberg summit, and then, behind the peaks, and almost lost, are broad, high-altitude valleys.

From a modern conservationist perspective, this dramatic scenery is breathtaking – the unpopulated expanses are today no different from what they were 140 years ago when Qing guided Orpen to rock shelters filled with images of another realm. But, taken together, those paintings and the myths that Qing recounted show us that the San saw and experienced far more in the landscape than we do. For them, the mountains and valleys were alive with beings and animals from another realm. They were where Cagn and Qwanciqutshaa lived with their families and foes.

It was also in that mountainous landscape that the first eland was created. The myth is significant.[3] Coti, Cagn's wife, took her husband's knife and sharpened her digging stick with it. He was angry and scolded her. Then she 'conceived and brought forth a little eland's calf'. She did not know what the creature was. On Cagn's orders she ground 'charms' (*buchu*) and he sprinkled them on the animal as he asked it whether it was this or that animal. When he asked it whether it was an eland (*Tsha*), it said, 'Aaaa'. Cagn took the young eland 'and folded it in his arms, and went and got a gourd, in which he put it, and took it to a secluded kloof enclosed by hills and precipices, and left it to grow there'.[4] While Cagn was away getting arrow poison from his nephew, his sons Gcwi and Cogaz together with other young men found the eland. They did not know what the new creature was. They tried to encircle it, but it broke through the circle. At last Gcwi killed it while it was asleep in the hidden place where Cagn had put it. They cut it up and took the meat and blood home. When Cagn returned and saw what had happened, he was angry. He pulled off Gcwi's nose and hurled it into the fire. Then he changed his mind and put his nose back on again and said: 'Now begin to try to undo the mischief you have done, for you have spoilt the elands when I was making them fit for use.' He told Gcwi to churn the eland's blood in a pot, but the blood that sprayed out turned into snakes. The next time he churned the blood he produced hartebeests, but they ran away. So Cagn called his wife Coti and told her to clean the pot and fill it with fresh eland blood and a new ingredient, fat from the eland's heart. He then sprinkled the mixture and the drops became eland bulls that 'pushed them with their horns'. Cagn drove these elands away. Finally, Cagn and Coti produced eland cows and 'multitudes of elands, and the earth was covered with them'.[5]

This myth is dense with meaning, but here we focus on some San beliefs about the spectacular landscape in which Cagn created the eland herds. In Qing's myths, we find that the mountains and the cliffs were where the San interacted with the spirit world. The peaks and precipices rose to meet unseen beings and animals – Cagn and Coti, their sons Gcwi and Cogaz, Qwanciqut-shaa and their great eland herds. As in Chapter 7, we find that the minds whose thinking we are trying to decipher articulated with their surroundings. In a sense, the landscape was a projection of the mind.

While we could be satisfied with an understanding of the San experience of mystical landscapes, it is illuminating to compare their view of the Drakensberg with the way in which some Native Americans thought about the land in which they lived. Despite the enormous spatial and cultural differences between the landscape and history of the Americans and the San, we encounter intriguing similarities between them, as we shall see on pp. 181–186, that take us beyond specific world views to parallels buried in our common humanity.

The San and mountains

Archaeological excavations conducted in rock shelters both above and below the Drakensberg escarpment have suggested that the San followed a seasonal lifestyle,[6] as indeed did the eland, their special antelope.

In the winter the high, upper reaches beyond the escarpment are dry and very cold: often snow blankets the land (Pl. 15).[7] At the beginning of winter, the San therefore left the heights and moved down into the valleys of the lowlands, where it is less cold, if rather dry. They spent the winters there in what are today known as the KwaZulu-Natal Midlands (Fig. 50). Some may even have travelled as far as the coast.[8] They lived in small scattered bands of about 20 people that were scattered across the Midlands. During the winter the eland, too, moved to the lower ground and lived in small groups, a couple of males together, and small groups of females with their young.

Then, with the first spring rains, the land is transformed. The thunderstorm clouds that the San thought of as rain-animals can be seen making their way along the summits of the mountain chain: the first storms are eagerly awaited. At this time, the eland move back up the slopes and through the passes. The new, sweet grass brought to life by the rains attracts them. The scattered eland unite to form large summer herds of sometimes well over 50 animals. The San followed these amalgamating eland: the people's small winter bands came together to form sizeable aggregations as they moved up to occupy the large rock shelters beneath the sandstone precipices. Transhumance was their way of life.

Patricia Vinnicombe and her archaeologist husband Patrick Carter studied these parallel human and animal movements.[9] They concluded that summer in the high mountains was not only a time of plenty: for the San, it was also a time for meeting people from whom they had been separated during the winter. Marriage brokering, large trance dances and rock painting were the order of the day. There are comparatively few painted rock shelters in the lower-lying land below the Drakensberg. It was with the higher reaches of the mountains that the San associated the complex ritual of painting. There, they felt close to Cagn and his eland herds.

50 A cross-section of the Drakensberg and Maloti mountains.

That is a broad picture of what happened. In practice, there was probably a good deal of variation from year to year.[10] One probable exception deserves closer attention because it ties in with something we find in the myths. It will be remembered that, when Joseph Millerd Orpen asked Qing where Cagn could be found, the young hunter replied:

We don't know, but the elands do. Have you not hunted and heard his cry, when the elands suddenly start and run to his call? Where he is, elands are in droves like cattle.[11]

Qing implied that the summer eland herds in the high mountains betokened the presence of Cagn. He protected them and, with 'his cry', warned them of approaching hunters. But there is more to it. At the beginning of August 1971, when she and her husband were excavating in the Sehonghong shelter (the one in which Qing showed Orpen the dual rain-animal capturing scene), Vinnicombe met two 'old patriarchs', Mosotho men who could remember San people living in the shelter. Both men had been born around 1880–81. One of them, Sello Mokoallo, said that when he was young, game was plentiful and eland were like cattle. As the Oxford archaeologist Peter Mitchell says, the similarity between Mokoallo's and Qing's statements about the eland being 'like cattle' is 'uncanny'.[12] In both Mokoallo's and Qing's words, we have a glimpse of a now long-gone world full of eland that the coming of the rifle and the horse destroyed.

Then Mokoallo added an interesting observation. He said that, when he was young, the eland herds of those high valleys were not seasonal: they stayed in that area all through the year. 'They grazed far away but always returned to their young.'[13] The other old man, Liselo Rankoli, explained:

There were many eland in those days. The eland used to choose warm places in the valleys during the winter. When it was warm, they grazed on the mountains and browsed on the many trees that were in the valleys.[14]

We should remember that the valleys of which he spoke are the high ones over the crest of the Drakensberg. On the coastal side of the escarpment, on and above the Midlands, the eland were almost certainly seasonal – as they still are today in the nature reserve that stretches the entire length of the KwaZulu-Natal Drakensberg.

The eland herds did not supply only meat. As we saw in the myth about Qwanciqutshaa (Chapter 7), an eland kill was also a reason for people to congregate and dance – which is still the case for the Kalahari San. Beyond highly desirable, plentiful food and the potency that the San could harness in a trance dance, eland also supplied blood, a key ingredient (along with fat) that Cagn used to make the first eland herds. The San also used eland blood in the making of paint. Mokoallo never saw San people actually painting, but 'the paintings were new at the time he was a young man'.[15] He added that 'they used the blood of killed animals for paint'.[16]

This important piece of information about blood and paint was corroborated and made more specific by another Mosotho man, Mapote. He had grown up with San people and had learned to paint with them in rock shelters. In the 1930s, he told Marion How, wife of the British district commissioner at the small Lesotho town of Qacha's Nek, that, if he was to make a painting in the traditional San manner, as she requested, he would require 'the blood of a freshly killed eland'.[17] In the event, Mapote had to be satisfied with ox blood obtained from the local butcher, the eland having been long since shot out of that area.

Then in the 1980s, Maqhoqha, a woman of mixed San descent whose father had been a shaman-artist, said that the old San had driven eland back to a sandbank in a stream opposite the rock shelter where she and her family lived. They killed the eland there. They then used their blood and fat to make paint, the same two substances that Cagn used to create the first eland herds. Standing in that shelter, she pointed to the sandbank and then danced before the paintings that her father had made 80 and more years earlier.[18]

Eland blood was one of the media, probably the most desired, that the San used to mix their paint. What of the pigment? Mapote offered information that again ties in with beliefs about the high mountains. He said that, in addition to eland blood, he required genuine San pigment that was known as *qhang qhang*. Unlike ordinary ochre, such as Marion How was able to buy at the local shop, *qhang qhang* 'glistened and sparkled'.[19] Sparkling has a long history. As long as 60,000 to 70,000 years ago, people collected 'strong-red' or glittering specularite ochres. This preference suggests that, even at that remote time, people were interested in the visual qualities of special ochres.[20] Significantly, Mopote added that *qhang qhang* could be obtained only in the high basalt summits of the Drakensberg mountains, where it was dug out of the rock.[21] Then he said that eland blood, and eland blood only, was mixed with *qhang qhang* to make the paint even more special. Farther to the west, the /Xam San spoke of red haematite (*ttò*) being obtained from a 'mine' that was guarded by mystical 'sorcerers'. When the /Xam approached these 'mines', they threw stones at them to warn the 'sorcerers' to hide themselves. If the 'sorcerers' looked at them, they believed that they would become ill.[22]

There is thus a remarkable coming together of information. When the eland were in droves like cattle and could be easily hunted, not only was the presence of Cagn readily felt: people could also frequently perform large trance dances and, moreover, obtain *qhang qhang* and eland blood to make special paintings. Once made, the images fed back into the highly charged ambience of that time and place. Maqhoqha said that when people who were dancing felt the need for more potency, they turned to face the images in the rock shelters. As they raised their hands before the images, potency flowed into them. Because the potency of eland was in their blood, the images became reservoirs of potency. No wonder, then, that in the 1870s George Stow routinely found dancing ruts in the floors of rock shelters and nearby (Chapter 2).

Dancing infiltrates Qing's creation myth in another subtle way that escapes most readers and was certainly missed by Orpen. When Cagn saw that Gcwi had killed the first eland, he told his son that he would punish him. It was then that he 'pulled his nose off and flung it into the fire'. The text demands close attention at this point:

> But he said 'No! I shall not do that', so he put his nose on again, and he said, 'Now begin to try to undo the mischief you have done, for you have spoilt the elands when I was making them fit for use.'[23]

We have seen on many occasions that the nose played a significant role in /Xam healing. Nasal bleeding was experienced by shamans in trance,[24] and they used their noses for sniffing sickness out of people, the practice known as *sũ*.[25] Moreover, a certain /Xam shaman of the rain was known as !Haunu, a word that means nasal mucus.[26] But a more precise clue to understanding what was meant by Cagn's pulling off Gcwi's nose is to be found in the Bleek and Lloyd manuscripts. A female shaman who was having no success in curing was told that other *!gi:ten* would take away her dangerous 'snoring power' because it was killing people. The /Xam word used here is /*nũnu*.[27] It means 'nose'.[28] At first, Lloyd translated the word thus, but, no doubt after consultation with the informant (Diä!kwain), she crossed out this translation and inserted instead 'snoring power', that is, the ability to heal people. At another point the informant said: 'And this is why her snoring-power [/*nũnu*] had become weak.'[29] The /Xam word for 'nose' was used to mean 'healing power'.

Although we do not have a phonetic transcription of Qing's San words, we can see that taking away Gcwi's nose was depriving him of his ability to heal. Cagn restored his son's status as a shaman so that he could 'undo the mischief' he had done. What was a puzzling incident thus turns out to be a 'building block', a 'coded' message about a person's ability to be a shaman.

In sum, there seems to be little doubt that, as the San moved up the passes to the summit of the Drakensberg (Pls 26, 27), their minds filled with richer thoughts than ours do. Beyond the freezing mist was the dwelling of Cagn and his vast herds of eland, herds that betokened massive stores of potency. Climbing up to their large summer aggregation rock shelters, San people were getting closer to Cagn and the healing potency that they desired. There, in the mountains, the San could – as did Qwanciqutshaa himself – kill an eland and 'purify' themselves in a place redolent with the scent of meat.

High and lifted up

A key concept that ran through the lives and landscape of the Drakensberg San was altitude. Even though, at any time, Cagn can, as //Kabbo put it, 'be by you, without your seeing him',[30] his presence was especially associated with summer in the high mountains. The divine, to put it broadly, was conceived as being up and above. The landscape itself, with its towering peaks and precipices, provided a ready-made template that human thought could transform into spiritual dimensions. Worldwide, beliefs about supernatural things are projected onto landscapes to give the various features meanings that are not readily apparent to outsiders.

Not all San live in such a dramatic landscape as the Drakensberg. Those whom the Bleek family interviewed in the 1870s came from the central parts of the subcontinent. As we have seen, this is a semi-arid plain dotted with comparatively low hills, most of which can be easily scaled in half an hour or less (Pl. 28). There is nothing here comparable to the altitudinal scale of the Drakensberg. There are no towering mountains in the land from which the Bleek family's /Xam San informants came. Nevertheless, from the summits of these hills the climber is able to gaze out across the vast flat terrain below.

Farther to the north there is even less in the way of altitudinal variation. In the sandy flat Kalahari Desert there are virtually no hills (the Tsodilo Hills in the north-west are an exception), no valleys, no rivers, except at unusual times of flood. The average rainfall is 200 mm (7.8 in), and protracted droughts are common.[31] Water is obtained from ephemeral pans in the rainy season and from melons, roots and tubers at other times of the year.

Did the San of these comparatively waterless plains hold beliefs in any way comparable to those of the Drakensberg San?

The Brinkkop

On the semi-arid plains where the /Xam San lived the small hills that are today known as 'koppies' assumed an importance beyond their size. The Afrikaans word *kop* means 'head' or 'hill'; the diminutive is *koppie*. (Afrikaans is the present-day form of Cape Dutch.) These hills are usually flat-topped, being capped with a stratum of dolerite. The /Xam used three words, *//xau:*, *!kaugen* and *!ka$o*, to mean a 'hill', that is, one of these koppies.[32] Interestingly, the word *!kaugen* is the plural of *!kau*, which means a 'stone'. The plural form probably derives from the abundance of dolerite boulders and stones scattered across the summits of these hills (Pl. 28).

In addition to 'hill', Lloyd also translated *//xau:* as 'Brinkkop', another Cape Dutch word. Janette Deacon, who has extensively studied the land from which the /Xam people came, has persuasively argued that 'Brinkkop' is a corruption of the Afrikaans word 'Bruinkop'.[33] *Bruin* means 'brown'. The first syllable of the Afrikaans word thus refers to the colour of the dolerite capping, the stones implied by *!kaugen*. In using the word 'Brinkkop', it seems that the informants were speaking of dolerite hills to which they went to make rain.[34]

When a thunderstorm was brewing, dark clouds gathered on the summit of Brinkkop hills, as they still do. Bleek and Lloyd's informant //Kabbo said: 'For the darkness is very dark on the Brinkkop's summit. The rain's darkness is black because the clouds are black…. Therefore the people do first, they fear; because they think that the houses will blow away.'[35] Again and again, /Xam people spoke of fearing the dark male rain, the thunderstorm. On another occasion, //Kabbo, himself a rain shaman, was able to reassure them: 'People think that the time of death must be come. Then the mountain tops are covered, but it is a shadow, it is not danger.'[36] He could control the rain and protect people from its wrath.

The tops of the hills were also more directly associated with water. A /Xam rain-maker's grandson remembered his grandfather saying: 'I will milk a she-rain, I will cut her, by cutting her I will let the rain's blood flow out, so that it runs along the ground.'[37] The grandson replied: 'I understand, for the she-rain is drawing her breath which resembles mist; you must please go and cut the rain at the great waterpits which are on the mountain.'[38] Thinking of how he would capture and control a rain-animal, the grandfather replied: 'I will really ride the rain up the mountain on top of which I always cut the rain. It is high, so the rain's blood flows down.'[39] As Deacon rightly points out, it is clear that /Xam rain-makers often went to hilltops to make rain.[40]

Another account is more oracle consultation than rain-making. An old woman climbed a 'small hill' and thrust her digging stick into the ground. Then she asked a chameleon for rain.[41] The chameleon was one of the rain's creatures: it changes colour, as do rain clouds.[42] 'And the chameleon looked at the ground, and when it had looked at the ground, it looked up to the sky, it knew that rain would fall.'[43] The swivelling of its eyes was believed to indicate whether rain would fall.

The statement that the 'great waterpits' are 'on the mountain' is significant. In this part of the subcontinent, waterholes, or springs, are found on the plains, not (at any rate in any significant size) on hilltops (Pl. 28). On the plains, the San camped near, but not at, waterholes in order not to frighten away animals that came to drink there.[44] //Kabbo stayed near a waterhole still today known as the Bitterpits, because the water there is brackish.[45] The normal location of waterholes on the plain leads us to suspect that the 'great waterholes' said to be on top of a hill are, principally if not exclusively, mystical entrances to the nether world where the rain-animal lived. If the rain-animal (a storm cloud) was observed to be frequently on top of the Brinkkop, it was reasonable for the San to believe that it must have emerged from a significant waterhole. Speaking of the 'great waterpits', the man used the /Xam word *!kerri*, the same word that another informant used to describe the 'great sorcerer' who led the dance and taught others how to 'learn sorcery' (Chapter 2). Not surprisingly, engravings of rain-animals are found on the rocky summits of some of these hills.[46]

That waterholes were thought of as entrances to the spirit world, in addition to being the place where shamans captured rain-animals, is explicitly seen in an account in which the angered rain sends lightning: 'they all disappeared in the waterpit, for the rain lightened putting them underground'.[47] The importance of verticality for the San is clearly evident here: the hills reach up to the sky, but on them are 'great waterholes' that are entrances to the underworld.

The elevation of the hills that the /Xam San knew, small as they are compared with the Drakensberg, was significant. It seems that we have a deeply embedded belief that associates height with spirituality. Even when the terrain does not dramatically lend itself to the development of ideas about altitude, people still think in those terms.

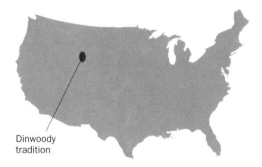

51 The Dinwoody tradition of rock art is situated in the American state Wyoming. It has certain elements in common with southern African San rock art.

Dinwoody
tradition

Animals, *puha* and place: an American landscape

Before we hazard a suggestion as to why, even in comparatively flat land-scapes, people think of verticality as a route to spirituality, we consider a case far from southern Africa. The Dinwoody rock art tradition is found in a fairly restricted region of Wyoming in the United States of America (Fig. 51). The images, or petroglyphs, as they are known in America, were made by pecking, or hammering, through the outer crust of rocks to leave the lighter-coloured inner rock. They have a counterpart in the San rock engravings that are found in the central parts of southern Africa.[48]

The Dinwoody images are intricate and highly varied. We describe only some of the principal forms. Prominent among them are anthropomorphs that have rectangular bodies with rounded corners.[49] The torsos are filled with designs, such as sets of dots and undulating or zigzagging parallel lines. Some-times the torsos have upper limbs that resemble wings; often the figures have large hands and feet with five or three digits; the frequent depiction of only three digits suggests avian associations (Fig. 52). Extra lines often encase the human figures or connect them one to another. There are also images of

52 Many Dinwoody figures have three digits, and wings that suggest avian creatures.

quadrupeds shown in profile; some are connected to scenes of other images by a pecked line. Some resemble dogs; more commonly, they are images of bison. Fewer depict bears, the larger ones having internal decoration resembling that of the human figures.

The makers of these distinctive images were the Mountain Shoshone. They were a hunter-gatherer people who, like the Drakensberg San, practised seasonal transhumance. In the summer, they followed herds of bighorn sheep as they grazed in the high mountains; in the winter they moved down to lower pastures. The identity of the Mountain Shoshone as the makers of the Dinwoody petroglyphs is established by a large body of ethnographic material that records their way of life, rituals and beliefs.[50]

One of the Shoshone ritual practices was vision questing. Young men seeking an empowering vision went to petroglyph sites, bathed in a stream or lake, and then sat fasting for several days waiting for the supernatural power they called *puha*. It is in many ways comparable to the *!gi:*, *//ke:n* or */ko:öde* of which the San spoke. The Shoshone vision-quest sites are often isolated, well away from living areas.[51] Fasting in isolation is one of the common ways of inducing an altered state of consciousness among North American shamans.

When the overpowering vision came, the shaman experienced visions of a fusion of animals and human beings:

There is the frightening trial, the manifestation of the spirit who tends to change forms – now a man, now an animal – the imparting of supernatural power, the conditions for the ownership of this power, and the regulations concerning ritual paraphernalia.[52]

Power also came from less fantastic creatures, such as eagles, rattlesnakes and bears, or even from natural forms, like strangely shaped rocks.

Julie Francis and Larry Loendorf, two archaeologists who have studied this art in detail, explain the relationship between visions induced by fasting or hallucinogens and the fantastic Dinwoody imagery:

Engravings and paintings were created the morning after a vision was received in order to preserve it, as forgetting the details of a vision could result in death or illness. Previously created panels were consulted to refresh the shaman's memory and to renew the connection to the supernatural.[53]

As with the San, the Shoshone rock art images were not simply pictures or decorations. They were made to be used by the visionary and by other people as well. They were intimately associated with supernatural potency and the acquisition of potency.

The Shoshone categorized the creatures they depicted into sky people, ground people and water people.[54] Even though they are animals, they are spoken of as people because the Shoshone routinely anthropomorphize animals: in their view, animals can speak and communicate with human beings. As is the case in many indigenous taxonomies, these three categories are not rigid, and creatures cross over from one to another. For example, water birds can fly and also walk on the land. Myths are attached to these various creatures.

We can now turn to the terrain in which the Shoshone made these images. The Dinwoody region is dominated by the Wind river, the upper reaches of which are at elevations of some 10,000 feet (3,048 m). The large petroglyph sites in this section are at about 7,000 feet (2,133 m). The middle course of the Wind river ranges at elevations of 6,000 to 5,500 feet (1,828 to 1,676 m). There are several sites in this section of the river. The lower Wind river and its tributaries are at elevations of 5,000 to 4,000 feet (1,524 to 1,219 m). There are numerous sites in this area, many clustered around the hot springs near the town Thermopolis.

Throughout the entire area, the petroglyphs were executed on sandstone with very uneven surfaces. Many images seem to enter natural cavities. Indeed, Francis and Loendorf believe that the more eroded surfaces were deliberately chosen above smoother surfaces. Dinwoody images were thus intentionally closely integrated with the rock on which they were made, as were so many southern African San images with the rock walls of rock shelters.

This American example may therefore be usefully compared with the Drakensberg San beliefs about landscape that we have discussed in this and the previous chapter. In both cases, we are able to consult ethnographic records of the peoples' beliefs. We do not have to imagine, or guess, how they may have conceived of the landscapes in which they lived. Indeed, Loendorf makes the point that the ethnographic record 'was extremely helpful in understanding the meaning and distribution of Dinwoody petroglyphs'[55] – as we found San ethnography to be in southern Africa.

We are therefore in a position to ask: Do the three broad taxonomic categories (sky people, ground people, water people) relate to the three levels of the landscape through which the Wind river runs? We will consider the three levels and their imagery in turn.

At the highest mountain sites, petroglyphs include many human-like figures and flying figures (see Fig. 52). There are few quadrupeds. Some of the flying figures are recognizable as Shoshone power birds that are associated

53 Left: *A Dinwoody engraving of a hummingbird. The Mountain Shoshone people equated the small hummingbird with eagles and the thunderbird as sources of power.*

54 Opposite: *A Dinwoody water-ghost being whose head appears to emerge from the rock. A projectile point hangs from the figure's left hand.*

with vision questing.[56] The one shown here (Fig. 53) is probably a transformed hummingbird. Other petroglyphs depict owls with prominent eyes. Some images with outstretched wings seem to be eagles. Both hummingbirds and eagles are associated with the thunderbird that is believed to gather water in clouds and cause thunder. The Shoshone consider lightning and the hummingbird to be at the top of their hierarchy of spirit powers. The eagle is immediately below them. In the rock art, zigzag lines around these flying creatures represent lightning.[57]

Sites in the middle reaches of the Wind river have significantly fewer anthropomorphic images with three digits than those in the upper reaches, but there is an increase in anthropomorphs with four or five digits. Humans with three-digit birdlike feet are more common at the higher altitudes. Likewise, clear depictions of birds decrease in frequency in the middle reaches of the Wind river. At the same time, horned figures and quadrupeds increase in frequency. So-called ground people are found at these sites. They include bears, beavers and buffalo. Loendorf sums up the significance of these differences in imagery between the upper and middle Wind river sites: 'The increase in quadrupedal animals and the decrease in birds suggest that the power found in the mountains and that found on the plains is represented differently in the petroglyphs.'[58]

Sites in the lower levels of the Wind river have images of so-called water-ghosts of different kinds that are surrounded by wavy lines that represent water (Fig. 54).[59] Water spirits were considered to be shamans' helpers. The theme of water is developed by images of frogs and turtles. All these supernatural creatures are associated with hot springs, which the Shoshone believed to be sources of *puha*. Flying creatures and three-digit anthropomorphs are

less common in lower-level sites than in the upper-level sites. The only images of snakes in the entire region occur at lower-level sites.

There is thus a distinct correlation between categories of engraved creatures and altitudinal levels (Fig. 55). Shamans desiring a particular kind of power went to fast and conduct their vision quests at the appropriate levels. For instance, a person who desired sky power would climb to the upper reaches of the landscape, experience the desired vision and then make an image of it.

The Shoshone, then, think of the world as divided into three parts and these parts structure much of their thought, myths and visionary experiences. In previous chapters we saw that the San inscribed their conception of the landscape into their myths and that their visionary journeys traversed the three levels of their cosmos. The same applies to the Shoshone. In 1881 the missionary Reverend John Roberts was given an account of a visionary experience that both parallels and differs from the accounts that Orpen and the Bleek family recorded in southern Africa. A Shoshone shaman had gone into the mountains to pray:

At the end of some days three animals appeared to him: an eagle, a bear and a badger. The eagle addressed him and, taking off one of his claws, gave it to him that by means of it he could command all the powers of the air. Then the bear addressed him and,

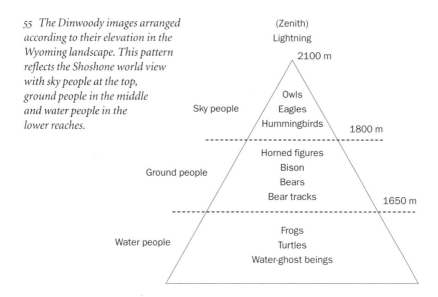

55 The Dinwoody images arranged according to their elevation in the Wyoming landscape. This pattern reflects the Shoshone world view with sky people at the top, ground people in the middle and water people in the lower reaches.

(Zenith)
Lightning
2100 m

Owls
Eagles
Hummingbirds

Sky people

1800 m

Horned figures
Bison
Bears
Bear tracks

Ground people

1650 m

Frogs
Turtles
Water-ghost beings

Water people

taking off one of his claws, gave it to him and told him that by means of it he could command all the powers of the earth. Finally the badger addressed him and, taking off one of his claws, gave it to him and told him that by means of it he could command all that was under the earth.[60]

Francis and Loendorf point out that the shaman supported his account by showing Roberts the three claws; he wore them around his neck. Significantly, Roberts added that the Indians visited 'pictured rocks' to obtain their power. The link between vision questing and Dinwoody rock art images can hardly be doubted.

The altitudinal pattern and the distinctive type of imagery seems to have endured for thousands of years,[61] though Francis and Loendorf point out that this does not mean that Dinwoody shamanism was monolithic and unchanging. There is in fact evidence to show clear changes in the relative frequencies of image types over time. Changes of this kind probably reflect the 'increasing importance of the shamans in the social and political areas of Shoshonean life'.[62] But, as in southern Africa, the arrival of new people, animals and artefacts did not have the impact we may have expected: '[T]he symbolism and beliefs expressed in the imagery were seemingly uninfluenced by the introduction of new forms.'[63] People can adopt new forms without fundamentally changing the overall structure of their beliefs and rituals.

People and the land

We emphasize that the parallel division of images and power by altitude in Dinwoody rock art is controlled by the people's culture. The Shoshone established the system of equivalences between images and landscape within the parameters of their own terrain and the creatures that live there. In other regions the distribution of imagery may be different, even inverted.[64] Landscape is therefore not deterministic in that it imposes beliefs on people. On the contrary, people transform the given mountains and valleys of their terrain into landscapes pregnant with meaning and inhabited by spirit beings and animals. There is an interaction between the human mind and landscape.

Yet, despite all the good intentions of researchers who quite rightly emphasize differences between belief systems, it seems clear that people all over the world and in markedly differing cultures have ideas about altitude. They imagine a vertical axis that runs from a spirit realm in the sky, through the level on which people live, down to a subterranean spirit realm. This is the so-called *axis mundi*, a phrase that researchers worldwide use to denote the vertical axis of the cosmos that shamans in a variety of different cultures scale to reach the spirit realm that they believe lies in, or beyond, the sky. In different cultures the *axis mundi* is conceived differently: sometimes it may be a tree, at other times it may be a mountain or simply an invisible 'ladder'. The *axis mundi* is one part of a broad cosmological framework. The traditional Christian (though now contested) notion of Heaven above and Hell below is but one example. In Old Testament times the 'children of transgression' went up 'a lofty and high mountain ... to offer sacrifice',[65] and Moses met God 'in a thick cloud' on Mount Sinai. The people themselves were forbidden to go up the mountain 'or to touch the border of it': anyone who did so 'shall surely be stoned, or shot through'.[66] Within each culture, the vertical divisions are given their own significances and even subdivisions.

One way of explaining the near universality of the importance of the vertical axis is to point to two experiences that, because they are wired into the human brain, are widely experienced.[67] One is the liberating sensation of flying; the other is the constricting sensation of entering a tunnel or passing under water.

Flight is a common metaphor for altered states of consciousness. In the Dinwoody rock art, it is represented by the avian images we have described.[68] In San rock art, flying creatures similarly represent *!gi:ten* on out-of-body journeys (Pls 12, 13). Diä!kwain spoke of a shaman who 'turns into a little bird, he comes to see us where we live and flies about our heads. Sometimes he sits on our heads.'[69]

Similarly, but moving down rather than up, a San *!gi:xa* told Megan Biesele how the giraffe, his spirit helper, took him to a 'wide body of water' and how he travelled under water. He expressed the restricting tunnel sensation by saying: 'My sides were pressed by pieces of metal. Metal things fastened to my sides.'[70] Then his 'protector' told him that he 'would travel far through the earth and then emerge at another place'. Having emerged, he began 'to climb the thread – it was the thread of the sky'; it took him up to the realm where god was believed to live.[71] The Shoshone also regarded lakes and springs as entrances to the underworld. Francis and Loendorf persuasively argue that figures surrounded by wavy lines probably depict beings under water.[72] Vertical movement was thus part of both Shoshone and San experience in altered states of consciousness, and these two peoples are by no means alone in this.

Probably, the functioning of the human brain in altered states contributed to the worldwide belief in spiritual realms above and below daily life. No matter what their cultural background, people who enter certain altered states of consciousness report two significant experiences. They speak of flying and of entering holes in the ground or tunnels. These experiences are wired into the brain.[73] But they form only the foundation for rich elaborations in each separate culture. Intense experiences are probably not part of everyone's lives; many people simply accept what they are taught about the cosmos, feeling that what they experience in their dreams guarantees the existence of spiritual realms. The details of those realms vary greatly.

Certainly, in deciphering accounts of religious experience projected onto landscapes we should bear in mind that our own perceptions of mountains and valleys are probably different from those that were entertained in the distant past. Nothing that we have said in this and the previous chapter about San and Shoshone beliefs could be recovered by a Westerner simply by contemplating the landscape.[74]

Parallels between widely separated peoples lead us to reconsider Lévy-Bruhl's notion of a 'primitive mentality'. In our final chapter, we therefore ask: How 'simple' were these 'primitive people' whose cosmos was multidimensional?

CHAPTER 9

'Simple' People?

What is most striking about this inquiry is what it reveals about
the way the !Kung think. The similarity of their thinking to our own
suggests that the logico-deductive model of science may be very ancient,
and may in fact have originated with the first fully human
hunter-gatherers in the Pleistocene.[1]

Some of the texts and imagery concerning 'sorcery' that we have tried to decipher may help us to understand why, at least in his early work, Lucien Lévy-
Bruhl thought that 'primitive' people were fantasists. Seated in his armchair
and reading accounts of small-scale societies from around the world, he
concluded that the minds of 'primitive' people were inundated by emotion
and imagination to a far greater extent than the sober Westerners he knew
in French academe. Part of the problem was that the early ethnographers
were more interested in what they considered outlandish beliefs than in the
practical, daily lives of the people whom they were studying. As a result, Lévy-
Bruhl concluded that 'primitive' people did not have a notion of rational
causality. The affairs of daily life were believed to be at the whim of unseen
beings and forces.

Paradoxically, continuing Western expansion into distant parts of the
world seemed to bring both a confirmation and contradiction of this propo-
sition. Inevitably, Westerners saw themselves as different from the people they
met in small-scale societies. That difference became a cornerstone in the for-
mulation of Westerners' own identity: the people they met were 'other' than
themselves. Hand in hand, two identities were built up: the rational Westerner
and the simple, 'primitive' native. Some of those 'primitives' were, at least in
Jean-Jacques Rousseau's 18th-century theory, solitary noble savages, who
stood apart from property and social inequality. Rousseau's idealism contra-
dicted Thomas Hobbes's earlier (and now more famous) view that, in their
natural state, human beings' lives are 'solitary, poor, nasty, brutish and short'
as they struggle with one another. Only strong, consensual government,
under which people voluntarily give up some of their freedom, can, as Hobbes
saw it, offer escape from decidedly unpleasant primitiveness.

Rousseau's and Hobbes's contrasting views of 'primitive' people tended to shape the outlook of Westerners as they encountered, rather than merely read about, people like the San. For some, such as the missionaries, the San were unspeakably debased. For others, there was a nobility in their stand against the incursions of the colonists. Neither position did the San much good. Inevitably, they were brought under colonial rule.

In more recent years, anthropologists began to see past these positions. They concluded that the 'primitives', *within their own terms*, were as rational as they themselves. On the other side of the coin, even Lévy-Bruhl came to realize that many Westerners are as irrational as anyone. Many still believe that special people can rise from the dead, that prayers to God can cause natural laws to be suspended and that, when they die, their souls will be transported to an eternal, blissful place.

The study of colonialism and the ways in which people construct their own identities is today a productive industry. Archaeology itself is sometimes alleged to be a weapon of colonialism, along with Christianity and capitalism. Insensitively constructed and handled, the archaeological past can indeed seem to widen the gap between the industrial West and indigenous people. If emphasis is placed on the degree of 'otherness', alienation is inevitable. Colonialism itself is, of course, not monolithic. Western expansion played itself out differently in different parts of the world. In some regions, the conflict between the past as pictured by, on the one hand, Western archaeology and, on the other, by indigenous histories is more acute than in others. As attempts to deal with this situation have become more and more sophisticated, prolix and jargon-ridden theory has unfortunately put up a smokescreen that sometimes conceals down-to-earth, practical issues. Often, it seems that many studies are strong on theory but thin on specifics.

In our investigation of San thought and art, we have found the complexity and deeply interrelated nature of the cosmology, myths, rituals and art that we have discussed sufficient to dispel any notion of a naïve, prosaic 'primitive mentality'. The lives of the San were not 'solitary, poor, nasty, brutish and short' in pre-colonial times.

Changing views

The colonial concept of the San changed over time.[2] Early on, they were deemed barbaric and 'untameable', inveterate thieves lacking in all subtlety of thought and religion. The 19th-century missionary Reverend Barnabas Shaw declared the San to be '*slaves of passion.* They are deeply versed in deceit, and treacherous in the extreme'[3] (original emphasis). In some quarters, this view lasted a long time. One of the most egregious examples of it was published as recently as 1973 in a book that bore the imprimatur of a cabinet minister in the then South African apartheid government. The author wrote: 'Actually, the Bushmen can almost be regarded as a link between man and the animal world. Man acts largely on pure reason: the animal world relies on blind instinct. The Bushman was midway between the two, often more animal than man, and many of his actions can only be explained on the basis of instinct.'[4]

Another 19th-century, though less pejorative, view developed under the influence of George Stow, on whose copies of rock paintings Wilhelm Bleek and Lucy Lloyd asked /Xam San people to comment. It portrayed the San as 'noble savages' bravely defending their land against the intrusions of 'stronger' people. Retaining the 'Bushman-as-inveterate-thief' concept, Stow added a heroic gloss in a now-famous passage:

The last known Bushman artist of the Malutis was shot in the Witteberg Native Reserve, where he had been on a marauding expedition, and had captured some horses…. Thus perished the last of the painter tribes of Bushmen! Thus perished their chiefs and artists ! [sic] after a continuous struggle to maintain their independence and to free their hunting grounds from the invaders who pressed in from every side for upwards of a couple of centuries, a period which commenced with the southern migration of the Hottentot hordes, and did not end until the last surviving clans had been exterminated with the bullet and the assegai, and their bones were left to bleach amid the rugged precipices of the Malutis.[5]

Those declamatory words were written towards the end of the 19th century. In the 20th century a new notion took hold. The San became known as child-like, highly spiritual conservationists living in harmony with Nature, a view propagated largely by Sir Laurens van der Post.[6] They came to be widely seen as an integral part of southern African ecology and a focus of sentimental philosophy:

Perhaps this life of ours, which begins as a quest of the child for the man, and ends as a journey by the man to rediscover the child, needs a clear image of some child-man, like the Bushman, where in [sic] the two are firmly and lovingly joined in order that our confused hearts may stay at the centre of their brief round of departure and return.[7]

In fact, van der Post's influence on the public's ideas about the San exceeded his actual contact with them. His knowledge of the Kalahari hunters and gatherers was slight, and he greatly exaggerated his first-hand contact with the San. His biographer J. D. F. Jones described him as 'a master fabricator',[8] but he still has many followers. Old ideas die hard, especially when they create distance between ourselves and other people and, as in this instance, foster warm paternalistic sentiments in well-to-do Westerners.

How do these changing views of the San stand up to the evidence we have uncovered?

First and foremost, we believe that San thought and art are intrinsically fascinating. Our 'Rosetta Stone' opened up, though by no means fully explored, vistas on a complex world of closely interwoven concepts and images. As we claimed in our Preface, San rock art is arguably more varied, more complex, more meticulous in its minute details and more technically sophisticated than any other rock art. But it is not just beautiful. It has profound symbolic and conceptual depths that we are still researching: we have not reached the end of our journey into San thought. The way in which it is possible to trace an idea, together with its transformations, through San mythology and art speaks of minds that are far from simple.

But we now need to ask in more comprehensive terms about the type, or, more accurately, types, of San thinking that we have come across. Our understanding of San thought is founded on context and a major distinction. An example illustrates this point. When Westerners tried to transmit human speech across immense distances, they thought rationally and came up with the telephone and the wireless. Even if they were religiously inclined, they did not implore God to send the message for them. Even if they believed that the miracles described in the Bible actually took place, they did not expect parallel miracles in their scientific work. But when anthropologists and colonists came to study small-scale societies, many tended to lay more emphasis on mythical thought and on indigenous 'superstitious' explanations than on the people's rationality in dealing with many practical situations. We therefore need to distinguish between San rationality in practical daily life and their thinking in what we see as non-real realms.

The 'science' of daily life

Fortunately for our inquiry into San thinking, two Harvard researchers studied Ju/'hoan knowledge in the early 1970s. They were Nicholas Blurton Jones, an ethologist who had studied the behaviour of preschool children as well as that of birds and mammals, and Melvin Konner, an anthropologist and psychologist.[9] Their work revealed striking parallels between Ju/'hoan thinking and what we recognize as Western scientific thinking.

Fundamentally, the Ju/'hoansi do not confuse the sort of thinking that is required to conduct a successful hunt with the thinking that underwrites non-rational beliefs about animals that come to the fore in myths (Fig. 57). The Ju/'hoansi realize that confusing the two ways of thinking would be disastrous. Non-rational beliefs play only a small role in people's practical interactions with animals.

In thinking about animal behaviour and, especially, the all-important task of tracking, the Ju/'hoansi are careful to distinguish between data and interpretation. Moreover, hunters discriminate between what they themselves observe and hearsay. Nor do they confuse the animal behaviour that they have inferred from their close observation of animal tracks with what they think may happen as the hunt unfolds. A concomitant point that Blurton Jones and Konner do not make is that a certain amount of 'theory', explicit or tacit, is necessary for someone to interpret, even simply to recognize, animal tracks. Still, the San do not confuse hypotheses with observable facts, and they seem uninterested in formulating overarching theories.

We reach an interesting point when we come to the explanations that Ju/'hoansi advance for animal behaviour. Why do animals behave in the sometimes strange and erratic ways that they do? This is where the issue of anthropomorphism enters. There has been a long-standing popular belief that, because the San are said to think of animals as people, they do not draw a distinct line between the two. But, as is so often the case, what Westerners think is a distinction between themselves and other peoples itself turns out to be false. Blurton Jones and Konner concluded that Ju/'hoan explanations for why animals behave in certain ways came close to the explanations that many Westerners advance. The San say that an animal does what it does simply because it wants to, thus imputing human-like characteristics to the animal. This does not mean that the Ju/'hoansi think that animals are people any more than Westerners think their dogs are people when they impute human-like motivations to them. In any event, in dealing with the animals they hunt, and other animals as well, the Ju/'hoansi are more interested in *what* animals do than in *why* they do it.

The skills needed to infer what an animal is doing, or will do, from its tracks is fundamental to hunter-gatherer life. They are learned in practice. The Ju/'hoansi do not teach in any formal way. Young men pick up much useful information as people sit around a fire in the evening to discuss the

56 *San tracking and hunting skills are legendary.* Opposite: *When they have killed an animal, here a gemsbok, they cut it up; it is the task of the man who owned the fatal arrow to distribute the meat.*

events of a hunt. But, apart from that, the Ju/'hoansi say, 'You teach yourself' by participating in hunts.[10] According to their egalitarian ideals, the notion of a person lecturing another, even if there is a marked age difference, is anathema.

Once hunters are onto an animal track they learn from one another and thus build up better understandings. As they follow the track, they discuss possible inferences from the details they are able to pick up, changing their minds as new evidence comes to light. As Blurton Jones and Konner remark, the hunters argue in a way not dissimilar to the discussions that they themselves had in their interviews with a number of Ju/'hoan individuals, or, for that matter, in seminars with Western students. The San's willingness to change their explanations in the light of new data parallels the way in which Western science works.

Non-rational beliefs about animals are, with few exceptions, kept distinct from practical knowledge. One exception is beliefs about infants being 'possessed' by birds while they are sleeping. If children clench their hands while asleep, the parents may conclude that they are doing what a bird does with its talons. Infant deaths are sometimes attributed to bird possession.[11] As a result, an elaborate ritual must be performed. But the important point is that the Ju/'hoansi never referred to this sort of belief, or to the many myths in which animals behave as if they were people, when they were telling Blurton Jones and Konner about tracking and the kind of animal behaviour that may be inferred from tracks. Nor did the San ever invoke the mythical, remote past.

There are a number of things that the San say must be avoided when out hunting. Many are purely practical, such as using gestures rather than noisy speech to communicate. Others come under the heading of what Westerners call superstitions. For example, /Xam hunters took care not to step on an eland's spoor.[12] Then, when they reached the carcass, they did not allow their shadows to fall on the animal because this was believed to make the eland 'lean'.[13] Today the Ju/'hoansi hold comparable beliefs. They say that a boy who has shot his first eland must not run fast after the wounded animal because 'if he runs fast, the eland will also run fast'.[14] Nor, as we saw in Chapter 3, should he urinate, because if he does so the eland is said to urinate and lose the poison. When the successful boy approaches the dead eland, he crouches

down behind an old man and places his arms around him – the position that is adopted by an experienced shaman and a novice who is learning to enter trance.[15] Approaching a dead eland with all its extreme potency is akin to approaching the spirit realm in the trance dance. *Tcheni* (dance), it will be remembered, is the Ju/'hoan respect word for eland.

Hunters need to respect many other observances, but these are kept separate from the actual business of tracking. The supernatural is not allowed to interfere with the efficiency required for survival in daily life. It is peripheral to the main business of tracking. In Western contexts, there are comparable practices: for instance, crossing oneself in a dangerous situation or not walking under a ladder. Some Westerners observe these superstitions, perhaps laughingly; others take them more seriously.

Observing these practices does not materially affect the outcome of a San hunt one way or the other. But, like so many comparable practices in the West, they may give the hunters a degree of self-confidence that is beneficial. The practices may not have material outcomes, but they may have psychological benefits.

Overall, Blurton Jones and Konner's findings were confirmed by Louis Liebenberg, who has had much experience with Kalahari San people. By going on a great many hunts with them he was able to compare the way they think with a Western philosophy of science.[16] Agreeing with what Richard Lee says in the epigraph to this chapter, he argues that the origin of scientific thinking lay in the very earliest human practice of tracking animals and that tracking contributed to the evolution of humans from pre-humans. Going further than Blurton Jones and Konner, Liebenberg believes that the ways in which hunters change their minds as new evidence comes to light presaged the hypothetico-deductive method whereby scientists make and modify (or reject) hypotheses in the light of new evidence.[17]

Another realm

When we leave practical daily life and the extraordinary skills that the San have in tracking animals, we encounter another sphere of thought. Here we are in the realm of myth and the supernatural. There is a central principle that helps us to understand this mode of thinking. It is transformation.

In mythology worldwide, people transform into animals and vice versa. 'They all become mantises' is a phrase we discussed in Chapter 3; we also learned that the Mantis himself can change into a snake, a louse, a hartebeest and 'a little green thing that flies'. Then, too, a lion can turn into a hartebeest.[18]

A /Xam *!gi:xa* could turn into a bird when he wished to find out what was happening in a distant part of the country.[19] Another transformation that a /Xam shaman could effect for the same purpose was into a jackal.[20] Are these beliefs about transformations markedly different from the Western tradition? No, they are not. In the Bible, Moses' staff transforms into a serpent[21] and the Holy Spirit can become a dove;[22] in Catholic ritual, wine and bread transform into the blood and flesh of Christ. In Greek mythology, Hippomenes and Atalanta are changed into lions, and King Minos kept a half-bull, half-man Minotaur in his labyrinth on Crete.

Transformations of this kind are not part of daily life – there is no empirical evidence for them. We therefore need to ask how human beings came to believe that they could change into animals or that one animal could change into another. Is it *merely* a matter of imagination, or is there more to it? To answer that question, we return to Chapter 1 and the San's great trance dance. The experiences of the dance – flying to distant places, seeing 'threads of light', passing under ground and under water – all originate in the human nervous system as it enters certain altered states, though they are elaborated and embroidered by those who experience them.[23]

We see this sort of neurologically created transformation in a classic Western instance: a man turns into a fox. The American psychologist and philosopher William James recorded the experiences of a friend who had ingested hashish: 'I thought of a fox, and instantly I was transformed into that animal. I could distinctly feel myself a fox, could see my long ears and bushy tail, and by a sort of introversion felt that my complete anatomy was that of a fox.'[24] Similarly, the French novelist Théophile Gautier, having ingested marihuana resin, wrote: 'After some moments of contemplation and by a strange miracle, I myself melted into the objects I regarded: I became that very object.'[25] In altered states, people can transform into animals or objects.

Having ingested mescaline, another Western subject reported as follows:

I see pulsating stars outlining the shape of a dog overlaying a spiral-tunnel of lights, changing to a real dog which is barking with the words 'Arf, arf' coming out of his mouth, changing into a toy dog on wheels changing into a sports car on the same wheeled platform in the desert with the sun high in the sky, changing back into the toy dog still barking, changing back to the sports car with the Road-Runner and another cartoon character driving in the same desert scene.[26]

Here we observe the shifting, mercurial nature of visions. This Western example reminds us of the Shoshone shaman's vision in which spirits change form, 'now a man, now an animal' (Chapter 8).[27] Changing hallucinations can be bewildering.

In yet another report, a Western subject blends not with an animal but with a lattice or fretwork: 'The subject stated that he saw fretwork before his eyes, that his arms, hands, and fingers turned into fretwork and that he became identical with the fretwork.... "The fretwork is I."'[28]

These reports (especially the last) parallel what Richard Katz found when he asked Ju/'hoan shamans to draw pictures of themselves, and men who had never experienced trance to do the same (see Chapter 3). Figure 19 A and C show the way that non-trancers drew themselves while B, D and E show the trancers' self-images. The bodily transformations that the shamans experience are clear: 'The fretwork is I.'

The Western transformation into fretwork and the San drawings that Katz obtained illustrate transformation into the iridescent geometrical visual percepts known as entoptic phenomena or form constants, one of which (bright sinuous lines) we saw was one of the 'things of sorcery' (see Chapter 3). We must not lose sight of the fact that these mental states need not be induced by psychotropic substances. They can also be caused by rhythmic movements, drumming, fasting, pain, meditation, and certain pathological conditions including migraine. San people in the sort of altered state that routinely occurs without hallucinogens in the dance see and blend with these neurologically produced forms, as they do with objects and creatures in the material world. The reported transformations take place during a dance that consciously focuses on altered consciousness: whatever role imagination may play in other contexts, in the dance it is human neurology that effects San shamans' transformations.

'Intellectual brilliance'

The upshot of this evidence is that transformation, among the San and indeed worldwide, is not merely a matter of a fertile imagination, though imagination clearly plays an important role. Although the neurological details may not be fully known, neuropsychological research has shown that the experience of transformation is indisputably wired into the human nervous system. All people, no matter what their cultural background, have the potential to experience culturally informed transformation.[29] Transformation is therefore 'real' to those who experience it, *and* it can be repeatedly induced.

So far, we have considered only instances in which subjects have experienced radically altered consciousness. But such transformations are also part of the dreams that everyone experiences. In dreams, people feel themselves changing into animals, other people and things. San transformations are therefore not exceptional: they are part of worldwide experience. The human brain is tuned to transformation.

All in all, the strangeness that many Westerners sense in much San mythology and art is no different from the strangeness of Western religious thought. In the Middle Ages and later, people living in Western communities were sometimes burnt alive because they refused to subscribe to the mental experiences of others. The San do not take such violent action. For them, everyone is entitled to believe whatever they choose to believe about the spirit realm, though there are, of course, experiential commonalities that produce beliefs to which everyone can respond. But they do not allow their religious experiences and beliefs to interfere with the normal round of daily life – for the San, hunting and gathering (Fig. 58). For them, their religious experiences were (and still are) 'real'. They just did not allow them to affect the outcome of the hunt. They do not necessarily know they are making this distinction; they do not draw an explicit distinction between the sacred and the secular. Non-real things are just not allowed to skew the tracking process.

Blurton Jones and Konner therefore concluded: 'The two areas seem to be completely different compartments of intellectual life.'[30] They went further and argued that, overall, the similarities between the thought processes of Westerners in general and the Ju/'hoansi suggest that '[w]e have gained little or nothing in ability or intellectual brilliance since the Stone Age…. Just as primitive life can no longer be characterized as nasty, brutish, and short, no longer can it be characterized as stupid, ignorant, or superstition-dominated.'[31]

This is our conclusion too. As we have tried to decipher the relationship between the endlessly intricate and varied San rock art and the often initially opaque statements about images that 19th-century researchers recorded, we have been repeatedly struck by the subtlety of San thought and its interrelatedness. The early San and their present-day descendants cannot be called 'simple'.

Indeed, the integration of San life, myth and art has been our theme. The art was not the sport of quirky individuals. One of the points that gave Egyptologists confidence in their decipherment of the Rosetta Stone was the parallelism between its three registers and, moreover, the way in which, together, they unlocked the hieroglyphics in so many Egyptian monuments.

57 Women are highly skilled in detecting signs of edible roots among the grasses of the Kalahari Desert. Back in the camp they prepare the roots and melons for consumption.

So, too, with the San. The verbatim 19th-century texts and the 20th- and 21st-century accounts of San life and thought mesh in detail with the art: central concepts and cognitive images run through the texts, paintings and myths (flight, travelling under ground, passing through water or mist, 'threads of light'). The ethnographic record and the painted images illustrate, illuminate and extend one another.

'Tactible' ideas

Can we say more than 'run through'? What happens when imagistic ideas are given materiality? Contemplating the diversity of art (visual and verbal), the influential anthropologist Clifford Geertz wrote: 'If there is a commonality [among all arts worldwide] it lies in the fact that certain activities everywhere seem specifically designed to demonstrate that ideas are visible, audible, and – one needs to make up a word here – tactible, that they can be cast in forms where the senses, and through the senses emotions, can reflectively address them.'[32] This is what San rock art images did: they made abstract ideas and mental experiences visible and 'tactible'. The complex, ritualized act of making the images brought ephemeral experiences under control and made them manipulable.

Geertz also made the point that, in looking at works of art, we need to ask what made them important to those who fashioned them or possessed them. He then added that the factors that brought about this importance 'are as varied as life itself'.[33] Questioning the existence of a 'universal sense of beauty' as a sufficient motive for making art, Geertz claimed, quite rightly in our view, that if we wish to go beyond 'an ethnocentric sentimentalism' we need some 'knowledge of what those arts are about or an understanding of the culture out of which they come'.

Today we know, at least in large measure, what San rock art 'is about': it deals with the vast web of San religion and cosmology. Once made, the images that were a part of that web and took on a life of their own. As performances of myths and shamans' accounts of their visits to the spirit realm fed back into and helped to shape that web, so too the images fed back into San concepts and, at the same time, impacted on social relationships. We have been able to use the three registers of our 'Rosetta Stone' to move beyond any superficial appeal to what Geertz calls a 'universal sense of beauty' and to situate painted San images in the web of San thought, a web that, like some spiders' webs, has a coherent pattern but no finality, neither a beginning nor an end.

Notes

PREFACE (PAGES 6–14)
1 e.g., Evans-Pritchard (1956, 1965); Malinowski (1922).
2 1912; cited in Barnard (2000, 107).
3 e.g., Renfrew & Zubrow (1994); Mellars & Gibson (1996); Mithen (1996); Lewis-Williams (2002b).
4 Barnard (2007, 93).
5 Mazel (2009a, 2009b).
6 Wendt (1976).
7 Lewis-Williams (1984); Lewis-Williams & Pearce (2008).

A NOTE ON PRONUNCIATION (PAGE 15)
1 Marshall (1976, p.xx).

1 BACK IN TIME (PAGES 16–50)
1 22 February 1850. Baines (1964, 19–20).
2 Baines (1964, 20).
3 Vinnicombe (1976); Campbell (1987); Wright and Mazel (2007); Blundell (2004); Challis (2008, 2009).
4 Sparrman (1789:2, 143).
5 Thunberg (1986 [1788], 290–91).
6 Anthing (1863, 4–5).
7 Philip (1828, p.xx).
8 Mitchell (2002, 161–91).
9 Mitchell (2002, 248–58); Phillipson (1977).
10 Alexander (1838, p.vi).
11 Alexander (1838, 123–25).
12 Deacon & Deacon (1999); Crawhall (2006); Soodyall (2006).
13 e.g., Guenther (1999); Katz (1982); Lee (1979); Marshall (1976, 1999); Marshall Thomas (2006); Schapera (1930); Shostak (1981); Silberbauer (1981); Wilmsen (1989).
14 Lewis-Williams (1981, 1992); Lewis-Williams & Biesele (1978); Barnard (1992).
15 Traill (1978); Barnard (1992, 17–18, 20–27).
16 Bleek & Lloyd (1911, p.xiii).
17 Chippindale et al. (2000); Barnard (2003).
18 Deacon & Dowson (1996); Lewis-Williams (2002a, 2008); Bennun (2004); Bank (2006); Skotnes (2007); Wessels (2010).
19 Spohr (1962, 33); on these raids, see Wright (1971) and Vinnicombe (1976); Challis (2008, 2009).
20 Skotnes (2007).
21 Orpen (1874).
22 Lewis-Williams (2003).

23 Bleek (1874).
24 Bleek (1874, 11).
25 Stow (1905).
26 Young (1908, 27–28); Dowson et al. (1994).
27 Bleek (1874, 12).
28 Theal (1905, p.v).
29 See Skotnes (2008).
30 Woodhouse & Lee (1976); Woodhouse (1979); Dowson et al. (1994).
31 Stow & Bleek (1930).
32 See, for example, Le Quellec (2004) and Skotnes (2008).
33 Dowson et al. (1994); Lewis-Williams & Dowson (2008).
34 Smith & Ouzman (2004).
35 Prins (1990); Challis (2008, 2009); Jolly (1986, 1995, 2006); Smith & Ouzman (2004).
36 Lewis-Williams & Pearce (2004a).
37 Wendt (1976); see also Thackeray (1983).
38 Mazel (2009a, 2009b); Mazel & Watchman (2003).
39 Wilman (1933); Dowson (1992); Fock & Fock (1979, 1984, 1989); Scherz (1970, 1975); Deacon & Foster (2005); Parkington et al. (2008).
40 Maggs (1995).
41 Lewis-Williams (1984); Mazel (2009b, 100).
42 Lewis-Williams (1984); Loubser & Laurens (1994); Pearce (2005).
43 Barnard (1992, 71); Barnard (2007).
44 Mazel (2009).
45 Dowson et al. (1994).
46 Bleek & Lloyd (1911, p.x).
47 Ibid.
48 L.V.1.3612.
49 L.VIII.1.6052.
50 Bleek & Lloyd (1911, 305); Deacon (1986).
51 Bleek & Lloyd (1911, 307).
52 L.V.24.5963 rev. Bleek & Lloyd (1911, p.xiv).
53 L.VIII.18.7608–7609.
54 Orpen (1874, 2).
55 Solway & Lee (1990, 120, 122).

2 DANCE OF LIFE, DANCE OF DEATH (PAGES 51–72)
1 Stow & Bleek (1930, caption to pl. 2a).
2 Arbousset & Daumas (1846, 247).
3 Arbousset & Daumas (1846, 246–47).
4 Stow (1905, 111).

5 Stow & Bleek (1930, caption to pl. 2a); L.V.22.5754 rev.

6 e.g., Schapera (1930); Marshall Thomas (1959, 2006); Marshall (1976, 1999); Howell (1979); Lee (1979, 1993); Shostak (1981); Katz (1982); Wilmsen (1989); Barnard (1992); Valiente-Noailles (1993); Guenther (1999); Keeney (1999, 2003); Gordon (1992).

7 Katz et al. (1997); Marshall (1999).

8 Biesele (1993); Guenther (1999); Barnard (1992).

9 Guenther (1999); Hewitt (2008).

10 Lewis-Williams (1992).

11 e.g., Guenther (1999); Hewitt (2008); cf. Lewis (1989).

12 Bleek (1956, 382).

13 Bleek (1956, 382).

14 Lewis-Williams & Pearce (2004a, 102).

15 Bleek (1956, 255).

16 Bleek (1956, 457).

17 Barnard (1985, 83, 85).

18 Katz et al. (1997, 26, 58, 110).

19 Bleek (1956, 422).

20 Marshall (1999, 48); Katz (1982, 118–40).

21 Biesele (1993, 75).

22 Barnard (1985, 84).

23 Bleek (1956, 569, 320).

24 Bleek (1935, 28–29).

25 Bleek (1935, 10–11).

26 Bleek (1956, 436–37).

27 Orpen (1874, 10).

28 Marshall (1999); Katz (1982); Biesele (1993); Lee (1993).

29 Biesele (1993, 109).

30 Arbousset & Daumas (1846, 247).

31 Kriel (1958).

32 Bleek (1956, 320); original parenthesis; cf. Butler (1997).

33 Bleek (1935, 12).

34 Lewis-Williams (1981, 88).

35 Bleek (1935, 22, 23).

36 Bleek (1956, 425).

37 Katz (1982).

38 L.V.10.4744–4750, 4755–4757.

39 Stow & Bleek (1930, caption to pls 13 and 14).

40 Lewis-Williams & Pearce (2004a, 97–98).

41 Bleek (1935, 45).

42 L.V.10.4745 rev.

43 Bleek (1933, 378).

44 Bleek (1935, 13).

45 Lewis-Williams (1981, 78).

46 Lewis-Williams & Pearce (2004a, 99).

3 'THESE ARE SORCERY'S THINGS' (PAGES 73–93)

1 Biesele (1993, 72).

2 Bleek (1956, 24).

3 Bleek (1935, 13).

4 Bleek (1928, 12); cf. Schapera (1930, 67).

5 Lewis-Williams et al. (2000).

6 See, e.g., Siegel (1977); Klüver (1966); Bressloff et al. (2000); for a summary see Lewis-Williams (2002b, 121–35), (2010).

7 Lewis-Williams (2010, 144–54).

8 Katz (1982, 235–36).

9 Lewis-Williams (2002, 121–35); Lewis-Williams & Pearce (2005, 39–59).

10 e.g., Schapera (1930, 198); Biesele (1993, 70–72); Keeney (2003).

11 Lewis-Williams (1997); Lewis-Williams & Pearce (2004, 189–91).

12 L.II.6.669 rev.

13 Keeney (1993, 105).

14 Katz et al. (1997, 112).

15 Katz et al. (1997, 24).

16 Biesele (1980, 56, 61).

17 England (1968, 431–32).

18 Guenther (1986, 219–20).

19 Katz et al. (1997, 108).

20 Ibid.

21 Lewis-Williams et al. (2000).

22 Lewis-Williams & Dowson (1990); Lewis-Williams & Pearce (2004a, 147, 181–82).

23 Schmidt (1973); Lewis-Williams (1981, 117–26); Hewitt (2008, 97–114).

24 Bleek (1924, 16, 33).

25 Bleek (1924, 16).

26 L.8.17.5434 rev.

27 Lewis-Williams (2002, 78, 89–91).

28 Bleek & Lloyd (1911, 25).

29 Bleek (1924, 27).

30 Bleek (1924, 41).

31 Bleek & Lloyd (1911, 361); Bleek (1935, 41).

32 Bleek (1935, 41).

33 Bleek & Lloyd (1911, 11); Campbell (1815, 29).

34 Bleek (1924, 45–46).

35 Bleek (1924, 44).

36 Campbell (1872: 2, 32–33).

37 Keeney (1999, 47).

38 Keeney (1999, 59–60).

39 Bleek (1932, 233–40); see also Silberbauer (1965, 49); Vinnicombe (1976, 300–01); Lewis-Williams & Biesele (1978); Lewis-Williams (1981, 55–67), (2002a, 229–32).

40 Lewis-Williams (2002a, 231).

41 Marshall Thomas (1959, 66).

42 Marshall Thomas (1959, 65, 660).
43 Bleek (1924, 10).
44 Bleek & Lloyd (1911, 3).
45 Marshall (1999, 77).
46 Lewis-Williams (1981, 14).
47 Arbousset & Daumas (1846, 256).
48 England (1968, 401).
49 Marshall (1962, 247); see also Marshall (1999, 148).
50 Bleek (1924, 12).
51 L.V.17.5265; Lewis-Williams (1981, 56–57).
52 Schmidt (1973, 119).
53 Bleek (1936, 143); Lewis-Williams (1996, 138, 140, fig. 3).
54 Bleek (1956, 315).
55 Katz et al. (1997).
56 Bleek & Lloyd (1911, 13).
57 Bleek (1956, 557); also Bleek (1924, 27).
58 Marshall (1962, 250), (1965, 272), (1999, 68); see also Marshall Thomas (1959, 130).
59 Marshall (1962, 228, 232–33); England (1968, 453).
60 L.2.27.2463 rev.
61 Arbousset & Daumas (1846, 253).
62 See, e.g., Johnson (1910, fig. 35); Rudner (1957, pl. xxvi); Rudner & Rudner (1970); How (1962, 28).
63 Lewis-Williams (1981, 124, 126).
64 Orpen (1874, 3).

4 DISCOVERING RAIN (PAGES 94–109)
1 Baines ([1850] 1964, 19).
2 Dornan (1925, 167).
3 Ibid.
4 Campbell (1815, 139).
5 Doke (1936, 469).
6 Barrow (1801:1, 284).
7 Alexander (1837, 314, 315).
8 Alexander (1837, 316).
9 Alexander (1837, 317).
10 Bleek (1875, 20).
11 Willcox (1963, 35).
12 Leeuwenburg (1970).
13 Ibid.
14 Bleek & Lloyd (1911, 395).
15 L.VIII.1.6063–6068; Lewis-Williams (1977), (2002a, 222–23); Lewis-Williams et al. (1993).
16 Bleek (1933); Lewis-Williams (1981, 103–16); Lewis-Williams & Pearce (2004a, 137–57).
17 L.VIII.1.6074–6077.
18 Keeney (1999, 60).
19 L.V.3.4993–4994.
20 Katz (1982); Marshall (1969, 363).

21 e.g., Lewis-Williams & Dowson (1999, figs 15, 20, 28, 29); Lewis-Williams & Pearce (2004a, figs 5.1, 5.3, 5.4, 6.5, 7.8).
22 L.V.3.4995.
23 Marshall (1969, 351–52); Katz (1982, 46, 168, 263); Lewis-Williams & Dowson (1999, 48–49).
24 L.V.13.4994–4995.
25 L.VIII.1.6063–6064.
26 Hollman (2004).
27 Lewis-Williams (1981, 1992); Lewis-Williams & Biesele (1978); Barnard (1992, 2007).
28 Bleek (1874).
29 Hollmann (2003, 2005).
30 e.g., Van der Riet et al. (1940, pl. 23); Rudner & Rudner (1970, figs 48b); Rudner & Rudner (1978, fig. 4.20).
31 Hollmann (2005, fig. 7).
32 e.g., Barber (1971, 103); Siegel (1977); Blanke et al. (2002).
33 Bleek (1935, 18).
34 L.V.21.5696–5707.
35 Bleek (1956, 465).
36 Bleek (1956, 296, 431).
37 L.V.21.5698–5699.
38 Biesele (personal communication).
39 L.V.21.5701–5702.
40 L.V.21.5706–5707.
41 L.VIII.1.6067–6068.
42 Hollmann (2003, table 3).
43 Fry (1988); Chantler (1999).
44 Hollmann (2005).

5 CAPTURING RAIN (PAGES 110–131)
1 Orpen (1874, 10).
2 Lloyd (1889, 28).
3 Vinnicombe (1976, 101), (2009).
4 Challis (2005).
5 Vinnicombe (1976, fig. 239).
6 Lewis-Williams (2000, 53).
7 Bleek (1875, 20).
8 Crause (personal communication, 2010).
9 B.XXVII.2540–2608; L.V.25.6008–6013; Bleek (1933, 375–78), (1935, 14–15).
10 Bleek (1933, 297–312, 375–92).
11 Bleek (1933, 375–76).
12 Orpen (1874, 10).
13 Bleek (1874, 12).
14 B.XXVII.2540–2608; Bleek (1875, 18).
15 See also Bleek (1933, 375–78).
16 cf. Vinnicombe (1976, 336); Lewis-Williams (1980).
17 Bleek & Lloyd MS, L.V.6.4385 rev.; Bleek (1933, 301).

18 Orpen (1874, 3).

19 Challis (forthcoming, 2011); Hoff (1997, 1998).

20 Schmidt (1979).

21 Orpen (1874, 2).

22 Orpen (1874, 3).

23 Mitchell & Challis (2008, 459).

24 Ibid.

25 Orpen (1874, 2).

26 Lewis-Williams (1980); Lewis-Williams & Pearce (2004a, 171–72); Solomon (1997).

27 Lewis-Williams (1980, 474).

28 Challis (2005).

29 Bleek (1935, 15).

30 Bleek (1935, 46), (1936, 144); Lewis-Williams (1981, 77).

31 Jolly (1995, 2006).

32 B.XXVII.2540 rev.

33 L.V.13.4989.

34 Bleek & Lloyd (1911, 193–99); Schmidt (1979); Hewitt (2008, 49–69).

35 Lewis-Williams (1981, 106–16), (2002a, 222–23).

36 Bleek (1933, 309).

37 Bleek (1933, 378).

38 Bleek (1936, 135).

39 Bleek (1875, 12).

40 Bleek (1933, 389).

41 B.27.2545–2546.

42 Bleek (1933, 376), (1956, 678).

43 Bleek (1936, 135).

44 Bleek (1956, 550).

45 Bleek (1874, 12).

46 Schmidt (1979); Lewis-Williams (1981, 41–53); Marshall (1999, 187–202); Hewitt (2008, 205–11).

47 Bleek (1933, 300).

48 Bleek (1933, 382).

49 Bleek (1935, 23).

50 Bleek (1935, 2, 4).

51 Bleek (1935, 14–15); L.5.25.6008–6013.

52 L.5.25.6007 rev.

53 Biesele (1993, 93–94).

54 Bleek (1956, 196).

55 L.5.25.6009.

56 On this point, see James (2001, 212).

57 Bleek (1935, 22–23).

58 L.5.3.4126 rev.

59 Bleek (1956, 425); Lewis-Williams (1981, 78).

60 Katz (1982); Marshall (1999, 88).

61 Bleek (1956, 238).

62 Bleek (1935, 15, 25).

63 Bleek (1935, 18).

64 Lewis-Williams *et al.* (2000).

65 Shapera (1930, 198).

66 e.g., Bamboo Mountain, Vinnicombe (1976, fig. 240); for a complete copy, see Lewis-Williams (2003, fig. 56).

67 Bleek (1924, 66).

68 Marshall (1999, 167).

69 Lewis-Williams & Pearce (2004a, 13–19).

70 Keeney (1999, 45).

71 Goodwin (1938, 253, pl. VIA); Lewis-Williams & Pearce (2004a, 63–65).

6 TRUTH HIDDEN IN ERROR (PAGES 132–152)

1 Stow & Bleek (1930, caption to pl. 12).

2 Stow (1905, p.xiv).

3 Stow & Bleek (1930).

4 Frobenius (1931, pl. 133).

5 Dowson *et al.* (1994).

6 Stow & Bleek (1930, pl. 12).

7 Stow & Bleek (1930, caption to pl. 12).

8 Alexander (1838:1, 289–90); Bleek (1932, 55, 56); Marshall Thomas (2006, 157–73); Marshall Thomas (1994, 119).

9 Woodhouse (1979, 133).

10 Alexander (1838:2, pl. 14, p.181).

11 e.g., Pager (1971).

12 e.g., Stow & Bleek (1930, pls 7, 16, 21, 32).

13 Vinnicombe (1976, 218, 332); Lewis-Williams (1981, 95–97), (1985); Hollmann (2004, 33–36).

14 Biesele (1996, 149).

15 Marshall Thomas (2006, 168).

16 Bleek (1932, 53, 57).

17 L.2.26.2339.

18 Bleek (1932, 233).

19 Bleek (1932, 61).

20 Ibid.

21 Bleek (1932, 58).

22 Bleek & Lloyd (1911, 267).

23 Bleek (1932, 47, 50, 60), (1933, 390).

24 Bleek (1932, 61); cf. Mackenzie (1871, 151).

25 Bleek (1932, 55).

26 Bleek (1932, 61).

27 Bleek (1956, 291).

28 Bleek (1932, 62–63); cf. Bleek (1911, 183, 187); Fourie (1928, 102).

29 Bleek (1932, 61).

30 Bleek (1911, 187).

31 Bleek (1935, 3).

32 Bleek (1935, 2).

33 Ibid.

34 Bleek (1935, 23).

35 Bleek (1936, 131–34); Bleek & Lloyd (1911, 236).

36 Bleek (1935, 132).
37 Bleek (1936, 131); Hollmann (2004, 279).
38 Katz (1982, 227); see also Lee (1967, 35).
39 Katz *et al.* (1997, 24).
40 Guenther (1999, 187).
41 Heinz (1975, 29).
42 Biesele (1993, 11).
43 Marshall (1999, 238).
44 Biesele (1993, 11).
45 Barnard (1985, 83).
46 Guenther (1999, 187).
47 Biesele (1993, 111).
48 Biesele (1993, 88, 109–11).
49 L.2.22–24.1548–1652.
50 Vinnicombe (1976, 210, 211, 259).
51 Bleek & Lloyd (1911, 27).
52 Bleek & Lloyd (1911, 85–98); on the Dawn's-Heart Star, see Hewitt (2008, 71–82).
53 Orpen (1874, 10).
54 Bleek (1936, 149).
55 Lee (1967, 33).
56 cf. Katz (1982, 106–07).
57 e.g., Marshall (1962, 251).
58 Marshall (1969, 352, 371, 378).
59 Lewis-Williams (1985).
60 Lewis-Williams (1981, 81); Lewis-Williams & Pearce (2004a, 90, 97–100, 112).
61 Katz (1982, 100).
62 Katz (1982, 165).
63 Lewis-Williams (1981, 84–100); Lewis-Williams & Pearce (2004a, 159–75).
64 Lewis-Williams (1981, 88).
65 Bleek (1935, 2).
66 Bleek (1924, 16); Lewis-Williams (1996, 128).
67 Bleek (1924, 33).
68 Katz (1982, 46).
69 Lewis-Williams (1985).
70 Pager (1971, 321); for comparable results, see Vinnicombe (1976, 215); Lewis-Williams (1972, 51); Lewis-Williams (1974).
71 Vinnicombe (1976, 215).
72 e.g., Fock & Fock (1989, 41).
73 Vinnicombe (1976, 218).
74 Biesele (1978, 927–28).
75 Lewis-Williams (1995b).
76 Lewis-Williams & Dowson (1990); Lewis-Williams & Pearce (2004a).
77 Lewis-Williams (1986); Lewis-Williams & Pearce (2004a, 147, 180–81, 200).
78 Lewis-Williams (1985).
79 Lewis-Williams & Pearce (2004a, 2004b).
80 Summers (1959, pls 28, 29, 30, 31, 50, 55, 57); Garlake (1995, pls xxi, xxii, xxiii, xxiv;

figs 102, 103, 104, 123, 127, 180); Walker (1996, figs 54, 75, 89).
81 Eastwood & Eastwood (2006, 127).
82 Frobenius (1931).
83 Holm (1957, 69).
84 Rudner & Rudner (1970, 86, 87).
85 Cooke (1969, 42).
86 Cooke (1969, 42); Pager (1971, 349–52), (1973).
87 Rudner & Rudner (1970, 87); Lee & Woodhouse (1970).
88 Garlake (1995, 96); on the *gebesi*, see Katz (1982, 45, 46).
89 Mguni (2005).
90 Bleek & Lloyd (1911, 199, 207, 259–61); Bleek (1924, 23–24, 51); Arbousset & Daumas (1846, 244).
91 Bleek (1936, 161).
92 Ibid.
93 Ibid.
94 Pager (1971, 1973, 1975).
95 Bleek (1924, 47).
96 Marshall Thomas (1969, 145).
97 Bleek (1875, 11).
98 Bleek & Lloyd (1911, 353–55).
99 Bleek & Lloyd (1911, pl. 19).
100 Bleek & Lloyd (1911, 353–59).
101 Bleek (1935, 13).
102 Bleek & Lloyd (1911, 355–57).
103 Marshall (1969, 362).
104 Marshall (1969, 370).
105 See also Bleek (1932, 246); Bleek & Lloyd (1911, 197).
106 Marshall (1962, 249).
107 Edwin Wilmsen (personal communication).
108 Marshall (1999, 73, 76–77).
109 Bleek (1924, 2).
110 Bleek (1933, 390–91).

7 THE IMAGISTIC WEB OF MYTH
(PAGES 153–171)

1 Orpen (1874, 6).
2 Orpen (1874, 2).
3 Orpen (1874, 3).
4 Orpen (1874, 10).
5 e.g., Propp (1968).
6 e.g., Leach (1969, 1974); Lévi-Strauss (1967).
7 Lewis-Williams (1996, 1997).
8 Macksey & Donato (1972).
9 For examples see Lewis-Williams (1983, 44–54), and more especially (1996, 1997); Lewis-Williams & Pearce (2005, 149–68); Vinnicombe (1975).

10 Lewis-Williams & Loubser (1986).
11 Whitehouse (2000).
12 Lensen-Erz (1989, 366–69); see Lewis-Williams (1990, 1992a) for further discussion.
13 Lewis-Williams (1972, 1974, 2006); Lewis-Williams & Pearce (2004a, 2008, 2009).
14 Lewis-Williams & Pearce (2004a, 99).
15 Biesele (1993, 72).
16 Biesele (1993, 74).
17 Lewis-Williams & Dowson (1990); Lewis-Williams & Pearce (2004a).
18 Lewis-Williams (1996, 2003); Lewis-Williams & Pearce (2004a, 51–55).
19 Orpen (1874, 3).
20 Bleek & Lloyd (1911, 198–205).
21 Summarized from Bleek & Lloyd (1911, 198–205).
22 Marshall (1999, 187–202); Lewis-Williams (1981, 41–54); Hewitt (2008, 205–21).
23 Lewis-Williams & Pearce (2004a, fig. 3.7).
24 On rain and mediators see Lewis-Williams & Pearce (2004a).
25 Orpen (1874, 10).
26 Dowson (1988); Dowson & Lewis-Williams (1999, 140).
27 e.g., Bleek & Lloyd (1911, 112–17).
28 Lewis-Williams & Dowson (1999, 88–89).
29 Bleek (1933, 303).
30 Orpen (1874, 8–9).
31 Bleek (1874, 11).
32 Orpen (1874, 8–9).
33 Bleek (1928, 7); Marshall (1962, 236, 243).
34 L.2.14.1365.
35 Biesele (1978, 927), (1993, 86–87).
36 Marshall (1962, 249).
37 Marshall (1999, 73).
38 Marshall (1999, 76–77).
39 Hahn (1870, 120); Stow (1905, 86); Marshall (1960, 336).
40 Stow (1905, 86); see also Borcherds (1861, 115); How (1962, 46).
41 See also Chapman (1868:1, 273).
42 Ellenberger (1953, 98).
43 Cumming (1850:2, 177).
44 Bleek (1924, 41).
45 L.2.14.1363.
46 Pager (1971, 345–52), (1975, 28, 94); see also Mazel (1982).
47 Lewis-Williams & Dowson (1999, 62–63, 108).
48 Biesele (1993, 72).
49 Biesele (1993, 71).
50 Lewis-Williams (1997).
51 Orpen (1874, 7–8).
52 Orpen (1874, 6, 3).
53 Orpen (1874, 6–7).
54 Lewis-Williams (1981).
55 Bleek (1924, 2–9).
56 Bleek (1924, 3).
57 Bleek (1924, 12).
58 Bleek (1924, 11).
59 Bleek & Lloyd (1911, 193); Bleek (1933, 309).
60 Lewis-Williams (1996, 1997).
61 Orpen (1874, 3).

8 INTO THE UNKNOWN (PAGES 172–188)
1 Orpen (1874, 4).
2 Orpen (1874, 8).
3 Orpen (1874, 3–4).
4 Orpen (1874, 4).
5 Ibid.
6 Wright & Mazel (2007).
7 Grab & Nash (2009).
8 Note: Seashells found in rock shelters on the far side of the escarpment were either taken there by people who had been to the sea or were traded from person to person until they found their way to the highest parts of the subcontinent; Mitchell (1996), (2002, 155–56).
9 Vinnicombe in Carter (1970); Vinnicombe (1976); Mitchell (2002, 169).
10 Wright & Mazel (2007).
11 Orpen (1874, 3).
12 Mitchell (2009, 183); notes to Vinnicombe (2009).
13 Vinnicombe (2009, 168).
14 Vinnicombe (2009, 172).
15 Vinnicombe (2009, 168).
16 Ibid.
17 How (1962, 37).
18 Jolly (1986); Lewis-Williams (1986); Jolly & Prins (1990).
19 How (1962, 37).
20 Watts (2002).
21 How (1962, 34).
22 Bleek & Lloyd (1911, 379).
23 Orpen (1874, 4).
24 Bleek (1935, 12, 19, 22, 34); cf. Bleek & Lloyd (1911, 113, 115); see also Marshall (1969, 374).
25 Bleek (1935, 1, 34); Lewis-Williams (1981, 78); Campbell (1815, 316).
26 Bleek & Lloyd (1911, 113).
27 L.V.4.4180.
28 Bleek (1956, 352).
29 L.V.4.4157.
30 L.II.27.2463 rev.

31 Hollmann (2004, 163).

32 Bleek (1956, 633); without the vowel-extending colon, //xau means 'to fly'; Bleek (1956, 632–33).

33 Deacon (1986, 1988, 1997); Deacon & Foster (2005).

34 Deacon (1997).

35 Passage omitted from Bleek (1933); L.II.24.2232–2233; Hollmann (2004, 156).

36 Bleek (1933, 308).

37 Bleek (1933, 309).

38 Ibid.

39 Bleek (1933, 310).

40 Deacon (1988, 1997).

41 Bleek (1936, 135–41).

42 Ibid.

43 Bleek (1936, 136).

44 Bleek (1924, p.viii).

45 Deacon (1986).

46 Deacon (1997).

47 Bleek (1933, 299).

48 Dowson (1992).

49 Loendorf (2004, 201–02).

50 Francis & Loendorf (2002); Loendorf & Stone (2006).

51 Francis & Loendorf (2002, 194).

52 Hultkrantz in Loendorf (2004, 205).

53 Francis & Loendorf (2002, 110); see also Loendorf (2004).

54 Loendorf (2004, 205).

55 Loendorf (2004, 214).

56 Loendorf (2004, 205).

57 Loendorf (2004, 206).

58 Loendorf (2004, 210).

59 Loendorf (2004, 211).

60 Culin (1901, 17); quoted in Francis & Loendorf (2002, 120).

61 Francis & Loendorf (2002, 123).

62 Francis & Loendorf (2002, 195).

63 Francis & Loendorf (2002, 123).

64 Whitley *et al.* (2004).

65 Isaiah 57:7.

66 Exodus 19:9, 12, 13.

67 Lewis-Williams (2002b, 2010); Lewis-Williams & Pearce (2005).

68 Francis & Loendorf (2002, 29–30).

69 Bleek (1935, 18).

70 Biesele (1993, 71).

71 Biesele (1993, 70–72).

72 Francis & Loendorf (2002, 30).

73 Lewis-Williams (2002b, 2010); Lewis-Williams & Pearce (2004a).

74 Smith & Blundell (2004).

9 'SIMPLE' PEOPLE? (PAGES 189–201)

1 Lee (1976, 17).

2 Gordon (1992, 1997); Lewis-Williams (1995a, 1995c); Bank (2006).

3 Shaw (1820, 25).

4 Pearse (1973, 7).

5 Stow (1905, 230).

6 Van der Post (1958, 1961).

7 Van der Post (1958, 13).

8 Jones (2001, 4).

9 Blurton Jones & Konner (1976).

10 Blurton Jones & Konner (1976, 339).

11 Blurton Jones & Konner (1976, 343–44).

12 L.V.17.5316 rev.

13 Bleek (1932, 238).

14 Lewis-Williams (1981, 58).

15 Lewis-Williams (1981, 59); Biesele (personal communication).

16 Liebenberg (1990).

17 Liebenberg (1990, 29, 153–65).

18 Bleek (1932, 62).

19 Bleek (1935, 18).

20 Bleek (1935, 15, 25).

21 Exodus 7:9, 10, 15.

22 Matthew 3:16; Mark 1:10.

23 Lewis-Williams (2002b); Lewis-Williams & Pearce (2005).

24 Siegel & Jarvik (1975, 104–05).

25 Siegel & Jarvik (1975, 107).

26 Siegel & Jarvik (1975, 132).

27 Hultkranz in Loendorf (2004, 205).

28 Klüver (1966, 71–72).

29 Lewis-Williams (2002b); Lewis-Williams & Pearce (2004a, 2005).

30 Blurton Jones & Konner (1976, 346).

31 Blurton Jones & Konner (1976, 348).

32 Geertz (1983, 119–20).

33 Geertz (1983, 119).

Bibliography and
Guide to Further Reading

Alexander, J. E. 1837. *Narrative of a Voyage of Observation among the Colonies of Western Africa, in the Flagship Thalia; and of a Campaign in Kaffir-land, on the Staff of the Commander-in-Chief, in 1835.* London: Henry Colburn.

Alexander, J. E. 1838. *An Expedition of Discovery into the Interior of Africa, through the Hitherto Undescribed Countries of the Great Namaquas, Boschmans, and Hill Damaras,* 2 vols. London: Henry Colburn.

Anthing, L. 1863. Report in message from His Excellency the Governor with enclosures, relative to affairs in the north-western districts of the Colony. Cape of Good Hope Parliamentary Paper, A-39 63.

Arbousset, T. & Daumas, F. 1846. *Narrative of an Exploratory Tour to the North-East of the Colony of the Cape of Good Hope.* Cape Town: A. S. Robertson.

Baines, T. 1964. *Journal of Residence in Africa, 1842–1853.* Cape Town: Van Riebeeck Society.

Bank, A. 2006. *Bushmen in a Victorian World: The Remarkable Story of the Bleek-Lloyd Collection of Bushman Folklore.* Cape Town: Double Storey, Juta.

Barber, T. X. 1971. Imagery and 'hallucinations': effects of LSD contrasted with the effects of 'hypnotic' suggestions. In Segel, S. J. (ed.) *Imagery: Current Cognitive Approaches,* pp. 101–29. New York: Academic Press.

Barnard, A. 1985. *A Nharo Wordlist with Notes on Grammar.* Durban: Department of African Studies, University of Natal, Occasional Paper No. 2.

Barnard, A. 1992. *Hunters and Herders of Southern Africa: A Comparative Ethnography of the Khoisan Peoples.* Cambridge: Cambridge University Press.

Barnard, A. 2000. *History and Theory in Anthropology.* Cambridge: Cambridge University Press.

Barnard, A. 2003. !Ke e: /xarra //ke – Multiple origins and multiple meanings of the motto. *African Studies* 62, 243–50.

Barnard, A. 2007. *Anthropology and the Bushman.* Oxford: Berg.

Barrow, J. 1801. *An Account of Travels into the Interior of Southern Africa.* London: Cadell & Davies.

Bennum, N. 2004. *The Broken String: The Last Words of an Extinct People.* London: Viking.

Biesele, M. 1978. Sapience and scarce resources: communication systems of the !Kung and other foragers. *Social Science Information* 17, 921–47.

Biesele, M. 1980. Old K"au. In Halifax, J. (ed.) *Shamanic Voices: A Survey of Visionary Narratives,* pp. 54–62. Harmondsworth: Penguin.

Biesele, M. 1993. *Women like Meat: The Folklore and Foraging Ideology of the Kalahari Ju/'hoan.* Johannesburg: Witwatersrand University Press.

Biesele, M. 1996. 'He stealthily lightened at his brother-in-law' (and thunder echoes in Bushman oral tradition a century later). In Deacon, J. & Dowson, T. A. (eds) *Voices from the Past: /Xam Bushmen and the Bleek and Lloyd Collection,* pp. 142–60. Johannesburg: Witwatersrand University Press.

Blanke, O. S., Ortigue, S., Landis, T. & Seeck, M. 2002. Stimulating illusory own-body perceptions. *Nature* 419, 269–70.

Bleek, D. F. 1924. *The Mantis and his Friends.* Cape Town: Maskew Miller.

Bleek, D. F. 1928. *The Nharon: A Bushman Tribe of the Central Kalahari.* Cambridge: Cambridge University Press.

Bleek, D. F. 1931. Customs and beliefs of the /Xam Bushmen: Part I: Baboons. *Bantu Studies* 5, 167–79.

Bleek, D. F. 1932. Customs and beliefs of the /Xam Bushmen. Part II: The lion. Part III: Game animals. Part IV: Omens, wind-making, clouds. *Bantu Studies* 6, 47–63, 233–49, 323–42.

Bleek, D. F. 1933. Customs and beliefs of the /Xam Bushmen: Part V: The rain. Part VI: Rain-making. *Bantu Studies* 7, 297–312, 375–92.

Bleek, D. F. 1935. Customs and Beliefs of the /Xam Bushmen: Part VII: Sorcerors [sic]. *Bantu Studies* 9, 1–47.

Bleek, D. F. 1936. Customs and beliefs of the /Xam Bushmen: Part VIII: More about sorcerors [sic] and charms. Special speech of animals and the moon used by /Xam Bushmen. *Bantu Studies* 10, 131–62, 163–99.

Bleek, D. F. 1956. *A Bushman Dictionary*. American Oriental Series, Vol. 41. New Haven, CT: American Oriental Society.

Bleek, W. H. I. 1874. Remarks on Orpen's 'A glimpse into the mythology of the Maluti Bushmen'. *Cape Monthly Magazine* (n.s.) 9, 10–13.

Bleek, W. H. I. 1875. Brief account of Bushman folklore and other texts. *Second Report Concerning Bushman Researches, Presented to both Houses of Parliament of the Cape of Good Hope*. Cape Town: Government Printer.

Bleek, W. H. I. & Lloyd, L. C. 1866–1913. MS. Manuscript collection. Cape Town: Jagger Library, University of Cape Town.

Bleek, W. H. I. & Lloyd, L. C. 1911. *Specimens of Bushman Folklore*. London: George Allen.

Blundell, G. 2004. *Nqabayo's Nomansland: San Rock Art and the Somatic Past*. Uppsala: Uppsala University Press.

Blurton Jones, N. & Konner, M. J. 1976. !Kung knowledge of animal behaviour (or: The proper study of mankind is animals). In Lee, R. B. & De Vore, I. (eds) *Kalahari Hunter-Gatherers: Studies of the !Kung San and their Neighbours*, pp. 325–48. Cambridge, MA: Harvard University Press.

Borcherds, P. B. 1861. *An Autobiographical Memoir*. Cape Town: Robertson.

Bressloff, P. C., Cowan, J. D., Golubitsky, M., Thomas, P. J. & Wiener, M. C. 2000. Geometric visual hallucinations, Euclidean symmetry and the functional architecture of the striate cortex. *Philosophical Transactions of the Royal Society, London*, Series B, 356, 299–330.

Butler, F. G. 1997. Nose-bleed in shamans and eland. *South African Field Archaeology* 6, 82–87.

Campbell, C. 1987. Art in crisis: contact period rock art of the south-eastern mountains of southern Africa. Unpublished M.Sc. thesis. Johannesburg: University of the Witwatersrand.

Campbell, J. 1815. *Travels in South Africa, Undertaken at the Request of the Missionary Society*. London: Black, Parry & Co.

Campbell, J. 1872. *Travels in South Africa Undertaken at the Request of the London Missionary Society; Being a Narrative of a Second Journey in the Interior of that Country*. London: Francis Westley.

Carter, P. L. 1970. Late Stone Age exploitation patterns in southern Natal. *South African Archaeological Bulletin* 25, 55–58.

Challis, S. (W.). 2009. Taking the rain: the introduction of the horse in the nineteenth century Maloti-Drakensberg and the protective medicine of baboons. In Mitchell, P. & Smith, B. W. S. *The Eland's People: New Perspectives in the Rock Art of the Maloti-Drakensberg Bushmen, Essays in Memory of Patricia Vinnicombe*, pp. 104–07. Johannesburg: Witwatersrand University Press.

Challis, S. (W.), Mitchell, P. & Orton, J. 2008. Fishing in the rain: control of rain-making and aquatic resources at a previously undescribed rock art site in Highland Lesotho. *Journal of African Archaeology* 6, 203–18.

Challis, W. 2005. 'The men with rhebok's heads; they tame elands and snakes': incorporating the rhebok antelope in the understanding of southern African rock art. *South African Archaeological Society Goodwin Series* 9, 11–20.

Challis, W. 2008. The impact of the horse on the Amatola 'Bushmen': new identity in the Maloti-Drakensberg mountains of southern Africa. Unpublished D.Phil. thesis, University of Oxford.

Chantler, P. 1999. Order Apodiformes. In del Hoyo, J., Elliott, A. & Sargatal, J. (eds) *Handbook of the Birds of the World*. Vol. 5, *Barn-Owls to Hummingbirds*, pp. 388–417. Barcelona: Lynx Edicions.

Chapman, J. 1868. *Travels in the Interior of South Africa*, 2 vols. London: Bell & Daldy.

Chippindale, C., Lewis-Williams, J. D., Blundell, G. & Smith, B. 2000. Archaeology and symbolism in the new South Africa. *Antiquity* 74, 467–68.

Cooke, C. K. 1969. *Rock Art of Southern Africa*. Cape Town: Books of Africa.

Crawhall, N. 2006. Languages, genetics and archaeology: problems and possibilities in Africa. In Soodyall, H. (ed.) *The Prehistory* of Africa: Tracing the Lineage of Modern Man, pp. 109–24. Johannesburg & Cape Town: Jonathan Ball.

Culin, S. 1901. A Summer Trip among Western Indians: The Wanmaker Expedition. Philadelphia: Bulletin of the Free Museum of Science and Art of the University of Pennsylvania 3 (1–3).

Cumming, R. G. 1850. Five Years of a Hunter's Life in the far Interior of South Africa, 2 vols. London: John Murray.

Deacon, H. J. & Deacon, J. 1999. Human Beginnings in South Africa. Cape Town: David Philip.

Deacon, J. 1986. 'My place is the Bitterpits': the home territory of Bleek and Lloyd's /Xam San informants. African Studies 45(2), 135–55.

Deacon, J. 1988. The power of a place in understanding southern San rock engravings. World Archaeology 20, 129–40.

Deacon, J. 1996. Archaeology of the Flat and Grass Bushmen. In Deacon, J. & Dowson, T. A. (eds) Voices from the Past: /Xam Bushmen and the Bleek and Lloyd Collection, pp. 245–70. Johannesburg: Witwatersrand University Press.

Deacon, J. 1997. 'My heart stands in the hill': rock engravings in the Northern Cape. KRONOS, Journal of Cape History 24, 18–29.

Deacon, J. & Dowson, T. A. 1996. Voices from the Past: /Xam Bushmen and the Bleek and Lloyd Collection. Johannesburg: Witwatersrand University Press.

Deacon, J. & Foster, C. 2005. My Heart Stands in the Hill. Cape Town: Struik.

Doke, C. M. 1936. Games, plays and dances of the ≠Khomani Bushmen. Bantu Studies 10, 461–71.

Dornan, S. S. 1925. Pygmies and Bushmen of the Kalahari. London: Seely, Service & Co.

Dowson, T. A. 1988. Revelations of religious reality: the individual in San rock art. World Archaeology 20, 116–28.

Dowson, T. A. 1989. Dots and dashes: cracking the entoptic code in Bushman rock paintings. South African Archaeological Society Goodwin Series 6, 84–94.

Dowson, T. A. 1992. Rock Engravings of Southern Africa. Johannesburg: Witwatersrand University Press.

Dowson, T. A. 1994. Reading art, writing history: rock art and social change in southern Africa. World Archaeology 25, 332–45.

Dowson, T. A. 1998. Rain in Bushman belief, politics and history: the rock-art of rain-making in the south-eastern mountains of southern Africa. In Chippindale, C. & Taçon, P. S. C. (eds) The Archaeology of Rock Art, pp. 73–89. Cambridge: Cambridge University Press.

Dowson, T. A. & Lewis-Williams, J. D. (eds) 1994. Contested Images: Diversity in Southern African Rock Art. Johannesburg: Witwatersrand University Press.

Dowson, T. A., Ouzman, S., Blundell, G. & Holliday, A. 1994. A Stow site revisited. In Dowson, T. A. & Lewis-Williams, J. D. (eds) Contested Images: Diversity in Southern African Rock Art, pp. 177–88. Johannesburg: Witwatersrand University Press.

Dowson, T. A., Tobias, P. V. & Lewis-Williams, J. D. 1994. The mystery of the Blue Ostriches: clues to the origin and authorship of a supposed rock painting. African Studies 53, 3–38.

Eastwood, E. & Eastwood, C. 2006. Capturing the Spoor: An Exploration of Southern African Rock Art. Cape Town: David Philip.

Ellenberger, V. 1953. La fin tragique des Bushmen. Paris: Amiot Dumont.

England, N. 1968. Music among the Ju/wa-si of South West Africa and Botswana. Harvard University, Ph.D. thesis.

Evans-Pritchard, E. E. 1956. Nuer Religion. Oxford: Clarendon Press.

Evans-Pritchard, E. E. 1965. Theories of Primitive Religion. Oxford: Clarendon Press.

Fock, G. J. & Fock, D. 1979. Felsbilder in Südafrika. Vol. 1: Die gravierungen auf Klipfontein, Kapprovinz. Köln: Bohlau Verlag.

Fock, G. J. & Fock, D. 1984. Felsbilder in Südafrika. Vol. 2: Die gravierungen auf Kinderdam und Kalahari. Köln: Bohlau Verlag.

Fock, G. J. & Fock, D. 1989. Felsbilder in Südafrika. Vol. 3: Die Felsbilder in Vaal-Oranje Becken. Köln: Bohlau Verlag.

Fourie, L. 1928. The Bushmen of South Africa. In Hahn, C. (ed.) The Native Tribes of South West Africa. Cape Town: Cape Times.

Francis, J. E. & Loendorf, L. 2002. Ancient

Visions: Petroglyphs and Pictographs of the Wind River and Bighorn Country, Wyoming and Montana. Salt Lake City: University of Utah Press.

Frobenius, L. 1931. *Madsimu Dzangara.* Graz: Akademische Druck.

Fry, H. C. 1988. Apodidae. Genus *Apus* Scopoli. In Fry, H. C., Keith, S., Urban, E. K. (eds) *The Birds of Africa*: Vol. 3, pp. 212–29. London: Academic Press.

Garlake, P. 1995. *The Hunter's Vision: The Prehistoric Art of Zimbabwe.* London: British Museum Press.

Geertz, C. 1983. *Local Knowledge: Further Essays in Interpretive Anthropology.* New York: Basic Books.

Goody, J. 2000. *The Power of the Written Tradition.* Washington, DC: Smithsonian Institution Press.

Gordon, R. J. 1992. *The Bushman Myth: The Making of a Namibian Underclass.* Boulder, CO: Westview Press.

Gordon, R. J. 1997. *Picturing Bushmen: The Denver Africa Expedition of 1925.* Athens, OH: Ohio University Press. Cape Town: David Philip.

Grab, S. W. & Nash, D. J. 2009. Documentary evidence of climate variability during cold seasons in Lesotho, southern Africa, 1833–1900. *Climate Dynamics* 34, 473–99.

Guenther, M. 1986. *The Nharo Bushmen of Botswana: Tradition and Change.* Hamburg: Helmut Buske Verlag.

Guenther, M. 1989. *Bushman Folktales: Oral Traditions of the Nharo of Botswana and the /Xam of the Cape.* Stuttgart: Franz Steiner Verlag.

Guenther, M. 1999. *Tricksters and Trancers: Bushman Religion and Society.* Bloomington, IN: Indiana University Press.

Hahn, T. 1870. Die Buschmänner. *Globus* 18, 5–8.

Heinz, H.-J. 1975. Elements of !Ko Bushman religious beliefs. *Anthropos* 70, 17–41.

Hewitt, R. 2008. *Structure, Meaning & Ritual in the Narratives of the Southern San.* Johannesburg: Witwatersrand University Press.

Hoff, A. 1997. The water snake of the Khoekhoen and /Xam. *South African Archaeological Bulletin* 52, 21–37.

Hoff, A. 1998. The water bull of the /Xam. *South African Archaeological Bulletin* 53, 109–24.

Hollmann, J. C. 2003. Indigenous knowledge and paintings of human-animal combinations: ostriches, swifts and religion in Bushman rock-art, Western Cape Province, South Africa. Unpublished MA thesis, University of the Witwatersrand.

Hollmann, J. C. 2005. 'Swift-people': therianthropes and bird symbolism in hunter-gatherer rock-paintings, Western and Eastern Cape Provinces, South Africa. *South African Archaeological Society Goodwin Series* 9, 21–33.

Hollmann, J. C. (ed.) 2004. *Customs and Beliefs of the /Xam Bushmen.* Johannesburg: Witwatersrand University Press.

Holm, E. 1957. Frobenius' cigars. *South African Archaeological Bulletin* 12, 68–69.

How, M. W. 1962. *The Mountain Bushmen of Basutoland.* Pretoria: van Schaik.

Howell, N. 1979. *Demography of the Dobe !Kung.* New York: Academic Press.

James, A. 2001. *The First Bushman's Path: Stories, Songs and Testimonies of the /Xam of the Northern Cape.* Pietermaritzburg: University of Natal Press.

Johnson, J. P. 1910. *Geological and Archaeological Notes on Orangia.* London: Longmans, Green.

Jolly, P. 1986. A first-generation descendant of the Transkei San. *South African Archaeological Bulletin* 41, 6–9.

Jolly, P. 1995. Melikane and Upper Mangolong revisited: the possible effects on San art of symbiotic contact between south-eastern San and southern Sotho and Nguni communities. *South African Archaeological Bulletin* 50, 68–80.

Jolly, P. 2006. The San rock paintings from the 'Upper cave at Mangolong' Lesotho. *South African Archaeological Bulletin* 61, 68–75.

Jolly, P. & Prins, F. 1994. M—a further assessment. *South African Archaeological Bulletin* 49, 16–23.

Jones, J. D. F. 2001. *Storyteller: The Many Lives of Laurens van der Post.* London: John Murray.

Katz, R. 1982. *Boiling Energy: Community Healing among the Kalahari San.* Cambridge, MA: Harvard University Press.

Katz, R., Biesele, M. & St. Denis, V. 1997. *Healing Makes Our Hearts Happy: Spirituality and Cultural Transformation among the Kalahari Ju/'hoansi.* Rochester, VT: Inner Traditions.

Keeney, B. 1999. *Kalahari Bushmen Healers*. Philadelphia, PA: Ringing Rocks Press.

Keeney, B. 2003. *Ropes to God: Experiencing the Bushman Spiritual Universe*. Philadelphia, PA: Ringing Rocks Press.

Klüver, H. 1966. *Mescal and Mechanisms of Hallucinations*. Chicago, IL: University of Chicago Press.

Kriel, T. J. 1958. *The New English-Sesotho dictionary*. Johannesburg: APB.

Leach, E. 1969. *Genesis as Myth and Other Essays*. London: Jonathan Cape.

Leach, E. 1974. *Lévi-Strauss*. London: Fontana.

Lee, D. N. 1972. Bushman folk-lore and rock paintings. *South African Journal of Science* 68, 195–99.

Lee, D. N. & Woodhouse, H. C. 1970. *Art on the Rocks of Southern Africa*. Johannesburg: Purnell.

Lee, R. B. 1967. Trance cure of the !Kung Bushmen. *Natural History* 78(40), 14–22.

Lee, R. B. 1976. Introduction. In Lee, R. B. & De Vore, I. (eds) *Kalahari Hunter-Gatherers:Studies of the !Kung San and their Neighbours*, pp. 3–24. Cambridge, MA: Harvard University Press.

Lee, R. B. 1979. *The !Kung San: Men, Women and Work in a Foraging Society*. Cambridge: Cambridge University Press.

Lee, R. B. 1993. *The Dobe Ju'/hoansi*. New York: Harcourt Brace.

Leeuwenburg, J. 1970. A Bushman legend from the George District. *South African Archaeological Bulletin* 25, 145–46.

Lensen-Erz, T. 1989. The conceptual framework for the analysis of the Brandberg rock paintings. In Pager, H. *The Rock Paintings of the Upper Brandberg: Part 1: Amis Gorge*. Cologne: Heinrich Barth Institute, pp. 361–69.

Le Quellec, J.-L. 2004. *Rock Art in Africa: Mythology and Legend*. Paris: Flammarion.

Lévy-Bruhl, L. 1912. *Les Fonctions mentales dans les sociétés inférieures*. Paris: Alcan. English trans. 1926. *How Natives Think*. London: George Allen & Unwin.

Lévy-Bruhl, L. 1922. *La Mentalité primitive*. Paris: Alcan. English trans. 1923. *Primitive Mentality*. Oxford: Clarendon Press.

Lévi-Strauss, C. 1968. The story of Asdiwal. In Leach, E. (ed.) *The Structural Study of Myth and Totemism*. London: Tavistock, pp. 1–47.

Lewis, I. M. 1989. South of north: shamanism in Africa. *Paideuma* 35, 181–88.

Lewis-Williams, J. D. 1972. The syntax and function of the Giant's Castle rock paintings. *South African Archaeological Bulletin* 27, 49–65.

Lewis-Williams, J. D. 1974. Superpositioning in a sample of rock paintings from the Barkly East District. *South African Archaeological Bulletin* 29, 91–103.

Lewis-Williams, J. D. 1977. Ezeljagdspoort revisited: new light on an enigmatic rock-painting. *South African Archaeological Bulletin* 32, 165–69.

Lewis-Williams, J. D. 1980. Ethnography and iconography: aspects of southern San thought and art. *Man* (n.s.) 15, 467–82.

Lewis-Williams, J. D. 1981. *Believing and Seeing: Symbolic Meanings in Southern San Rock Paintings*. London: Academic Press.

Lewis-Williams, J. D. 1983. *The Rock Art of Southern Africa*. Cambridge: Cambridge University Press.

Lewis-Williams, J. D. 1984. Ideological continuities in prehistoric southern Africa: the evidence of rock art. In Schrire, C. (ed.) *Interfaces: The Relationship of Past and Present in Hunter-Gatherer Studies*, pp. 225–52. New York: Academic Press.

Lewis-Williams, J. D. 1985. Testing the trance explanation of southern African rock art depictions of felines. *Bollettino del Centro Camuno di Studi Preistorici* 22, 47–62.

Lewis-Williams, J. D. 1986. The last testament of the southern San. *South African Archaeological Bulletin* 41, 10–11.

Lewis-Williams, J. D. 1990. Documentation, analysis and interpretation: problems in rock art research. *South African Archaeological Bulletin* 45, 126–36.

Lewis-Williams, J. D. 1992a. Ethnographic evidence relating to 'trance' and 'shamans' among northern and southern Bushmen. *South African Archaeological Bulletin* 47, 56–60.

Lewis-Williams, J. D. 1992b. *Vision, Power and Dance: The Genesis of a Southern African Rock Art Panel*. Fourteenth Kroon Lecture. Amsterdam: Stichting Nederlands Museum voor Anthropologie en Praehistorie.

Lewis-Williams, J. D. 1995a. Perspectives and traditions in southern African rock art research. In Helskog, K. & Olsen, B. (eds) *Perceiving Rock Art: Social and Political Perspectives*, pp. 65–86. Oslo: Novus forlag.

Lewis-Williams, J. D. 1995b. Modelling the production and consumption of rock art. *South African Archaeological Bulletin* 50, 143–54.

Lewis-Williams, J. D. 1995c. Some aspects of rock art research in the politics of present-day South Africa. In Helskog, K. & Olsen, B. (eds) *Perceiving Rock Art: Social and Political Perspectives*, pp. 317–37. Oslo: Novus forlag.

Lewis-Williams, J. D. 1996. A visit to the Lion's house: the structure, metaphors and socio-political significance of a nineteenth-century Bushman myth. In Deacon, J. & Dowson, T. A. (eds) *Voices from the Past: /Xam Bushmen and the Bleek and Lloyd Collection*, pp. 122–41. Johannesburg: Witwatersrand University Press.

Lewis-Williams, J. D. 1997. The Mantis, the Eland and the Meerkats: conflict and mediation in a nineteenth-century San myth. In McAllister, P. (ed.) *Culture and the Commonplace: Anthropological Essays in Honour of David Hammond-Tooke*, pp. 195–216. Johannesburg: Witwatersrand University Press.

Lewis-Williams, J. D. 2000. *Discovering Southern African Rock Art*. Cape Town: David Philip.

Lewis-Williams, J. D. 2002a. *Stories that Float from Afar: Ancestral Folklore of the San of Southern Africa*. Cape Town: David Philip.

Lewis-Williams, J. D. 2002b. *The Mind in the Cave: Consciousness and the Origins of Art*. London and New York: Thames & Hudson.

Lewis-Williams, J. D. 2003. *Images of Mystery: Rock Art of the Drakensberg*. Cape Town: Double Storey.

Lewis-Williams, J. D. 2006. Rock art and ethnography: a case in point from southern Africa. In Keyser, J. D., Poetschat, G. and Taylor, M. W. (eds) *Talking with the Past*, pp. 30–48. Portland, OR: Oregon Archaeological Society.

Lewis-Williams, J. D. 2008. A nexus of lives: how a heretical bishop contributed to our knowledge of South Africa's past. *Southern African Humanities* 20, 463–75.

Lewis-Williams, J. D. 2010. *Conceiving God: The Cognitive Origin and Evolution of Religion*. London and New York: Thames & Hudson.

Lewis-Williams, J. D. & Biesele, M. 1978. Eland hunting rituals among northern and southern San groups: striking similarities. *South African Archaeological Bulletin* 48, 117–34.

Lewis-Williams, J. D., Blundell, G., Challis, W. & Hampson, J. 2000. Threads of light: re-examining a motif in southern African rock art. *South African Archaeological Bulletin* 55, 123–136.

Lewis-Williams, J. D. & Dowson, T. A. 1990. Through the veil: San rock paintings and the rock face. *South African Archaeological Bulletin* 45, 5–16.

Lewis-Williams, J. D. & Dowson, T. A. 1999. *Images of Power: Understanding San Rock Art*. Cape Town: Struik.

Lewis-Williams, J. D. & Dowson, T. A. 2008. The case of the 'Blue Ostriches': an archaeological *cause célèbre* reopened. *The Digging Stick* 25(3), 1–5.

Lewis-Williams, J. D., Dowson, T. A. & Deacon J. 1993. Rock art and changing perceptions of southern Africa's past: Ezeljagdspoort reviewed. *Antiquity* 67, 273–91.

Lewis-Williams, J. D. & Loubser, J. H. N. 1986. Deceptive appearances: a critique of southern African rock art studies. *Advances in World Archaeology* 5, 253–89.

Lewis-Williams, J. D. & Pearce, D. G. 2004a. *San Spirituality: Roots, Expression and Social Consequences*. Walnut Creek, CA: AltaMira Press. Cape Town: Double Storey.

Lewis-Williams, J. D. & Pearce, D. G. 2004b. Southern African rock paintings as social intervention: a study of rain-control images. *African Archaeological Review* 21, 199–228.

Lewis-Williams, J. D. & Pearce D. G. 2005. *Inside the Neolithic Mind: Consciousness, Cosmos and the Realm of the Gods*. London: Thames & Hudson.

Lewis-Williams, J. D. & Pearce, D. G. 2008. From generalities to specifics in San rock art. *South African Journal of Science* 104, 428–30.

Lewis-Williams, J. D. & Pearce, D. G. 2009. Constructing spiritual panoramas: order and chaos in southern African San rock art panels. *South African Humanities* 21, 41–61.

Liebenberg, L. 1990. *The Art of Tracking: The Origin of Science*. Cape Town: David Philip.

Lloyd, L. C. 1889. *A Short Account of Further Bushman Material Collected. Third Report Concerning Bushman Researches, Presented to both Houses of Parliament of the Cape of Good Hope by Command of His Excellency the Governor.* London: David Nutt.

Loendorf, L. 2004. Places of power: the placement of Dinwoody petroglyphs across the Wyoming landscape. In Chippindale, C. & Nash, G. (eds) *Pictures in Place: The Figured Landscapes of Rock-Art*, pp. 201–16. Cambridge: Cambridge University Press.

Loendorf, L. & Stone, N. M. 2006. *Mountain Spirit: The Sheep Eater Indians of Yellowstone.* Salt Lake City, UT: University of Utah Press.

Loubser, J. H. N. & Laurens, G. 1994. Depictions of domestic ungulates and shields: hunter/gatherers and ago-pastoralists in the Caledon River valley area. In Dowson, T. A. & Lewis-Williams, J. D. (eds) *Contested Images: Diversity in Southern African Rock Art Research*, pp. 83–118. Johannesburg: Witwatersrand University Press.

Mackenzie, J. 1871. *Ten Years North of the Orange River: A Story of Everyday Life and Work among the South African Tribes from 1859–1869.* London: Frank Cass & Co.

Macksey, R. & Donato, E. (eds) 1972. *The Structuralist Controversy: The Languages of Criticism and the Sciences of Man.* Baltimore, MD: The Johns Hopkins Press.

Maggs, T. M. O'C. 1995. Neglected rock art: the rock engravings of agriculturalist communities in South Africa. *South African Archaeological Bulletin* 50, 132–42.

Malinowski, B. 1922. *Argonauts of the Western Pacific: An Account of Native Enterprise and Adventure in the Archipelagoes of Melanesian New Guinea.* London: George Routledge & Sons.

Marshall, L. 1960. !Kung Bushman bands. *Africa* 30, 325–55.

Marshall, L. 1962. !Kung Bushman religious beliefs. *Africa* 32, 221–51.

Marshall, L. 1965. The !Kung Bushmen of the Kalahari Desert. In Gibbs, J. L. (ed.) *Peoples of Africa.* New York: Holt, Rinehart & Winston.

Marshall, L. 1969. The medicine dance of the !Kung Bushmen. *Africa* 39, 347–81.

Marshall, L. 1976. *The !Kung of Nyae Nyae.* Cambridge, MA: Harvard University Press.

Marshall, L. 1999. *Nyae Nyae !Kung Beliefs and Rites.* Cambridge, MA: Harvard University Press.

Marshall Thomas, E. 1959. *The Harmless People.* London: Secker & Warburg. Reprinted 1988, Cape Town: David Philip.

Marshall Thomas, E. 1994. *The Tribe of the Tiger: Cats and their Culture.* New York: Simon & Schuster.

Marshall Thomas, E. 2006. *The Old Way: A Story of the First People.* New York: Farrar Straus & Giroux.

Mazel, A. D. 1982. Distribution of painted themes in the Natal Drakensberg. *Annals of the Natal Museum* 25(1), 67–82.

Mazel, A. D. 1989. People making history: the last ten thousand years of hunter-gatherer communities in the Thukela basin. *Natal Museum Journal of Humanities* 1, 1–168.

Mazel, A. D. 2009a. Images in time: advances in the dating of Maloti-Drakensberg rock art since the 1970s. In Mitchell, P. & Smith, B. W. (eds) *The Eland's People: New Perspectives in the Rock Art of Three Maloti-Drakensberg Bushmen. Essays in Memory of Patricia Vinnicombe*, pp. 81–85, 88–97. Pietermaritzburg: University of Natal Press.

Mazel, A. D. 2009b. Unsettled times: shaded polychrome paintings and hunter-gatherer history in the southeastern mountains of southern Africa. *Southern African Humanities* 21, 85–115.

Mazel, A. D. & Watchman, A. L. 2003. The dating of paintings in the Natal Drakensberg and the Biggarsberg, KwaZulu-Natal, South Africa. *Southern African Humanities* 15, 59–73.

Mellars, P. & Gibson, K. (eds) 1996. *Modelling the Early Mind.* Cambridge: McDonald Institute for Archaeological Research.

Mguni, S. 2004. Cultured representation: understanding 'formlings', an enigmatic motif in the rock-art of Zimbabwe. *Journal of Social Archaeology* 4, 181–99.

Mguni, S. 2005. A new iconographic understanding of formlings, a pervasive motif in Zimbabwean rock art. In Blundell, G. (ed.) *Further Approaches to Southern African Rock Art Goodwin Series* 9, 34–44.

Mitchell, P. 1996. Sehonghong: the late Holocene assemblages with pottery. *South African Archaeological Bulletin* 51, 17–25.

Mitchell, P. 2002. *The Archaeology of Southern Africa*. Cambridge: Cambridge University Press.

Mitchell, P. & Challis, S. 2008. A 'first' glimpse into the Maloti Mountains: the diary of James Murray Grant's expedition of 1873–4. *Southern African Humanities* 20, 399–461.

Mithen, S. 1996. *The Prehistory of the Mind: A Search for the Origins of Art, Religion and Science*. London: Thames & Hudson.

Mostert, N. 1992. *Frontiers: The Epic of South Africa's Creation and the Tragedy of the Xhosa People*. London: Pimlico.

Orpen, J. M. 1874. A glimpse into the mythology of the Maluti Bushmen. *Cape Monthly Magazine* (n.s.) 9(49), 1–13.

Ouzman, S. 1998. Towards a mindscape of landscape: rock-art as expression of world-understanding. In Chippindale, C. & Taçon, P. S. C. (eds) *The Archaeology of Rock-Art*, 30–41. Cambridge: Cambridge University Press.

Pager, H. 1971. *Ndedema*. Graz: Akademische Druck.

Pager, H. 1973. Rock paintings in southern Africa showing bees and honey gathering. *Bee World* 54, 61–68.

Pager, H. 1975. *Stone Age Myth and Magic, as Documented in the Rock Paintings of South Africa*. Graz: Akademische Druck.

Parkington, J. 2002. *The Mantis, the Eland and the Hunter*. Cape Town: Creda Communications.

Parkington, J. 2003. *Cederberg Rock Paintings*. Cape Town: Creda Publications.

Parkington, J. 2006. *Shorelines, Strandloopers, and Shell Middens*. Cape Town: Creda Publications.

Parkington, J., Morris, D. & Rusch, N. 2008. *Karoo Rock Engravings*. Cape Town: Creda Communications.

Pearce, D. G. 2005. Iconography and interpretation of the Tierkloof painted stone. *South African Archaeological Society Goodwin Series* 9, 45–53.

Pearse, R. O. 1973. *Barrier of Spears: Drama of the Drakensberg*. Cape Town: Howard Timmins.

Philip, J. 1828. *Researches in South Africa*. London: James Duncan.

Phillipson, D. W. 1977. *The Later Prehistory of Eastern and Southern Africa*. London: Heinemann.

Prins, F. E. 1990. Southern-Bushman descendants in the Transkei—rock art and rain-making. *South African Journal of Ethnology* 13, 110–16.

Propp, V. 1968. Morphology of the folktale. Austin, TX: University of Texas Press.

Reichel-Dolmatoff, G. 1978. Drug induced optical sensations and their relationship to applied art among some Colombian Indians. In Greenhalgh, M. & Megaw, V. (eds) *Art in Society*, pp. 289–304. London: Duckworth.

Renfrew, C. & Zubrow, E. B. W. (eds) 1994. *The Ancient Mind: Elements of Cognitive Archaeology*. Cambridge: Cambridge University Press.

Rudner, J. 1957. The Brandberg and its archaeological remains. *Journal of the South West Africa Scientific Society* 127–44.

Rudner, J. & Rudner, I. 1970. *The Hunter and his Art: A Survey of Rock Art in Southern Africa*. Cape Town: Struik.

Rudner, J. & Rudner, I. 1978. Bushman art. In Tobias, P. V. (ed.) *The Bushmen: San Hunters and Herders of Southern Africa*, pp. 57–75. Cape Town: Human & Rousseau.

Schapera, I. 1930. *The Khoisan Peoples of South Africa*. London: Routledge & Kegan Paul.

Scherz, 1970. *Felsbilder in Südwest-Afrika, Teil I*. Köln: Bohlau Verlag.

Scherz, 1975. *Felsbilder in Südwest-Afrika, Teil II*. Köln: Bohlau Verlag

Schmidt, S. 1973. Die Mantis religiosa in den Glaubensvorstellungen der Koesan-Völker. *Zeitschrift für Ethnologie* 98, 102–27.

Schmidt, S. 1979. The rain bull of the South African Bushmen. *African Studies* 38, 201–24.

Shaw, B. 1820. *Memorials of South Africa*. Reprint 1970: Cape Town: Struik.

Shostak, M. 1981. *Nisa: The Life and Words of a !Kung Woman*. London: Allen Lane.

Siegel, R. K. 1977. Hallucinations. *Scientific American* 237, 132–40.

Siegel, R. K. & West, L. J. (eds) *Hallucinations: Behaviour, Experience and Theory*, pp. 81–161. New York: Wiley.

Silberbauer, G. B. 1965. *Report to the Government of Bechuanaland on the Bushman Survey*. Gaberones, Botswana: [government printer].

Silberbauer, G. B. 1981. *Hunter and Habitat in the Central Kalahari Desert*. Cambridge: Cambridge University Press.

Skotnes, P. 2007. *Claim to the Country: The Archive of Wilhelm Bleek and Lucy Lloyd.* Cape Town: Jacana. Athens, OH: Ohio University Press.

Skotnes, P. 2008. *Unconquerable Spirit: George Stow's History Paintings of the San.* Johannesburg: Jacana.

Smith, B. & Ouzman, S. 2004. Taking stock: identifying Khoekhoen herder rock art in southern Africa. *Current Anthropology* 45(4), 499–526.

Smith, B. S. & Blundell, G. 2004. Dangerous ground: a critique of landscape in rock-art studies. In Chippindale, C. & Nash, G. (eds) *Pictures in Place: The Figured Landscapes of Rock-Art*, pp. 239–62. Cambridge: Cambridge University Press.

Solomon, A. C. 1997. The myth of ritual origins? Ethnography, mythology and interpretation of San rock art. *South African Archaeological Bulletin* 52, 3–13.

Solomon, A. C. 2008. Myth, making, and consciousness: differences and dynamics in San rock arts. *Current Anthropology* 49, 59–86.

Solway, J. S. & Lee R. B. 1990. Foragers, genuine or spurious? Situating the Kalahari San in history. *Current Anthropology* 31, 109–122.

Soodyall, H. (ed.) 2006. *The Prehistory of Africa: Tracing the Lineage of Modern Man.* Johannesburg and Cape Town: Jonathan Ball.

Sparrman, A. 1789. *A Voyage to the Cape of Good Hope.* London: Lackington.

Spohr, O. H. 1962. *Wilhelm Emmanuel Bleek: A Bibliographical Sketch.* Cape Town: University of Cape Town Libraries.

Steyn, P. 1996. *Nesting Birds: The Breeding Habits of Southern African Birds.* Vlaeberg, South Africa: Fernwood Press.

Stow, G. W. 1905. *The Native Races of South Africa: A History of the Intrusion of the Hottentots and Bantu into the Hunting Grounds of the Bushmen, the Aborigines of the Country.* London: Swan Sonnenschein.

Stow, G. W. & Bleek, D. F. 1930. *Rock Paintings in South Africa: from Parts of the Eastern Province and Orange Free State, copied by George William Stow, with an Introduction and Descriptive Notes by Dorothea F. Bleek.* London: Methuen.

Summers, R. (ed.) 1959. *Prehistoric Rock Art of the Federation of Rhodesia and Nyasaland.* Salisbury: National Publications Trust.

Thackeray, A. I. 1983. Dating the rock art of southern Africa. *South African Archaeological Society Goodwin Series* 4, 21–26.

Thunberg, C. P. 1986 (1788). *Travels in Europe, Africa and Asia Made between the Years 1770 and 1779.* London: F. & C. Rivington. Cape Town: Van Riebeeck Society.

Traill, A. 1978. The languages of the Bushmen. In Tobias, P. V. (ed.) *The Bushmen: San Hunters and Herders of Southern Africa*, pp. 137–47. Cape Town: Human & Rousseau.

Valiente-Noailles, C. 1993. *The Kua: Life and Soul of the Central Kalahari Bushmen.* Rotterdam: Balkema.

Van der Post, L. 1958. *The Lost World of the Kalahari.* London: Hogarth Press.

Van der Post, L. 1961. *The Heart of the Hunter.* London: Hogarth Press.

Van der Riet, J., van der Riet, M. & Bleek, D. F. 1940. *More Rock-Paintings in South Africa from the Coastal Belt between Albany and Piquetberg.* London: Methuen.

Vinnicombe, P. 1972. Myth, motive, and selection in southern African rock art. *Africa* 42, 192–204.

Vinnicombe, P. 1975. The ritual significance of eland (*Taurotragus oryx*) in the rock art of southern Africa. In Anati, E. (ed.) *Les religions de la préhistoire*, pp. 379–400. Capo de Ponte (Brescia): Centro Camuno di Studi Preistorci.

Vinnicombe, P. 1976. *People of the Eland: Rock Paintings of the Drakensberg Bushmen as a Reflection of their Life and Thought.* Pietermaritzburg: University of Natal Press.

Vinnicombe, P. 2009. Basotho oral knowledge: the last Bushman inhabitants of the Mashai District, Lesotho (with additional notes by Peter Mitchell). In *The Eland's People: New Perspectives in the Rock Art of the Maloti-Drakensberg Bushmen. Essays in Memory of Patricia Vinnicombe*, pp. 165–69, 172–90. Johannesburg: Witwatersrand University Press.

Walker, N. 1996. *The Painted Hills: Rock Art of the Matopos, Zimbabwe.* Gweru: Mambo Press.

Watts, I. 2002. Ochre in the Middle Stone Age of southern Africa: ritualized display or hide preservation? *South African Archaeological Bulletin* 57, 1–14.

Wendt, W. E. 1976. 'Art mobilier' from the Apollo 11 Cave, South West Africa: Africa's oldest dated works of art. *South African Archaeological Bulletin* 31, 5–11.

Wessels, M. 2010. *Bushman Letters: Interpreting the /Xam Narratives of the Bleek and Lloyd Collection*. Johannesburg: Witwatersrand University Press.

Whitehouse, H. 2000. *Arguments and Icons: Divergent Modes of Religiosity*. Oxford: Oxford University Press.

Whitley, D. S., Loubser, J. H. N. and Hann, D. 2004. Friends in low places: rock-art and landscape on the Modoc Plateau. In Chippindale, C. & Nash, G. (eds) *Pictures in Place: The Figured Landscapes of Rock-Art*, pp. 217–38. Cambridge: Cambridge University Press.

Willcox, A. R. 1963. *The Rock Art of South Africa*. London: Nelson.

Wilman, M. 1933. *The Rock Engravings of Griqualand West and Bechuanaland, South Africa*. Cambridge: Cambridge University Press.

Wilmsen, E. N. 1989. *Land Filled with Flies: A Political Economy of the Kalahari*. Chicago, IL: University of Chicago Press.

Winkleman, M. & Dobkin de Rios, M. 1989. Psychoactive properties of !Kung Bushman medicine plants. *Journal of Psychoactive Drugs* 21, 50–59.

Woodhouse, B. 1979. *The Bushman Art of Southern Africa*. Cape Town: Purnell.

Woodhouse, H. C. 1979. Interpretation of certain rock paintings in South Africa: a second opinion. *South African Archaeological Bulletin* 34, 133–37.

Woodhouse, H. C. & Lee, D. N. 1976. The rediscovery of rock paintings recorded by George W. Stow in the 1870s. *South African Archaeological Bulletin* 31, 29–30.

Wright, J. & Mazel, A. 2007. *Tracks in a Mountain Range: Exploring the History of the uKhahlamba-Drakensberg*. Johannesburg: Witwatersrand University Press.

Wright, J. B. 1971. *Bushman Raiders of the Drakensberg*. Pietermaritzburg: University of Natal Press.

Yates, R, Parkington, J. & Manhire, A. 1990. *Pictures from the Past: A History of the Interpretation of Rock Paintings and Engravings of Southern Africa*. Cape Town: Centaur Publications.

Young, R. B. 1908. *The Life and Work of George William Stow*. London: Longmans, Green.

Acknowledgments

We thank colleagues and friends who usefully commented on parts of the text: Janette Deacon, Jeremy Hollmann, Peter Mitchell, Tom Challis, Larry Loendorf and David Pearce. Victor Biggs took us to many sites – particularly those first copied by George Stow – in the Eastern Cape. He and his wife Linda extended great hospitality to several field teams. Jeremy Hollmann accompanied Sam Challis to trace the Rain Snake Shelter at Sehonghong, Lesotho, and shared with us his thoughts and images of swift-people in the Western Cape. Sven Ouzman took Sam Challis to the Free State and Eastern Cape, and in particular to the site that may have inspired George Stow's 'Blue Ostriches'. Mark McGranaghan and Jamie Coreth took time from their studies at Oxford University to help conduct fieldwork in the Free State and Eastern Cape. Natalie Edwards helped create the image of the South African 'Rosetta Stone'. Dirk and Lynette Kotze arranged site visits to several farms in the Rouxville area of the Free State. Louis Alberts helped us to search for the lost Stow site on the Aasvoëlberg, Zastron. We also thank landowners and field contacts: Russell Suchet, Willem and Christine Cronje, Liesel Foster, Dawn Green, Jan van Ronge, Will and Gill Pringle, Steve Bassett, Tommie Jordaan, Jack and Kollie Botha, Vaughan Victor and Qamo Thoola. Kevin Crause at the Fingerprints In Time project generously shared with us some of the results of the image-enhancing techniques that he has developed for clarifying very faint rock paintings. Azizo da Fonseca and David Duns of the South African Rock Art Digital Archive (SARADA) assisted greatly with the provision of images housed at the Rock Art Research Institute (RARI) and with permissions from other collections. We thank our colleagues at the Rock Art Research Institute: Benjamin Smith, David Pearce, Catherine Namono, John Wright, Edith Mkhabela, and colleagues Karim Sadr, Iain Burns, Peter Mitchell, Siyakha Mguni and Paolo dos Santos. Individual friends and family who have given their support to RARI and to this project: Susan Ward, Elizabeth Marshall Thomas. Sam Challis thanks his wife, Kristy.

The Rock Art Research Institute is funded by the National Research Foundation, the University of the Witwatersrand, the Andrew W. Mellon Foundation and African World Heritage Fund.

We thank the editorial team at Thames & Hudson for their unfailing support, critical eye and meticulous editing. They brought order and consistency to our chaotic efforts and saved us much embarrassment.

Sources of Illustrations

Plates 1 Sam Challis; 2 Museum Africa; 3 Richard Katz; 4, 5 John Hone, Natal Museum Collection; 6 Janette Deacon; 7 John Hone, Natal Museum Collection; 8 Sam Challis; 9 Geoff Blundell, RARI archive; 10, 11 Neil Lee, RARI archive; 12 Sam Challis; 13 Jeremy Hollmann, RARI archive; 14 RARI archive; 15 Sam Challis; 16, 17, 18 George Stow, IZIKO South African Museum; 19 Neil Lee, RARI archive; 20 George Stow, IZIKO South African Museum; 21 Sam Challis; 22, 23, 24 Jeremy Hollmann, RARI archive; 25 Harald Pager, RARI archive; 26 Nick Page; 27 Sam Challis; 28 Janette Deacon; 29 Ghilraen Sherman-Laue, RARI archive.

Figures 1 Natalie Edwards and Sam Challis; 2 Sam Challis; 3 RARI archive; 4 John Hone, Natal Museum Collection; 5 Sam Challis, RARI archive; 6 Pippa Skotnes; 7 George Stow, IZIKO South African Museum; 8 Pippa Skotnes; 9 Lorna Marshall (centre left: Jurgen Schadeberg); 10 Geoff Blundell (inset tracing RARI archive); 11 Joe Alfers, Analysis of Rock Art in Lesotho (ARAL) project (inset tracing RARI archive); 12 George Stow, IZIKO South African Museum; 13 RARI archive; 14 Jeremy Hollmann; 15, 16 RARI archive; 17 George Stow, IZIKO South African Museum; 18 Aron Mazel, Natal Museum Collection; 19 left: Richard Katz, right: Aron Mazel, Natal Museum Collection; 20 RARI archive; 21 George Stow, IZIKO South African Museum; 22 Harald Pager, RARI archive; 23 left: David Pearce, RARI archive, right: Neil Lee, RARI archive; 24 after Alexander 1837; 25, 26, 27, 28 RARI archive; 29 Franda Zondagh (from Hollmann 2005); 30 RARI archive; 31 Sam Challis after Vinnicombe 1976; 32 Sam Challis; 33 RARI archive; 34 above: Neil Lee, RARI archive; below: RARI archive; 35, 36 RARI archive; 37 Sam Challis; 38 Alexander 1838 opp. p. 180; 39 Roger de la Harpe/Africa Imagery; 40, 41 RARI archive; 42 Siyakha Mguni; 43 Sam Challis; 44 RARI archive; 45 Lorna Marshall; 46 George Stow, IZIKO South African Museum; 47, 48, 49 RARI archive; 50, 51 Sam Challis; 52 Francis & Loendorf 2002, fig. 6.32; 53 Loendorf 2004, fig. 10.2; 54 Francis & Loendorf 2002, fig. 6.20; 55 After Loendorf 2004, fig. 10.10; 56, 57 Lorna Marshall.

Index